NEW DIMENSIONS IN LITERATURE

A STUDY OF NONFICTION

Albert G. Craz

Editorial Board   Don M. Wolfe
John R. Arscott
Hardy R. Finch

McCORMICK-MATHERS   PUBLISHING   COMPANY

Florence, Kentucky 41042

McCORMICK-MATHERS PUBLISHING COMPANY

New York   **Florence, Kentucky**

CONTENTS

INTRODUCTION

Sit still and pay attention to *nothing!* Sound impossible? Promote the sale of prunes by telling about the ugly wrinkles and messy pits! Sound laughable? Grab a lion by the tail! Sound insane? Not for you? Perhaps not, but you can do all of these things and much more through reading nonfiction.

Grabbing a lion by the tail, for instance—only a handful of adventurers and hunters in each generation see a Masai spearman actually hold a lion by the tail. But that doesn't mean thousands more cannot at least share in such a fantastic adventure by reading a well-written eye witness account. Such an account is in this book.

Nonfiction is several things. It is a magic carpet carrying readers to Madison Avenue, New York, to write advertisements or to Barcelona, Spain, to report on a war. Nonfiction is a time machine capable of reaching back tens or thousands of years: describing the comical crossing of the United States in the 30s by two teenage adventurers from New Jersey; recounting the words of Socrates in Athens, Greece, 399 B.C., as he prepared to carry out his own death sentence.

Nonfiction is a switchboard. It can connect you with the thoughts of hundreds of people, living or dead: Eleanor Roosevelt, Samuel Hayakawa, Malcolm X, Joan Baez. Autobiographies, diaries, journals, letters, and essays can provide truly fascinating reading experiences which can put the reader in touch with the ideas and philosophies of people who help shape our world. Why should anyone

1

have to hear secondhand what a great man or woman has said? Let these people speak to you through their own writings.

The variety of topics and authors in this volume gives an idea of the range of nonfiction literature. It includes authors and subjects from earliest recorded history to today's newspaper stories. It includes people from various nationalities, backgrounds, cultures, and continents. The selections are very serious, or extremely humorous, or bitingly satirical, but always, always informative.

At its best, nonfiction brings the reader close to important matters or events which have affected human existence. Like television, it opens a window to the real world. Nonfiction may not always come as close to real events as the television camera, but it can become at times so close, become so absorbing and gripping, that for the reader there will come that rare moment when all else is forgotten. And it is at that moment that the eyes will leave the printed page and begin to look through a window gradually opening upon a new, strange, but very real world.

Albert Craz is currently a professor at Dowling College, Long Island, New York, and has 27 years experience teaching high-school literature.

J. A. Hunter lived through, or hunted through, all of his tales before he wrote them. Appropriately, the name of the book from which "Masai Spearmen" comes is titled *Hunter* (1952). Scottish-born into a hunting family, Mr. Hunter established himself as one of the most famous European hunters in Africa. His account of the Masai hunters describes an admirable group who daily expect they might have to put their lives on the line to protect their village, homes, and livestock. Here is writing which ranges far from practically any reader's normal experience.

MASAI SPEARMEN: THE BRAVEST OF THE BRAVE

J. A. Hunter

I SAW my first spear hunt when I was staying in a small Masai[1] community not far from Lake Magadi.[2] The night before, a lion had jumped the twelve-foot boma[3] that surrounded the village, seized a cow, and leaped back over the barrier with the cow in his mouth. I know this feat sounds incredible, as the cow probably weighed nearly twice that. Yet a male lion can perform this exploit with no more trouble than a fox has in carrying off a chicken.

A lion shows a special knack in getting partly under the carcass and shifting the weight onto his back while still

---

[1]*Masai:* the name of a pastoral and hunting people in Kenya and Tanzania
[2]*Lake Magadi:* lake in Kenya in eastern Africa, near the northern border of Tanzania
[3]*boma:* a fence

holding the cow's throat in his mouth. When jumping the barricade, the lion's tail becomes absolutely rigid and seems to act as a balance. The Masai have assured me that a lion without a tail could not possibly perform this feat.

I was prepared to start out on the lion's trail the next morning, but the moran[1] in this community told me somewhat contemptuously that my help was not needed. They would handle the situation themselves. At that time, I found it hard to believe that a group of men could kill an adult lion with spears. I asked if I could go along and bring my gun. Permission was politely granted me. That night I loaded my .416 Rigby magazine rifle, never doubting that it would fall to my lot to kill any lions that we might find.

We started off at daybreak. I followed the spearmen. There were ten of them. Magnificent-looking men, slender but finely muscled, not one under six feet. To give their limbs free play, each man removed his one garment, the long piece of cloth they wear draped over their shoulders, and wrapped it around his left arm. They carried their brightly-painted shields balanced on their shoulders. Their spears were in their right hands. The warriors wore their ostrich-plume headdresses as though going into battle and bracelets of fur around their ankles. Otherwise, they were completely naked.

We picked up the spoor of the lion and the moran began to track. The lion had gorged on the cow during the night and was lying up in some dense cover. They threw stones into the bushes at random until the savage growls of the lion showed he had been hit. When the moran had spotted the cat by his angry grunts and snarls, they began to throw stones in good earnest; then the bushes began to shake. Suddenly the lion burst out a hundred yards from us and went bounding away across the plains, his gorged belly swinging from side to side as he ran.

---

[1] *moran:* another name for a Masai hunter

Instantly the Masai were after him, giving their wild cries as they sped through the tall, yellow grass. The lion, still heavy with his great meal, did not run far. He stopped and turned at bay. The spearmen spread out to encircle him. The lion stood in the middle of the ring, looking this way and that, snarling in a way to make one's blood run cold as the spearmen slowly closed in.

The lion allowed the men to come within forty yards. Then I could tell that he was preparing to charge. His head was held low, just above his outstretched forepaws. His hindquarters were slightly arched so he could bring his rear legs well forward and get the maximum spring behind his rush. He began to dig his claws into the ground, much as a sprinter digs in with his spiked shoes to make sure he does not slip when he makes his first jump.

I concentrated on the sinister inverted curve of the lion's tail. Just before he charges, a lion always twitches the tasseled tip of his tail three times in rapid succession. On the third twitch he comes for you at amazing speed, going so fast he seems only a small part of his real size.

The spearmen knew as well as I did that the lion was preparing to attack. By what seemed to be a single impulse, all their spear arms moved back together for the cast. The men were so tense with excitement that their taut shoulder muscles twitched slightly, making ripples of sunlight play along the spear blades. You could have driven a nail into any one of them without his feeling it.

Suddenly the tip of the lion's tail began to twitch. One! Two! Three! Then he charged for the ring of spearmen. At once half a dozen spears leaped through the air toward him. I saw one plunge into his shoulder and the next instant the spear head broke through the hide on his other side. The lion never paused in his stride. In his path stood one of the moran, a youngster on his first hunt. The boy never flinched. He braced himself to meet the charge, holding his shield in front of him and swaying back slightly so as to put the whole weight of his body into his spear thrust. The lion sprang for the boy. With one blow he knocked the young moran's shield out of his hand as though it were cardboard. Then he reared up, trying to sweep the boy toward him with his outstretched paws.

The boy drove his spear a good two feet into the lion's chest. The mortally wounded beast sprang on him, fixing his hind claws in the boy's belly to insure his grip while at the same time he seized the boy's shoulder in his jaws.

The young warrior went down under the weight of the great cat. Instantly all the other moran were around the dying lion. It was too close quarters for spears. The men used their double-edged simis, heavy knives about two feet long. Shouldering each other out of the way, they hacked like madmen at the lion's head. In a matter of seconds, they had sliced the head to pieces, starting with the muzzle and shearing off an inch or so at a time. I saw one man deliver a terrible blow that split the lion's skull open, but whether the animal was still alive at the moment I can hardly say.

I had been quite unable to use my gun during this battle. A man with a gun is a positive menace at such times. Once the frenzied warriors begin to circle the lion, a rifleman cannot fire without running a grave chance of hitting them.

I examined the wounded boy. His wounds were truly frightful yet he seemed completely indifferent to them. I sewed him up with a needle and thread. He paid no more attention to the process than if I were patting him on the back.

The hide of the lion was so perforated with spear thrusts and simi-slashes that it was worthless as a trophy. It was simply a cut and bloody mass of dirty yellow hair. The dignity and majesty of the noble beast had completely departed, leaving only a sorry remnant.

When we returned to the Masai manyatta or village, the wounded boy was urged to eat great quantities of raw beef and then given cattle blood as a purgative so he could gorge himself again. Some of the other moran had been clawed by the lion but they made no attempt to guard against infection, except to wash their wounds with water. Later I saw some Masai communities soak the root of a bush called the "olki-lorite" in water, which gives it a permanganate of potash[1] color. It seems to act as an antiseptic and promotes healing.

I hope the lad recovered. He certainly held top honors for the day, and the young girls were looking at him with such admiration that, if he lived, he would have no trouble picking out a suitable sweetheart.

The Masai believe that the bravest act a man can perform is to grab a lion by the tail and hold the animal so the other warriors can close in with their spears and simis. Any man who performs this feat four times is given the title of "me-lombuki" and ranks as a captain. It is also an unwritten law among them that any man who gains this title must be willing to fight anything living. I doubt if more than two out of a thousand Masai ever become melombuki, although the competition among the moran to gain this honor is very keen.

I have seen several of these "tail pullings" during Masai lion hunts and it is a wonder to me that the men attempting the feat ever come out alive. I remember one hunt in which fifty or more spearmen were involved. They had put up two lions and a lioness. The animals tried to reach some heavy scrub[2] but the warriors cut them off. The lions retreated into a small clump of bush near a dry, sandy watercourse. When possible, a pursued lion nearly always makes for one of these dry stream beds with its canopies of overhanging bush. In a matter of minutes, the moran had the thicket surrounded and began to move forward for the kill.

As the circle of yelling warriors closed in, the concealed lions began to growl. Then without any warning, the largest

[1] *permanganate of potash:* mild antiseptic of purple color used to treat minor cuts and bruises

[2] *scrub:* small shrub

of the lions broke from the cover and made a rush for freedom. He was a fine sight as he dashed along the stream bottom, tail down and going all out at a gallop. He was headed straight for two moran, who raised their spears and prepared to meet his charge. But the big male had no desire to fight; he wished only to escape. He gave a mighty bound straight over the heads of the two spearmen, spinning one of them around sideways with a blow from his flank.

The other moran made tongue-clicking sounds of disapproval, partly because the two young men had allowed the lion to escape and partly because the lion had refused to fight. I have often noticed that the old lions with the finest manes are more reluctant to give battle than young males or females. The same is true of elephants. An old bull with fine ivory is shyer than a young bull or cow. I suppose they learn discretion with the years. It has also seemed to me that lions are able to tell young, inexperienced moran and will deliberately direct their attack at these youngsters. This may be nothing but my imagination yet the younger men are apt to be hesitant and uncertain in their actions and I believe the lions can detect it.

As the spearmen closed in around the thicket, they bunched together, jostling each other in their desire to be first to spill blood. The remaining two lions were clearly visible in the bush, standing shoulder to shoulder and both giving grating roars. When the moran were within ten yards of the lions, spears began to fly. One of the spears struck the lioness in the loin and she came out with a scream of rage and pain. For an instant she stood up on her hind legs, pawing the air like the crest on a coat of arms. Then she dropped to bite at the spear in her flank. At that moment, one of the moran threw down his spear and, rushing forward, grabbed her by the root of her tail. A moran never grabs a lion by the tasseled end of the tail. A lion can make his tail as stiff as a gun barrel, and a man would be swept aside by a single jerk.

At once the moran's comrades dashed in, slashing with their simis. At moments like this, the spearmen work themselves up to a pitch of blind frenzy. They seem to be mere automatic stabbers. Their faces are expressionless. There is no teamwork; each man is out to do the killing by himself. The lioness was digging her hind feet into the ground to get purchase forward and the tail puller was dragging her back. Suddenly the lioness went up on her hind legs, striking left and right with her paws at the men around her. Although I saw her blows go home, the men never flinched. They told me afterward that they never feel any pain at the time of a mauling—they are at too high a pitch of excitement. Apparently neither does the lion. Both sides continue to fight until one drops from loss of blood.

Slowly the lioness fell to the ground. Then all I could see were the flashing blades of the simis as the men hacked away in their blind fury. When it was over, the animal's head was cut into shreds. There must have been a dozen spears in the body. It looked like a bloody pincushion.

From the noise on the other side of the clump of bush, I knew another group of spearmen were busy with the second lion. I saw a warrior kneel and hold out his shield in a taunting fashion. The next instant the lion had leaped on it, knocking the man flat. The prone warrior tried vainly to get in a spear thrust while the lion mauled his exposed shoulder. I shouted to the other men to keep back and let me get in a shot, but nothing could be heard above the wild, falsetto yells of the warriors and the deep grunts of the lion as he lacerated the prostrate man. I saw two spears plunge into the lion's body and then the moran fell on the raging beast with their simis.

Before the lion was dead, he had seriously wounded one of the attacking moran besides ripping open the shoulder of the warrior lying under the shield. I did what I could for the injured men. They both had deep claw and fang incisions and were losing considerable blood. As I sewed up one man's injuries, he glanced down casually at the terrible cuts and made the same contemptuous clicking sound with his tongue that the moran had made when they saw the first lion escape.

The warrior's attitude seemed to be "What a nuisance!" yet a white man in a similar situation would have been wild with pain.

Strangely enough, I have never heard of any bones being broken by the lion's teeth. The wounds are all flesh wounds. Apparently the lion's fang teeth are wide enough apart to close around the bones. Yet when a lion grabs a man by the shoulder, his fangs often meet in his victim's body. If you pour disinfectant into one wound, it will run out the other.

The spearmen have assured me that a lion's most dangerous weapon is neither his teeth nor his claws proper but what might be called his dewclaws. On the inside of each lion's forelegs is an extra claw about two inches long. These claws roughly correspond to a man's thumbs. They are curved and very sharp. The dewclaws are usually kept folded against the lion's legs and are difficult to see, but the lion can extend them at will so they stand out almost at right angles. These two claws are keen as brush hooks and very strong. A lion slashes with them and can disembowel a man with one blow of these terrible hooks.

The Masai spears are made by native smiths from bits of iron ore picked up in the streams. The smiths do not understand the art of tempering the metal so the spears are soft. A man can easily bend the blade over his knee. But the moran are able to throw their weapons with such skill that the spear will sometimes pass completely through an animal. If the spear strikes a bone, it will bend almost at right angles. The owner never straightens the blade until he returns to the village. The bent spear is proof positive that he was in at the kill, and so is highly prized.

While I was in the reserve, I also saw the Masai spear leopards. I consider this an even greater feat than killing lions. Although a leopard does not weigh more than two hundred pounds, he is far quicker and more aggressive than a lion. Leopards are cunning beasts and will lie quietly until you are almost on top of them. Then they will suddenly charge with the deadliest speed and determination. Also, leopards lie up in caves and other dark recesses, while lions prefer the open bush. A man crawling among boulders after a leopard is in an unenviable position.

I accompanied three spearmen who were after a leopard that had been killing their goats. Unlike the noble lions, a leopard will kill for the sheer lust of killing. This cat had left several dead goats behind him, never even bothering to eat their flesh. After considerable tracking, the moran finally marked the animal down in a narrow belt of high grass. If the cat had been a lion, a few stones would have brought him out charging or at least forced him to growl and show his hiding place. But a leopard is a wily brute and, although we threw a bushel of stones into the grass, he gave no sign. Unfortunately, I did not have my dogs with me so there was nothing for it but to drive the animal out.

With only three spearmen, I was able to use my gun without fear of hitting one of the men. I told the moran to spread out on either side of me and keep well back. I knew when the leopard came, he would come fast. I was sure that the men would not have time to use their spears, and I would have scarcely time for a quick snap shot at the cat as he sprang. I was underrating the moran, but I still did not realize their marvelous skill with their long, delicate blades.

We moved slowly through the waist-high grass, much as though beating for pheasants. The moran kept a few paces behind me, their shields held before them and their spears raised for the cast. We moved forward a foot at a time, stopping constantly to look around for the big cat. The strip of grass was not long, but this slow progress was nerve-racking, especially as we were all at a high point of tension.

Suddenly the leopard exploded out of the grass a yard or so in front of me and to my right. He made a great bound for me. Before I could get my rifle up, the moran on my right had transfixed the beast with his spear. The leopard had scarcely left the ground before the thin blade was through him. The spear hit the leopard between the neck and shoulders, pinning him to the ground. He lay there squirming and snarling, unable to free himself. Immediately the moran drew his simi and leaped forward to finish him off. I had great difficulty restraining him until I had time to put a bullet into the skewered animal and save a good skin from being slashed to ribbons.

When a moran is about to throw his spear, he takes up a position just like a shooting stance with his left foot slightly advanced for balance. When he throws, the whole weight of his body goes into the cast. The spear seems to shiver as it flies through the air. Most of the spears have a narrow ridge on either side of the blade and I believe this may cause the spear to rotate slightly in flight, somewhat like a rifle bullet. A moran is absolutely accurate with his spear up to twenty yards, even when throwing at a moving target.

At the end of three months, I started back to Nairobi with two oxcarts full of lion hides. In ninety days, I had shot eighty-eight lions and ten leopards—a record which I believe has never been approached and, I sincerely hope, will never be approached again. The natives had filled a hundred-weight drum with lion fat. I had a box full of lion "floating bones." These curved bones vary in size up to four inches and are found in the last shoulder muscle tissue. They are not attached to any other bones in the lion's body and apparently act as regulators, preventing shoulder rack when the lions make their great bounds. They are much in demand among the East Indians, who set them in gold and make ornaments out of them.

Only twenty of the lions I killed had really prime manes. The rest were either lionesses or had manes ruined by the thick brush. If I had been shooting only to get good trophies, I could have obtained more first-rate hides, but I was more interested in destroying cattle killers. Often these beasts had poor manes, for they were old or diseased, which may well be why they had turned to killing cows instead of their natural prey.

When the Masai heard I was leaving, they were greatly distressed. The elders of the tribe assembled and, after much jabbering, came to me with a proposition. They wanted to buy me from the Game Department. After due consideration, they had settled on five hundred cows as the price. As a good wife costs only three cows, I felt highly flattered.

Questions and Comments

1. In several passages Hunter mentions facts about lions and hunting which he obviously learned from close observation and experience. State at least three such facts.

2. What is a "melombuki"? What is the unwritten law among the Masai about a melombuki?

3. What does the author consider more dangerous to spear, a lion or a leopard? Why?

4. What is the Masai attitude toward injury and pain? Does this seem reasonable to you? Why or why not? Might such an attitude have developed through necessity over the centuries?

5. What impression do you get of the Masai people from the author's account of their hunts? What impression do you get of the author from this selection? Point out passages in the selection that help to give you an idea of his character.

Word Study

1. *Antiseptic, antifreeze, antiaircraft* and *antidote* should together give you a good idea as to what *anti* means. Look up *septic* in a dictionary and put its meaning with that of *anti*. List five more words which begin with *anti*.

2. *Trans* means "across," "beyond," "over," or "through" and is one of the common Latin prefixes used in English. Which of the given prefix meanings would you put with *fix* in order to fit the context in the account by Mr. Hunter: "the moran on my right had *transfixed* the beast with his spear"?

3. *Purchase* is a common word but is used here in an uncommon way. What does it mean in the context "The lioness was digging her hind feet into the ground to get *purchase* forward"?

4. Guess at the meanings of the following words from their context. Check your guesses against dictionary meanings.

   "We picked up the *spoor* of the lion and the moran began to track." (page 4)

   ". . . the wounded boy was urged to eat great quantities of raw beef and then given cattle blood as a *purgative* so he could *gorge* himself again." (pages 6–7)

   ". . . nothing could be heard above the wild *falsetto* yells of the warriors and the deep grunts of the lion as he *lacerated* the prostrate man." (page 9)

   "A lion slashes with them and can *disembowel* a man with one blow of these terrible hooks." (page 10)

Composition

1. In a brief essay discuss the merit of film accounts versus written accounts of the same incident. Discuss which method you feel can achieve greater truth, greater dramatic impact.

2. Discuss Masai attitudes toward pain and personal courage. Contrast these attitudes with your own beliefs on the same subjects.

3. Discuss in a short essay your own feelings concerning the hunt.

H. Allen Smith was an extremely humorous writer whose essays regularly appeared in all the top American magazines. "The Bright Side of Pessimism" comes from *A Short History of Fingers* (1960), in which he writes, "I discovered in putting this book together that I am a miscellaneous writer. Why? Because I'll tackle anything." His essays range from Fetridge's Law (things which are supposed to happen never do, especially when someone is looking) to the use of whiskey for snakebite.

THE BRIGHT SIDE
OF PESSIMISM

H. Allen Smith

MEMBERS of my family tell me that when I was a boy I had uncombed reddish hair and freckles, went barefooted all summer, and usually wore faded corduroy knickerbockers[1] and a frayed blue shirt (known then, even among boys, as a waist). I must have presented just such a charming picture on that warm day when I saw my first shell game in a downtown park in Decatur, Illinois.

The fast-talking grifter was shifting the walnut shells around with eye-dazzling rapidity and then challenging the adult yokels to pick the shell with the pea beneath it. I had never seen a shell game in operation before. I knew nothing about the evil ways of the world and yet something caused me to pipe up in a shrill adolescent voice: "Maybe it ain't under none ubbem!" (That is the way I talked when I was a kid; that is the way I still talk).

---

[1] *knickerbockers:* boys' pants which end below the knee and clasp tightly around the leg

A silence fell on the proceedings and the yentzer[1] glared at me a long time and then delivered a loud public denunciation of me. "Ladies and genmun," he said, "this here boy you see before you, this here miserable little boy, he is gonna grow up to be a pessimist. He is already a pessimist and he will grow up to be a worse one. And if you didn't already know it, ladies and genmun, there is nothing on earth as lowdown as a pessimist." I feel sure that nobody in that audience knew what a pessimist was. Certainly I did not. I can remember that when the pitchman first began directing his eloquence against me I felt a momentary glow, a warm sense of importance, but pretty soon I was cringing beneath his bitter tongue-lashing (you see the pea really *wasn't* under none ubbem) and I crept away from the scene, for the people were beginning to glare at me as if I were an anarchist with a bomb in my waist.

This experience remained strong in my memory and eventually I looked up the word pessimist to find out what I was. I do know that since that time I have been a pessimist in almost everything I do. For years I believed that the shell game man was responsible for my condition—that I was a pessimist because he had called me one at a time when I was impressionable. But now I know better. I don't necessarily want to be a pessimist; I never sat down and decided that I would be one. I'm pessimistic by nature; I believe that true cynicism and skepticism and pessimism are characteristics that are not studied and deliberate—they are bred deep in the bone. The person possessing them cannot help himself; it is the same as being a Socialist or a Barnburner[2] or a Zen Buddhist[3] or the Life of the Party.

The dictionary definition of pessimism which fits me best is: "The tendency to expect misfortune or the worst outcome

[1] *yentzer:* a swindler or cheater

[2] *Barnburner:* member of a reform group of the Democratic party of New York in the 1840's, named for a man who burned his barn to rid it of rats

[3] *Zen Buddhist:* a member of a school of Buddhism that teaches self-discipline, meditation, and knowledge through direct intuitive insight

in any circumstances; practice of looking on the dark side of things." It is as if the dictionary people were writing my biography.

I contend that I lead a much more sensible life, because of my pessimism, than I would otherwise. I even make so bold as to say that I lead a more sensible life than my optimistic neighbors. I am always and forever anticipating misfortune and disaster, large and small. I am continually amused by people who have "premonitions" about airplanes crashing with themselves or their loved ones aboard. We read in the newspapers that a man who was killed in a crash told his friends or his family before take-off that he had a strong premonition of tragedy. Or, one of his friends or a member of his family had the premonition. Even the newspapers hint that there is something truly supernatural about these affairs. But I know better. I'm quite sure in my own mind that there is no extrasensory perception involved. *Every damn time I climb into a plane I murmur a sad and silent farewell to the world.* And I'm sure that there are many others like me. I feel quite positive that *this is it.* That this is the time I get it. And I have the same sensations each time I take friends or relatives to the airport and put them on a plane. I give each of them a final lingering look, knowing deep inside of me that it is the last time I'll see them alive.

What's good about this attitude? Why, you can't imagine how superbly elated I feel when they arrive safely at their destination. And as for me—I feel absolutely ecstatic when *I* make it.

To a somewhat lesser degree the same emotions are present when I start on an automobile trip. I prepare for every emergency that the human mind can possibly anticipate, even though I know that such precautions will never save me. I have flares that will guide rescue workers to the wreck of my car in the canyon, and rope for getting out of inaccessible gullies; I carry knives and a hatchet and a first-aid kit

big enough for the U.S. Marine units in the Iwo Jima[1] land-
ings. Even with all this I have a strong feeling that I am on
my final expedition and I usually give my house a last
affectionate look just before driving away from it. I must
confess that I am not at all logical about my automobile
premonitions; if I'm making only a short trip, say downtown
to the beer store, I don't contemplate anything more serious
than a concussion and perhaps a broken leg; if I'm driving
merely to the corner, I figure on just a few minor cuts.

I live in the country three miles from the nearest
firehouse. I always knew that some day my house would
catch on fire. I always figured that it would burn to the
ground and burn me and my family with it. In my anticipa-
tory, pessimistic thinking I was certain that when the dire
moment came I would panic. Occasionally I would speculate
on just how it would happen. How would it start? Would
the roof take fire from the chimney? Would the nearby
woods burn and throw flaming embers onto my house and
set it afire? Would the electrical wiring be responsible? And
what would I do when the fire was discovered? Would I faint
dead away, or throw a fit, or just start running in a westerly
direction? One thing I knew: my behavior in the crisis would
be so shameful that I would stand embarrassed before the
world. That is, if I survived. Which I wouldn't.

And so one December morning it happened. The thermom-
eter stood at ten above zero and a high wind was blowing.
The house caught fire from a defective oil burner. My family
still talks proudly of how I behaved. I was noble, almost
heroic. I took charge. I did everything exactly as it should
have been done, and in the proper sequence. I telephoned
for the fire department. I quickly instructed my family in
what to do for safety's sake. I got the cars out of the garage
where the fire was centered and I had a garden hose hooked
up and a stream playing on the flames before the first fire
truck arrived. I'm inclined to think that my pessimism was

[1]*Iwo Jima:* a small island in the Pacific; site of a famous landing and battle
during World War II

responsible for my exemplary behavior during the emergency. If I had never once thought of the possibility of fire, if I had never considered ways and means of coping with it, *then* I think I'd have been helpless when it came.

My pessimism extends into my business. I write books and magazine articles. Whenever I finish the long rough job of writing a book I sit and shudder a while, thinking of the horrible things the critics will say about it, thinking of how book buyers will ignore it from coast to coast. Thus, when I do get nasty reviews they don't bother me—I expected them; if I happen to get some praise it comes as a surprise and makes me happy. And if the book is a flop in sales, okay—I knew all along that it would be. On the other hand if it should sell well and make me a lot of money, my pleasure is almost beyond describing. I've written scores of magazine articles and short stories and each time I finish one of them I read it over and arrive at the conclusion that no editor could possibly be so stupid as to buy it. When an editor does, I'm the happiest man in forty square miles.

I can give you a concrete example of how my pessimism works in my favor in the business world. One summer afternoon my agent telephoned me and told me to get a firm grip on something solid and then he said, "Mike Todd[1] has agreed to buy the movie rights to your novel for . . . hold on now! . . . *one hundred thousand dollars.*"

"That's nice," I said. This was at a time when a hundred thousand dollars was almost top price for the movie rights to a book. "Listen," I said. "I'm watching a hot ball game and the Giants have the bases loaded. Let me call you back later for the details."

My agent still tells people about my casual manner, my almost total lack of response, my excitement over a baseball game in the face of such splendid news. Actually, it was my devout pessimism at work. The sum of a hundred thousand dollars was, and still is, almost astronomical to my mind, yet

[1] *Mike Todd:* famous movie producer, now deceased

I knew what it meant. At the same time I didn't believe a word of it. My mind told me that nothing on earth could ever happen that would fetch me a hundred thousand dollars all in a lump. So I went back to my ball game and put Mike Todd and his money out of my mind.

Later on I had a meeting with Todd, and a contract was drawn and signed by him, and then I signed it in my agent's office. It was placed in an envelope and mailed and the next step, on the following day, would be the delivery to me of the hundred thousand. It was never delivered. The following morning, perhaps an hour before that envelope arrived in Mike Todd's office, somebody went to court and forced him into bankruptcy. I never got a penny out of him. But it was all right. I had known all along that I wouldn't.

James Branch Cabell[1] once uttered an interesting definition of pessimism: "The optimist proclaims that we live in the best of all possible worlds; and the pessimist fears this is true." And somebody else said: "A pessimist is one who feels bad when he feels good for fear he'll feel worse when he feels better."

These definitions jibe with my own philosophy, in a way. I seldom suffer the awful disappointments that are the lot of most people. An optimist refuses to let himself dwell on tragedies to come. A pessimist thinks of them all the time. Let us consider a tragedy that may seem trivial to people who are not dog owners. Almost from the moment I acquired my dog I knew that the time would come when he would die—probably on my order. I often thought of that eventuality, and felt sad about it, but I knew it had to happen and when it came it wasn't nearly as rough as it has been with some of my neighbors. I had prepared myself for it; I had, in effect, lived through the death of my dog many times before it happened.

My pessimism covers almost every phase of my day-to-day life. If I should make a bet on a horse or a ball game I have

[1] *James Branch Cabell:* American humorist, novelist, and essayist (1879-1958)

no hope whatever of winning—it is just as if I had taken the money and thrown it to the winds; and if I do win I am delirious with joy. If I get a pimple or some sort of minor interior ache I race for the doctor's office, knowing in advance what his diagnosis will be: malignant. These and countless other pessimistic judgments and conclusions make me, in the long run, a happy and contented man.

The true pessimist has great material to work with nowadays. I have reference to The Bomb.[1] I can't truthfully say that I'm ready for it, though I know for certain that it is on the way. Optimistic people scoff at me and exclaim, "Why, don't be ridiculous, nobody is going to drop The Bomb!" And my answer to them is: "Somebody did. Twice."

In common with most of my fellow citizens I am doing nothing about it. Sometimes I try to think of a way to escape, but my mind always returns to the shrewd Australian who figured out, well in advance, the course that World War II would take, then chose a spot for himself where reason and logic told him no shot would ever be heard: the island of Guadalcanal.[2]

Being convinced that The Bomb will fall, I decided for a while that I would go to Mexico and take up residence in one of that country's mountain-girt valleys. I felt that in some place like Taxco I would escape the fiery blast and that if the fallout got me, it would be comparatively gentle, maybe like twilight sleep. Then my pessimism asserted itself. I knew that if I got into a Mexican valley, one of those tremendous rockets would leap from its pad at Cape Canaveral and, instead of following its prescribed course out over the Atlantic, it would somehow twist itself around, arc into Mexico and land right on my adobe hacienda.

I can't win but I have a lot of fun losing. And when I realize that many other people, who anticipate only eventualities

---

[1] *The Bomb:* atomic or H-Bomb

[2] *Guadalcanal:* an island in the Pacific; site of prolonged and heavy fighting during World War II

that are pleasant and healthful, spend much of their time groaning and whining about the unpredictable cruelty of fate, then I feel good; I get to feeling downright optimistic about my pessimism.

Questions and Comments

Titles of other books Mr. Smith has written are *The Pig in the Barber Shop, How to Write Without Knowing Nothing,* and *Two-Thirds of a Coconut Tree.*

1. Why does the author say that even as a child he was a pessimist?

2. The author claims that he leads a more sensible life because of his pessimism. Why?

3. Cite three examples the author gives which illustrate the bright side of pessimism.

4. What is the deeper meaning of James Branch Cabell's definition of pessimism?

5. At what point in the selection do you become aware that this is going to be a humorous essay?

Word Study

1. *Grifter* is a slang expression which the author uses to describe the operator of the shell game. What do you think a grifter probably is? Look up *grifter* in a dictionary.

2. *Loquor* is a Latin word meaning "speak," "say," "talk." It appears, in part, in *eloquence* on page 16, but is also contained in several other English words such as *loquacious, colloquialism, soliloquy,* and *ventriloquist.* What does *eloquent* mean? Look up the other words.

3. *Anarchist* is a simple word to analyze. *An,* "no," and *archos,* the Greek word for "ruler," together mean "no ruler" or "no government"—a good definition of *anarchy.* What does *anarchist* mean? Can you think of other words having to do with government which have the form *archy* in them?

4. The author states, "I believe that true *cynicism* and *skepticism* and pessimism are characteristics that are not studied and deliberated—they are bred deep in the bone." Look up the italicized words in a dictionary and distinguish between their meanings.

5. *Extrasensory perception,* or ESP, is an expression used by psychologists to describe perceptive powers that can not be scientifically explained. What other word in the essay is used to mean somewhat the same thing? See page 17.

6. *Adobe* and *hacienda* came into English, particularly American English, from the Spanish. What is an adobe hacienda? What other words of Spanish origin are commonly used in the southwestern United States? Why do you think this Spanish influence is so common there?

Composition

1. At the conclusion of his essay the author says, "I can't win but I have a lot of fun losing." Discuss your opinion of this remark and tell whether you feel that the lesson taught by the author is a valuable one.

2. Study your own outlook on life. Which are you? Pessimist or optimist? A little of both? In a brief essay explain your outlook.

Eleanor Roosevelt (1884-1962) was a world famous humanitarian and the wife of Franklin Delano Roosevelt, thirty-second president of the United States. In this chapter from her autobiography, Eleanor Roosevelt writes of a trip she and her granddaughter Nina made to Israel and Iran in the spring of 1959. The visit worried Mrs. Roosevelt, particularly the reluctance of Middle Eastern nations to accept democratic traditions. She wrote, "We must be prepared, like the suitor in *The Merchant of Venice*—and, I might point out, the successful suitor—to give and hazard all we have." She wrote of her faith in the young people of the world and set down for young Americans her concept of the American Dream. Rather than a dream, however, her concept becomes a striking challenge to young Americans, a challenge they must volunteer to accept if the American Dream is to survive.

THE AMERICAN DREAM

Eleanor Roosevelt

WHAT I had learned on these two trips was much on my mind when I returned home. Why, I wondered, were we not more successful in helping the young nations and those in transition to become established along democratic lines? Why was it that the Russians were doing so much better? The answer can be oversimplified and an oversimplification is false and misleading. But part of the answer, and I thought a major part, was that Russia had trained its young people to go out into the world, to carry their services and skills to backward and underdeveloped countries, to replace the missing doctors and teachers, the scientists and technicians; above all, to fill the vacant civil service jobs, prepared not only by training for the job itself but by a complete briefing in the customs, habits, traditions and trend of thought of the people, to understand them and deal with them. Where they go, of course, they take with them their Marxist[1] training, thinking and system.

And our young Americans? Were they being prepared to take their faith in democracy to the world along with their skills? Were they learning the language and the customs and the history of these new peoples? Did they understand how to deal with them, not according to their own ideas but according to the ideas of the people they must learn to know if they were to reach them at all? Had they acquired an ability to live and work among peoples of different religion and race and color, without arrogance and without prejudice?

Here, I believe, we have fallen down badly. In the past few years I have grasped at every opportunity to meet with the young, to talk with college students, to bring home as strongly as I can to even young children in the lower grades our responsibility for each other, our need to understand and respect each other. The future will be determined by the young and there is no more essential task today, it seems to me, than to bring before them once more, in all its brightness, in all its splendor and beauty, the American Dream, lest we let it fade, too concerned with ways of earning a living or impressing our neighbors or getting ahead or finding bigger and more potent ways of destroying the world and all that is in it.

No single individual, of course, and no single group has an exclusive claim to the American Dream. But we have all, I think, a single vision of what it is, not merely as a hope and an aspiration but as a way of life, which we can come ever closer to attaining in its ideal form if we keep shining and unsullied our purpose and our belief in its essential value.

That we have sometimes given our friends and our enemies abroad a shoddy impression of the Dream cannot be denied, much as we would like to deny it. *The Ugly*

[1]*Marxist:* relating to the philosophies of Karl Marx, co-author with Friedrich Engels, of the *Communist Manifesto*

American,[1] impressive as it was, struck me as being exaggerated. True, one of the first American ambassadors I ever met in an Eastern country was appallingly like the title character in the novel. There are doubtless many others, too many others; men who accept—and seek—the position of representative of their government abroad with no real interest or respect for the country they go to, and no real interest or respect for the image of their country which they present to other people.

Such men buy their position by gifts of money to their party or seek them because of the glamorous social life they may lead in exotic places.

"Oh, you must go there. You'll have a wonderful time. And the polo is top-notch."

They often do not know the language of the country; they are not familiar with its government or its officials; they are not interested in its customs or its point of view.

The Russians—and I say it with shame—do this better. They are trained in the language, history, customs and ways of life of a country before they go to it. They do not confine themselves to official entertaining but make a point of meeting and knowing and establishing friendly relations with people of all sorts, in every class of society, in every part of the country.

When we look at the picture of Russian greed in swallowing one satellite nation after another and contrast it with the picture of American generosity in giving food, clothing, supplies, technical and financial assistance, with no ulterior motive in acquiring new territory, it is stupid and tragic waste that the use of incompetent representatives should undo so much useful work, so great an expense, so much in the way of materials of every kind.

Of course, what the Russians have accomplished in training their young people for important posts in the underde-

[1]The Ugly American: a novel by William J. Lederer and Eugene Burdick which shows the American diplomat in a very poor light; later a movie

veloped countries—which, I must repeat, may affect the future course of these countries—has been done by compulsion. That's the rub. For what we must do is to achieve the same results on a voluntary basis. We do not say to our young people: "You must go here and take such a job." But we can show them that where we fail the Russians will win, by default. We can show them the importance of acquiring the kind of training that will make them useful and honorable representatives of their country wherever they may go abroad.

Perhaps the new frontier today is something more than the new revolution in textiles and methods and speed and goods. It is the frontier of men's minds. But we cannot cast an enduring light on other men's minds unless the light in our own minds burns with a hard, unquenchable flame.

One form of communication we have failed abjectly in: the teaching of languages. Most school children have several years of inadequate teaching in one language or another. I say inadequate because the study of a language, after all, is inadequate if one cannot learn to read and write it, to speak and to understand it. During World War II the government found a simplified and most effective method of teaching such difficult languages as Japanese and Chinese to American GIs. In a matter of weeks they had mastered more of the language than formerly they would have acquired in the same number of years. And yet in our schools the old, cumbersome, unproductive methods are still in use.

It seems to me so obvious that it should not need to be said that we must increase and improve the teaching of languages to our young people, who will otherwise find themselves crippled and sorely handicapped in dealing with people of foreign races and different cultures.

These are things our children should be told. These are the conditions they are going to have to meet. They ought to be made to understand exactly what competition they will encounter, why they must meet it, how they can meet it best. Yet I rarely find, in talking with them, that they have been given the slightest inkling of the meaning of the Soviet infiltration of other countries, or that the future the Soviets are helping to build is the one with which they will have to contend. I rarely find that anyone has suggested that our own young people should have any preparation whatsoever to cope with the problems that are impending.

That is why, in the course of the past several years, I have fitted into my schedule, wherever I could, occasions to talk with the young. Sometimes they come up to Hyde Park[1] by the busload to ask questions or to discuss problems. Sometimes I talk at their schools or colleges.

Last year, in co-operation with Brandeis University, I ex perimented with a new idea. I agreed to do a series of nine television programs, which were then sold to education television stations throughout the country. It worked so well that this year I have agreed to do ten programs.

In addition to this, I lectured to a class given by Dr. Fuchs on international law and international organization at Brandeis. There were only thirteen in the class, all students who hoped to go into foreign service either for business or for the government, five of them students from foreign countries. I was a little staggered by this assignment, as I felt sure that many of these young people were better versed in questions of international organization than I was. But at least I could discuss with them the tangled problems of foreign politics.

This, of course, was a specialized sort of lecture course, and I found it interesting and stimulating, as I have always found teaching. But what I would have preferred to say to these young people was something like the following:

Today our government and the governments of most of the world are primarily concerned—obsessed—by one idea: defense. But what is real defense and how is it obtained? Of

---

[1] *Hyde Park:* New York residence of President and Mrs. Franklin Delano Roosevelt

course, a certain amount of military defense is necessary. But there comes a point where you must consider what can be done on an economic and cultural basis.

It seems to me that, in terms of atomic warfare, we should henceforth have a small professional army[1] of men who have voluntarily chosen military service as an obligation to their country. But what then? What about the hundreds of thousands of young people who leave school every year, either from high school or from college? Are they, from now on, to have no participation in contributing to the welfare of their country?

Far from it. As matters stand, we draft young men into the service, train them until they are useful, and then let them go. This seems to me monstrous waste.

It has long been my personal conviction that every young person should be given some basic training that might, eventually, be useful to his country. As I thought about it, it seemed to me that this could be handled either in school or at college, and instead of calling all young men up for compulsory military service, we could offer an alternative along these lines:

Whether you finish college, or high school, you may, if you do not want to spend two years of compulsory military training, decide what country you would like to spend two years in. You will be given two years of basic training, either during school hours or in the evenings. If you want to go, say, to Africa or to other underdeveloped countries, you will, from the age of fifteen to seventeen, be taught the language, the history, the geography, the economic background of the country. You will be prepared to take with you a skill, or be trained for the most crying need in many transition nations, to fill the civil service jobs that Russia is now so rapidly filling. Or, if you are preparing for a profession, you may make use of that.

New industries are needed in these countries, there are

---

[1] *a small professional army:* the United States repealed the Draft Law in 1973 and maintains an all-volunteer army

technical needs in almost all areas. The economy has to be bolstered in countless ways. New techniques are required in agriculture. And nearly all of these countries need teachers badly.

I was greatly interested and pleased to hear that Chester Bowles's[1] son turned down a scholarship at Oxford University to go to Nigeria, where he plans to teach in high school for two years.

What is saving Ghana today is that Sir Robert Jackson[2] remained in the country after the withdrawal of Great Britain. He is using all his great experience and intelligence on behalf of the people as economic adviser to the Volta River Project.[3] He is also being aided by his brilliant wife, the famous economist, Barbara Ward.

For people in young nations, which are still in a transition stage and setting up governments, such help could be more valuable than a large standing army or economic aid, particularly when in the new country there are few people capable of administering it effectively.

As I have said, this training and use of our young has been long in my mind. Wherever and whenever I could I have advocated it. Recently with the announcement of the Peace Corps, it appears that a similar plan will at least have a fair trial. Some of our young people will be given the opportunity to take up the slack in underdeveloped countries, and to bring our skills and our attitudes and our principles to them as free men. I am delighted that this has been done, and am hopeful that it may prove to be one of the most fruitful ways we have found of sharing our American Dream with others.

President Kennedy has initiated a Peace Corps through which he hopes the ideals of young, and perhaps not so

[1] *Chester Bowles:* famous American diplomat and ambassador to India

[2] *Sir Robert Jackson:* chairperson of the Ghana Development Commission at that time

[3] *Volta River Project:* a power project on the Volta River in French West Africa

young, Americans may be expressed to people throughout the world, particularly in the underdeveloped countries which need help at the present time. The methods of choosing people and arranging with the recipient governments are still being worked out. Colleges and universities that have programs for exchange will be aided where their programs seem to be worthwhile. This will be an educational job for Americans, giving them an opportunity to get a better idea of the world in which they live and at the same time will show a spirit of service which is prevalent in this generation of Americans but which has not had great opportunity so far for expression.

A suggestion has also been made for a younger U.S. group of older high-school age to work on forestry and soil conservation throughout the U.S. This would seem to me of great value but as yet this is not even in the active planning stage as far as I know, though I hope it will materialize before very long.

I have said that the Russians have accomplished by compulsion what we must accomplish voluntarily. But there is one element of this Russian training that I have neglected to mention. I don't see why I neglected it, because it is of paramount importance. They have taught their young to feel that they are needed, that they are important to the welfare of their country. I think that one of the strongest qualities in every human being is a need to feel needed, to feel essential, to feel important. Too often our own youngsters do not feel that they are really essential to their country, or to the scheme of things. We have not had enough imagination to show them how very much we need every one of them to make us the kind of country that we can be.

In Austria, a short time ago, Mr. Khrushchev[1] said that he expected a Communist world in his lifetime. We have no time to waste.

[1] *Mr. Khrushchev:* **Premier of Russia 1958-1964**

All this, you may say, is far from the American Dream. Not at all. The American Dream can no more remain static than can the American nation. What I am trying to point out is that we cannot any longer take an old approach to world problems. They aren't the same problems. It isn't the same world. We must not adopt the methods of our ancestors; instead, we must emulate that pioneer quality in our ancestors that made them attempt new methods for a New World.

For instance, we are pioneers today in the field of automation. There is no possibility of holding back automation, but we can, at least, profit by the mistakes of the past in dealing with it. The industrial revolution, which began in Great Britain, put machinery into the mills and threw out the people to starve.

Eventually Great Britain was much better off as a result of the industrial revolution. But, because it was not prepared to cope with it at the time, a far-reaching and unexpected thing happened. Out of the industrial revolution and its abuses came Karl Marx.[1]

With automation we have a new situation and on the way we cope with it will depend the attitude of the world. Here we are the undisputed leaders. But we cannot handle it without planning. We must learn to foresee results before we act. We cannot afford, today, to throw a lot of people out of work without making some provision for them. True, the conscience of the people is different now; we would no longer sit by and let people starve and die. But if we are going to cope successfully, if we are to make this new technique a blessing to society and not a disaster, we have to make plans. We cannot blunder along, hoping things "will come out all right." Government, industry, labor, all these must use their best brains, must be aware of and accept their full responsibility for the situation.

[1] *Karl Marx:* German political philosopher and author of the Communist Manifesto; regarded as the father of modern communism

With decreased work hours there will come more leisure. What is to be done with it? Masses of people now working at machines, without any opportunity for self-improvement or bettering their condition, will be afforded new opportunities. But, unless we give them a background of education, they will not know how to make use of this opportunity for advancement. If they have no capacity for development, and no enterprise beyond sitting glued to a television screen, they will deteriorate as human beings, and we will have a great mass of citizens who are of no value to themselves or to their country or to the world.

It is a new industrial revolution that we are pioneering. The eyes of the world are on us. If we do it badly we will be criticized and our way of life downgraded. If we do it well we can become a beacon light for the future of the world.

And now, I see, my new concept of the American Dream is only the old one, after all. For, while those who started our government and fought for our right to be free may have thought in Old World terms to some extent, they, too, had a conception of the Dream being universal. The Thomas Jeffersons thought of education not for a handful, not even for their own country alone, but looked forward to the day when everyone, everywhere, would have the same opportunities. Today we have achieved so much more, in many ways, than our ancestors imagined that sometimes we forget that they dreamed not just for us but for mankind.

The American Dream is never entirely realized. If many of our young people have lost the excitement of the early settlers who had a country to explore and develop, it is because no one remembers to tell them that the world has never been so challenging, so exciting; the fields of adventure and new fields to conquer have never been so limitless. There is still unfinished business at home, but there is the most tremendous adventure in bringing the peoples of the world to an understanding of the American Dream. In this attempt to understand, to give a new concept of the relationships of mankind, there is open to our youngsters an infinite field of exciting adventure where the heart and the mind and the spirit can be engaged.

Perhaps the older generation is often to blame with its cautious warning: "Take a job that will give you security, not adventure." But I say to the young: "Do not stop thinking of life as an adventure. You have no security unless you can live bravely, excitingly, imaginatively; unless you can choose a challenge instead of a competence."

Questions and Comments

1. Why does Mrs. Roosevelt say that the Russians are more successful than the Americans in attracting young, underdeveloped nations to their political philosophy? What important difference does she point out between the Soviet and American approaches designed to help young nations develop?

2. According to Mrs. Roosevelt, what concerns of some Americans might get in the way of the American Dream?

3. What criticism does Mrs. Roosevelt make of some American representatives in foreign countries? Why does she claim that Russia's training of foreign representatives is superior to our own?

4. What is Mrs. Roosevelt's opinion of the teaching of foreign languages in our schools? Do you think she is right? Why?

5. Why does Mrs. Roosevelt feel that compulsory military training is a "monstrous waste"? What does she suggest as an alternative to the draft? What is her idea about maintaining a standing professional army?

6. What does Mrs. Roosevelt mean when she says, "We must emulate that pioneer quality in our ancestors"? In what field does she say we are pioneers today? What are some of

the dangers she feels exist for us as we develop this field?

7. Name some of the new fields of human activity in which America leads. What challenges do these fields constitute for the future?

8. What does Mrs. Roosevelt mean when she says, "And now, I see, my new concept of the American Dream is only the old one, after all"?

9. Who does Mrs. Roosevelt blame for the overcautious attitude of young people today? What is her advice to young people?

Word Study

1. Guess at the meanings of the following italicized words from the context of the selection and then check your guesses in a dictionary.

   "Had they acquired an ability to live and work among peoples of different religion and race and color, without *arrogance* and without prejudice?" (page 25)

   "That we have sometimes given our friends and our enemies abroad a *shoddy* impression of the Dream cannot be denied, much as we would like to deny it." (page 25)

   "Today our government and the governments of most the world are primarily concerned—*obsessed*—by one idea: defense." (page 28)

   "The economy has to be *bolstered* in countless ways." (page 29)

2. The Latin prefix *ab* means "from," "away from," or "down." *Jectus* is a Latin root meaning "cast." With this information make up your own definition of *abjectly* as in "One form of communication we have failed *abjectly* in."

3. *Impending* is a French adaptation of the Latin *pendere* meaning "to hang." Today *impending* means something a bit different: "threatening to occur soon," "approaching."

You should still be able to see the connection of present meaning with the former Latin meaning. What is it?

4. *Capio* is a Latin word meaning "hold," "take," or "seize," and appears in modern English words as *cap, capt, cip, cep.* What does a "recipient government" connected with our Peace Corps mean? List ten or more other words formed from *capio.*

Composition

1. Your personal opinion might clash with some of the statements made in this essay by Mrs. Roosevelt. In that case write a composition in which you take issue with some of Mrs. Roosevelt's beliefs and defend your own ideas.

2. Discuss your reaction to some of Mrs. Roosevelt's criticisms of American education and suggest what steps might be taken to improve it.

3. Discuss the part you hope to play some day in the American Dream.

James Baldwin (1924—) wrote in *Notes of a Native Son*, "I want to be an honest man and a good writer." He began plotting novels when he first began to read. Two books he read again and again were, *Uncle Tom's Cabin* and *A Tale of Two Cities*. When he was twelve he won his first prize for a short story. When a young man he was awarded many literary fellowships and awards.

This essay comes from *Nobody Knows My Name* (1954) which was written, says Baldwin in its "Introduction," ". . . over the past six years, in various places and in many states of mind." Other books by Baldwin are: *Go Tell it on the Mountain*, and *If Beale Street Could Talk*.

THE DISCOVERY
OF WHAT IT MEANS
TO BE AN AMERICAN

James Baldwin

"It is a complex fate to be an American," Henry James[1] observed, and the principal discovery an American writer makes in Europe is just how complex this fate is. America's history, her aspirations, her peculiar triumphs, her even more peculiar defeats, and her position in the world—yesterday and today—are all so profoundly and stubbornly unique that the very word "America" remains a new, almost completely undefined and extremely controversial proper noun. No one in the world seems to know exactly what it describes, not even we motley millions who call ourselves Americans.

I left America because I doubted my ability to survive

[1]*Henry James:* American novelist (1843-1916)

the fury of the color problem here. (Sometimes I still do.) I wanted to prevent myself from becoming *merely* a Negro; or, even, merely a Negro writer. I wanted to find out in what way the *specialness* of my experience could be made to connect me with other people instead of dividing me from them. (I was as isolated from Negroes as I was from whites, which is what happens when a Negro begins, at bottom, to believe what white people say about him.)

In my necessity to find the terms on which my experience could be related to that of others, Negroes and whites, writers and non-writers, I proved, to my astonishment, to be as American as any Texas G.I. And I found my experience was shared by every American writer I knew in Paris. Like me, they had been divorced from their origins, and it turned out to make very little difference that the origins of white Americans were European and mine were African— they were no more at home in Europe than I was.

The fact that I was the son of a slave and they were the sons of free men meant less, by the time we confronted each other on European soil, than the fact that we were both searching for our separate identities. When we had found these, we seemed to be saying, why, then, we would no longer need to cling to the shame and bitterness which had divided us so long.

It became terribly clear in Europe, as it never had been here, that we knew more about each other than any European ever could. And it also became clear that, no matter where our fathers had been born, or what they had endured, the fact of Europe had formed us both, was part of our identity and part of our inheritance.

I had been in Paris a couple of years before any of this became clear to me. When it did, I, like many a writer before me upon the discovery that his props have all been knocked out from under him, suffered a species of breakdown and was carried off to the mountains of Switzerland. There, in that absolutely alabaster landscape, armed with two Bessie Smith[1] records and a typewriter, I began to try to re-create the life that I had first known as a child and from which I had spent so many years in flight.

It was Bessie Smith, through her tone and her cadence, who helped me to dig back to the way I myself must have spoken when I was a pickaninny, and to remember the things I had heard and seen and felt. I had buried them very deep. I had never listened to Bessie Smith in America (in the same way that, for years, I would not touch watermelon), but in Europe she helped to reconcile me to being a "nigger."

I do not think that I could have made this reconciliation here. Once I was able to accept my role—as distinguished, I must say, from my "place"—in the extraordinary drama which is America, I was released from the illusion that I hated America.

The story of what can happen to an American Negro writer in Europe simply illustrates, in some relief, what can happen to any American writer there. It is not meant, of course, to imply that it happens to them all, for Europe can be very crippling, too; and, anyway, a writer, when he has made his first breakthrough, has simply won a crucial skirmish in a dangerous, unending and unpredictable battle. Still, the breakthrough is important, and the point is that an American writer, in order to achieve it, very often has to leave this country.

The American writer, in Europe, is released, first of all, from the necessity of apologizing for himself. It is not until he *is* released from the habit of flexing his muscles and proving that he is just a "regular guy" that he realizes how crippling this habit has been. It is not necessary for him, there, to pretend to be something he is not, for the artist does not encounter in Europe the same suspicion he encounters here. Whatever the Europeans may actually

[1]*Bessie Smith:* Black American jazz singer; also known as the "Empress of the Blues" (1898-1957)

think of artists, they have killed enough of them off by now to know that they are as real—and as persistent—as rain, snow, taxes or businessmen.

Of course, the reason for Europe's comparative clarity concerning the different functions of men in society is that European society has always been divided into classes in a way that American society never has been. A European writer considers himself to be part of an old and honorable tradition—of intellectual activity, of letters—and his choice of a vocation does not cause him any uneasy wonder as to whether or not it will cost him all his friends. But this tradition does not exist in America.

On the contrary, we have a very deep-seated distrust of real intellectual effort (probably because we suspect that it will destroy, as I hope it does, that myth of America to which we cling so desperately). An American writer fights his way to one of the lowest rungs on the American social ladder by means of pure bull-headedness and an indescribable series of odd jobs. He probably *has* been a "regular fellow" for much of his adult life, and it is not easy for him to step out of that lukewarm bath.

We must, however, consider a rather serious paradox: though American society is more mobile than Europe's, it is easier to cut across social and occupational lines there than it is here. This has something to do, I think, with the problem of status in American life. Where everyone has status, it is also perfectly possible, after all, that no one has. It seems inevitable, in any case, that a man may become uneasy as to just what his status is.

But Europeans have lived with the idea of status for a long time. A man can be as proud of being a good waiter as of being a good actor, and in neither case feel threatened. And this means that the actor and the waiter can have a freer and more genuinely friendly relationship in Europe than they are likely to have here. The waiter does not feel, with obscure resentment, that the actor has "made it," and the actor is not tormented by the fear that he may find himself, tomorrow, once again a waiter.

This lack of what may roughly be called social paranoia causes the American writer in Europe to feel—almost certainly for the first time in his life—that he can reach out to everyone, that he is accessible to everyone and open to everything. This is an extraordinary feeling. He feels, so to speak, his own weight, his own value.

It is as though he suddenly came out of a dark tunnel and found himself beneath the open sky. And, in fact, in Paris, I began to see the sky for what seemed to be the first time. It was borne in on me—and it did not make me feel melancholy—that this sky had been there before I was born and would be there when I was dead. And it was up to me, therefore, to make of my brief opportunity the most that could be made.

I was born in New York, but have lived only in pockets of it. In Paris, I lived in all parts of the city—on the Right Bank and the Left, among the bourgeoisie[1] and among *les misérables*,[2] and knew all kinds of people, from pimps and prostitutes in Pigalle[3] to Egyptian bankers in Neuilly.[4] This may sound extremely unprincipled or even obscurely immoral: I found it healthy. I love to talk to people, all kinds of people, and almost everyone, as I hope we still know, loves a man who loves to listen.

This perpetual dealing with people very different from myself caused a shattering in me of preconceptions I scarcely knew I held. The writer is meeting in Europe people who are not American, whose sense of reality is entirely different from his own. They may love or hate or admire or fear or envy this country—they see it, in any case, from another point of view, and this forces the writer to reconsider many things he had always taken for granted. This

---

[1]*bourgeoisie:* the middle class; property owners
[2]*les miserables:* the poor, poverty stricken of Paris
[3]*Pigalle:* theater, bar, and restaurant district of Paris
[4]*Neuilly:* upper-class residential suburb of Paris

reassessment, which can be very painful, is also very valuable.

This freedom, like all freedom, has its dangers and its responsibilities. One day it begins to be borne in on the writer, and with great force, that he is living in Europe as an American. If he were living there as a European, he would be living on a different and far less attractive continent.

This crucial day may be the day on which an Algerian taxi-driver tells him how it feels to be an Algerian in Paris. It may be the day on which he passes a café terrace and catches a glimpse of the tense, intelligent and troubled face of Albert Camus.[1] Or it may be the day on which someone asks him to explain Little Rock and he begins to feel that it would be simpler—and, corny as the words may sound, more honorable—to *go* to Little Rock than sit in Europe, on an American passport, trying to explain it.

This is a personal day, a terrible day, the day to which his entire sojourn has been tending. It is the day he realizes that there are no untroubled countries in this fearfully troubled world; that if he has been preparing himself for anything in Europe, he has been preparing himself—for America. In short, the freedom that the American writer finds in Europe brings him, full circle, back to himself, with the responsibility for his development where it always was: in his own hands.

Even the most incorrigible maverick has to be born somewhere. He may leave the group that produced him—he may be forced to—but nothing will efface his origins, the marks of which he carries with him everywhere. I think it is important to know this and even find it a matter for rejoicing, as the strongest people do, regardless of their station. On this acceptance, literally, the life of a writer depends.

The charge has often been made against American writers that they do not describe society, and have no interest in it.

---

[1] *Albert Camus:* French author and Nobel prize winner (1913–1960)

They only describe individuals in opposition to it, or isolated from it. Of course, what the American writer is describing is his own situation. But what is *Anna Karenina*[1]
describing if not the tragic fate of the isolated individual,
at odds with her time and place?

The real difference is that Tolstoy was describing an
old and dense society in which everything seemed—to the
people in it, though not to Tolstoy—to be fixed forever.
And the book is a masterpiece because Tolstoy was able
to fathom, and make us see, the hidden laws which really
governed this society and made Anna's doom inevitable.

American writers do not have a fixed society to describe.
The only society they know is one in which nothing is fixed
and in which the individual must fight for his identity.
This is a rich confusion, indeed, and it creates for the American writer unprecedented opportunities.

That the tensions of American life, as well as the possibilities, are tremendous is certainly not even a question.
But these are dealt with in contemporary literature mainly
compulsively; that is, the book is more likely to be a symp-
tom of our tension than an examination of it. The time
has come, God knows, for us to examine ourselves, but
we can only do this if we are willing to free ourselves of
the myth of America and try to find out what is really happening here.

Every society is really governed by hidden laws, by un-
spoken but profound assumptions on the part of the people,
and ours is no exception. It is up to the American writer to
find out what these laws and assumptions are. In a society
much given to smashing taboos without thereby managing
to be liberated from them, it will be no easy matter.

It is no wonder, in the meantime, that the American
writer keeps running off to Europe. He needs sustenance
for his journey and the best models he can find. Europe
has what we do not have yet, a sense of the mysterious

[1]*Anna Karenina:* famous novel written by Russian author, Leo Tolstoy (1828-
1910)

and inexorable limits of life, a sense, in a word, of tragedy. And we have what they sorely need: a new sense of life's possibilities.

In this endeavor to wed the vision of the Old World with that of the New, it is the writer, not the statesman, who is our strongest arm. Though we do not wholly believe it yet, the interior life is a real life, and the intangible dreams of people have a tangible effect on the world.

Questions and Comments

1. What does Baldwin discover about American black and white writers in Europe? How long did it take him to discover these ideas?

2. What were some of the major differences Baldwin describes between Europe and America?

3. What is the full meaning of "He may leave the group that produced him . . . but nothing will efface his origins, the marks of which he carries with him everywhere"?

4. Baldwin says, "The time has come, God knows, for us to examine ourselves, but we can only do this if we are willing to free ourselves of the myth of America and try to find out what is really happening here." What did Baldwin's years in Europe have to do with his making this statement? What does Baldwin mean in this statement? Has anything happened in recent years since this book was written to show that America is freeing itself from some of the myths?

Word Study

1. *Aspirations* comes from the Latin *aspiratus* "breathed on."
   Profoundly comes from the Latin *profundus* "deep."
   Unique comes from the Latin *unus* "one," "single."

   Using these Latin clues see how well you can deduce the meaning of each. Check yourself with the dictionary.

2. *Motley* is an interesting word which unexplainedly derives from the Middle-English word *mote* which means "speck." Find its modern meaning.

3. Tone and *cadence* are both basic "musts" for a singer. What do you think *cadence* means? Check your dictionary.

4. *Pickaninny* is a Negro Pidgin English version of a Portuguese word *pequenino* which means "very little." That clue should make it easy for you to figure out its meaning.

5. Check the following words as they appear in the essay and see if you can figure out their meanings from the context clues:

reconciliation (p. 39)	maverick (p. 42)
crucial (p. 39)	efface (p. 42)
skirmish (p. 39)	unprecedented (p. 43)
unpredictable (p. 39)	compulsively (p. 43)
paradox (p. 40)	taboos (p. 43)
preconceptions (p. 41)	sustenance (p. 43)
sojourn (p. 42)	inexorable (p. 44)
incorrigible (p. 42)	tangible (p. 44)

Be sure to look into the stories behind *taboo* and *maverick*.

Composition

1. Compose an essay in which you describe three or four American traits which a European would not know about typical Americans, but which native Americans readily recognize in themselves.

2. One of America's myth is the "best" myth: that anything American is best. Another myth is the "biggest" myth: the biggest cars, tallest buildings, largest cities, etc. Using these or other myths, choose one and discuss the actual truth of the matter and why these myths sometimes get in the way of Americans realizing who and what they really are.

3. Baldwin states that ". . . European society has always been

divided into classes in a way that American society never has been." Do you agree or disagree with this statement and why?

4. Discuss why Baldwin states at the end of the essay, "In this endeavor to wed the vision of the Old World with that of the New, it is the writer, not the statesman, who is our strongest arm."

5. Baldwin feels that the future promise of America is great. Can you describe your own dream of America's future, the kind of America you would like to see for your adult life and the life of your children?

Sojourner Truth (1797–1883) was illiterate and hence did not write the speech which follows; it was recorded by a listener. Sojourner Truth was a native New Yorker freed from slavery in 1827. Being black and a northerner did not help her popularity when she appeared in other states to speak in behalf of women and the rights of blacks. However, once she began to speak, her audience was compelled to listen. Not only what she said but the *way* she said it seemed to have a hypnotic effect on the audience.

AIN'T I A WOMAN?

Sojourner Truth

WELL, children, where there is so much racket there must be something out of kilter. I think that 'twixt the negroes of the South and the women at the North, all talking about rights, the white men will be in a fix pretty soon. But what's all this here talking about?

That man over there says that women need to be helped into carriages, and lifted over ditches, and to have the best place everywhere. Nobody ever helps me into carriages, or over mud-puddles, or gives me any best place! And ain't I a woman? Look at me! Look at my arm! I have ploughed and planted, and gathered into barns, and no man could head me! And ain't I a woman? I could work as much and eat as much as a man—when I could get it—and bear the lash as well! And ain't I a woman? I have borne thirteen children, and seen them most all sold off to slavery, and when I cried out with my mother's grief, none but Jesus heard me! And ain't I a woman?

Then they talk about this thing in the head; what's this they call it? [Intellect, someone whispers.] That's it, honey.

What's that got to do with women's rights or negro's rights? If my cup won't hold but a pint, and yours holds a quart, wouldn't you be mean not to let me have my little half-measure full?

Then that little man in black there, he says women can't have as much rights as men, 'cause Christ wasn't a woman! Where did your Christ come from? Where did your Christ come from? From God and a woman! *Man had nothing to do with Him.*

If the first woman God ever made was strong enough to turn the world upside down all alone, these women together ought to be able to turn it back, and get it right side up again! And now they is asking to do it, the men better let them.

Obliged to you for hearing me, and now old Sojourner ain't got nothing more to say.

Questions and Comments

1. There is a strong emotional appeal in Sojourner Truth's words; but there is also a strong and reasonable logic as well. Give examples of both the emotion and logic and explain how the combination creates a more effective argument.

2. What effective devices used in speaking and writing does Truth use in the second paragraph?

Word Study

Kilter is used frequently in conversation and informal usage. What does it mean, and how do you think it came into the language? Check its etymology in the *Oxford English Dictionary*.

Composition

1. Write a short up-to-date speech which a twentieth century

Sojourner Truth might make about a current controversial social issue.

2   Sojourner Truth uses ungrammatical, dialectical, informal levels of language in her speech. In a short essay explain why this use of language can be effective. Try to find public figures who still use this same approach; give some examples of their language use.

Virginia Woolf (1882-1941) was born into a British literary family. Her godfather, however, was a popular American poet, James Russell Lowell. Early in her marriage, she and her husband bought an old hand-press and began setting and handprinting their own stories and the works of several other contemporary writers who later became quite famous. T. S. Eliot and Katherine Anne Porter are two examples.

Virginia Woolf attained international fame for her novels, essays, and literary criticism. She was always interested in that "oppressed minority"—women—and in 1929 she wrote *A Room of One's Own*, which contains many of her opinions and ideas concerning that "oppressed half of the human race." Two of her most famous novels are *Mrs. Dalloway* (1925) and *To A Lighthouse* (1927). These are now considered modern classics.

The professor in this excerpt is someone she refers to as Professor von X, author of *The Mental, Moral, and Physical Inferiority of the Female Sex*. The professor, however, symbolizes anyone who could take such a title seriously.

from A ROOM OF ONE'S OWN

Virginia Woolf

SOME previous luncher had left the lunch edition of the evening paper on a chair, and, waiting to be served, I began idly reading the headlines. A ribbon of very large letters ran across the page. Somebody had made a big score in South Africa. Lesser ribbons announced that Sir Austen

Chamberlain[1] was at Geneva. A meat axe with human hair on it had been found in a cellar. Mr. Justice —— commented in the Divorce Courts upon the Shamelessness of Women. Sprinkled about the paper were other pieces of news. A film actress had been lowered from a peak in California and hung suspended in mid-air. The weather was going to be foggy. The most transient visitor to this planet, I thought, who picked up this paper could not fail to be aware, even from this scattered testimony, that England is under the rule of a patriarchy.[2] Nobody in their senses could fail to detect the dominance of the professor. His was the power and the money and the influence. He was the proprietor of the paper and its editor and sub-editor. He was the Foreign Secretary and the Judge. He was the cricketer; he owned the racehorses and the yachts. He was the director of the company that pays two hundred per cent to its shareholders. He left millions to charities and colleges that were ruled by himself. He suspended the film actress in mid-air. He will decide if the hair on the meat axe is human; he it is who will acquit or convict the murderer, and hang him, or let him go free. With the exception of the fog he seemed to control everything. Yet he was angry. I knew that he was angry by this token. When I read what he wrote about women I thought, not of what he was saying, but of himself. When an arguer argues dispassionately he thinks only of the argument; and the reader cannot help thinking of the argument too. If he had written dispassionately about women, had used indisputable proofs to establish his argument and had shown no trace of wishing that the result should be one thing rather than another, one would not have been angry either. One would have accepted the fact, as one accepts the fact that a pea is green or a canary yellow. So be it, I should have said. But I had

[1]*Sir Austen Chamberlain:* (1863–1937) British diplomat, author of *Peace in Our Time*

[2]*patriarchy:* a society based on male supremacy

been angry because he was angry. Yet it seemed absurd, I thought, turning over the evening paper, that a man with all this power should be angry. Or is anger, I wondered, somehow, the familiar, the attendant sprite on power? Rich people, for example, are often angry because they suspect that the poor want to seize their wealth. The professors, or patriarchs, as it might be more accurate to call them, might be angry for that reason partly, but partly for one that lies a little less obviously on the surface. Possibly they were not "angry" at all; often, indeed, they were admiring, devoted, exemplary in the relations of private life. Possibly when the professor insisted a little too emphatically upon the inferiority of women, he was concerned not with their inferiority, but with his own superiority. That was what he was protecting rather hot-headedly and with too much emphasis, because it was a jewel to him of the rarest price. Life for both sexes—and I looked at them, shouldering their way along the pavement—is arduous, difficult, a perpetual struggle. It calls for gigantic courage and strength. More than anything, perhaps, creatures of illusion as we are, it calls for confidence in oneself. Without self-confidence we are as babes in the cradle. And how can we generate this imponderable quality, which is yet so invaluable, most quickly? By thinking that other people are inferior to oneself. By feeling that one has some innate superiority—it may be wealth, or rank, a straight nose, or the portrait of a grandfather by Romney[1]—for there is no end to the pathetic devices of the human imagination—over other people. Hence the enormous importance to a patriarch who has to conquer, who has to rule, of feeling that great numbers of people, half the human race indeed, are by nature inferior to himself. It must indeed be one of the chief sources of his power. But let me turn the light of this observation on to real life, I thought. Does it help to explain some of those psychological puzzles that one notes

[1]*George Romney:* famous for painting the portraits of English nobility (1734–1802)

in the margin of daily life? Does it explain my astonishment the other day when Z, most humane, most modest of men, taking up some book by Rebecca West[1] and reading a passage in it, exclaimed, "The arrant feminist! She says that men are snobs!" The exclamation, to me so surprising—for why was Miss West an arrant feminist for making a possibly true if uncomplimentary statement about the other sex?—was not merely the cry of wounded vanity; it was a protest against some infringement of his power to believe in himself. Women have served all these centuries as looking-glasses possessing the magic and delicious power of reflecting the figure of man at twice its natural size. Without that power probably the earth would still be swamp and jungle. The glories of all our wars would be unknown. We should still be scratching the outlines of deer on the remains of mutton bones and bartering flints for sheepskins or whatever simple ornament took our unsophisticated taste. Supermen and Fingers of Destiny[2] would never have existed. The Czar and the Kaiser would never have worn their crowns or lost them. Whatever may be their use in civilised societies, mirrors are essential to all violent and heroic action. That is why Napoleon and Mussolini[3] both insist so emphatically upon the inferiority of women, for if they were not inferior, they would cease to enlarge. That serves to explain in part the necessity that women so often are to men. And it serves to explain how restless they are under her criticism; how impossible it is for her to say to them this book is bad, this picture is feeble, or whatever it may be, without giving far more pain and rousing far more anger than a man would do who gave the same criticism. For if she begins to tell the truth, the figure in the

---

[1]*Rebecca West:* English critic and novelist (1892–   )

[2]*Supermen and Fingers of Destiny:* each are representative phrases from philosophies developed in the 19th century by men and making little or no reference to women

[3]*Czar, Kaiser, Napoleon, Mussolini:* kings or dictators in Russia, Germany, France, and Italy, in that order

looking-glass shrinks; his fitness for life is diminished. How is he to go on giving judgement, civilising natives, making laws, writing books, dressing up and speechifying at banquets, unless he can see himself at breakfast and at dinner at least twice the size he really is? So I reflected, crumbling my bread and stirring my coffee and now and again looking at the people in the street. The looking-glass vision is of supreme importance because it charges the vitality; it stimulates the nervous system. Take it away and man may die, like the drug fiend deprived of his cocaine. Under the spell of that illusion, I thought, looking out of the window, half the people on the pavement are striding to work. They put on their hats and coats in the morning under its agreeable rays. They start the day confident, braced, believing themselves desired at Miss Smith's tea party; they say to themselves as they go into the room, I am the superior of half the people here, and it is thus that they speak with that self-confidence, that self-assurance, which have had such profound consequences in public life and lead to such curious notes in the margin of the private mind.

But these contributions to the dangerous and fascinating subject of the psychology of the other sex—it is one, I hope, that you will investigate when you have five hundred a year[1] of your own—were interrupted by the necessity of paying the bill. It came to five shillings[2] and ninepence.[3] I gave the waiter a ten-shilling note and he went to bring me change. There was another ten-shilling note in my purse; I noticed it, because it is a fact that still takes my breath away—the power of my purse to breed ten-shilling notes automatically. I open it and there they are. Society gives me chicken and coffee, bed and lodging, in return for a certain number of pieces of paper which were left me by an aunt, for no other reason than that I share her name.

[1] *five hundred a year:* five hundred pounds; at that time worth $2500, enough to live comfortably

[2] *shilling:* about $.25 in 1929; there are twenty shillings to a pound

[3] *pence:* plural in Britain for penny; a penny in Britain was half a shilling

Questions and Comments

1. Describe how Virginia Woolf proves the power of the patriarchs/professors.

2. Since this book was published in 1929, could her idea about man's concern for his superiority over women now be challenged? Why or why not?

3. Do women still play the "looking glass" role for men?

4. If men gain their self-confidence by thinking the female half of the human race is inferior, what is the source of women's self-confidence?

5. Virginia Woolf makes a very strong claim about what would have happened in human history if women had not reflected ". . . the figure of man at twice its natural size" (page 53). Do you think that this is an exaggeration? Why or why not?

Word Study

1. The prefix "dis" usually means the reversal of meaning of the word it precedes ie. *dis*honest, *dis*locate, etc. What is the meaning of *dispassionately* on page 51? Check with your dictionary.

2. *Sprite* on page 52 comes from the Old French *esprit* which comes from the Latin *spiritus* meaning "to breathe" or "blow." *Sprite* has two dictionary meanings: (1) ghost, shade; (2) elf, goblin, fairy. Which do you think fits best in the sentence where it is used?

3. Trace the Latin derivation of *exemplary* in a dictionary; you will have to go back to another English word before you are through.

4. *Arduous* should be easy to guess from its use on page 52. Check with your dictionary.

5. *Innate* combines two Latin parts—*in* which means "in," and *natus* which means "born." Put them together and you have the word's meaning.

6. *Arrant* on page 53 should be easy to figure out from the context. Check with your dictionary.

Composition

1. Describe Virginia Woolf's "looking glass" theory to a few of your friends, both male and female. Organize their reactions and opinions in a report.

2. Examine a recently published news magazine or newspaper and see if the male gender still dominates the content as it did in the author's day. Organize your findings in the same manner as the author in the beginning of her essay.

3. If you feel strongly about the current "women's movement," pro or con, react in an essay of your own.

4. Examine your community and school; then describe the effects the new social attitudes towards women have had locally. For example: has the high school sports program been affected?

Between a school's stated purpose and its actual performance can lie some interesting disparities. In *High School Students Speak Out* (1962) are some student's views on purpose and performance in their schools. Mr. Mallery visited eight high schools, the eight a mixture of public, private, denominational, small town, big city, just boys, just girls, and coeducational schools. The population in these schools varied from 450 to 5000 students. The regions visited were New England, Middle Atlantic, and Middle West.

During the course of a week's visit at a school, Mr. Mallery would provoke discussions by asking such questions as: "What are some of the things that have mattered most to you in your experience in this school?" "What are some of the things that you think account for the changes in you between, say, three years ago and now?" "What do you see as some of the real strengths of this school?"

YOU SACRIFICE LEARNING
FOR MARKS!

David Mallery

SCHOOL is not a place to get educated in. It's to get you into college.

I heard many comments like this in five of the eight schools I visited. These schools were situated in communities where the students and their parents were anxiety-ridden about the intense competition for admission to "prestige" colleges. In contrast, the students in the other three schools seemed puzzled when I mentioned the idea of tension about college admission.

seemed puzzled when I mentioned the idea of tension about college admission.[1]

The students in the schools where the tension was evident seemed to be torn by conflicting objectives. As one boy put it, "Our real aim—to grow intellectually—is blocked by this terrific marks-for-college hassle." In his school, an all-academic public high school with selective admissions, this idea of growing intellectually was expressed so frequently that I could only assume that the students were vitally concerned about it. Yet to them this objective seemed to be at odds with what one girl bitterly called "the neurotic obsession with college admission around here," and with what one boy called "this insane overemphasis on preparation for college."

The pressure starts early. It isn't just a matter of a little stimulating competition in the high school years. One description of the beginnings of the pressure reads like this:

I guess it began around the sixth grade in our community. The principal of the high school came over to our school to talk to us about college. I remember going home that night and asking my family if they thought I'd be able to get into college. That kind of thing pretty well conditions you from the sixth grade on. If you get it bad enough, there is really no room for intellectual expansion. You sacrifice learning for marks.

REGENTS[2] TENSIONS

Several New York schools offered conspicuous examples of the effects of pressures on the intellectual life of students. In these schools, students and teachers spoke of increased tensions which they attributed to the Regents examinations sys-

[1]*Author's note:* There is less pressure in private schools concerning college admission due to the social and economic advantages of those able to attend private schools, which can make a difference in entry to the expensive, prestige colleges

[2] *Regents:* a three-hour New York State exam given in June and January in each subject area. A student who qualifies by passing enough Regents in a variety of subject areas receives a Regents diploma.

tem. Some students described the constricting, frustrating routine of "boning up for the Regents." The kind of penetrating study that ambitious students and teachers said they would like to see in their classes seemed out of the question because of the combined effects of the college crush and the examinations.

The notion that "every tenth of a point is crucial in college admissions" would crop up in class after class. And with it would come talk about the Regents examinations' tendencies to dampen student interest and discourage intellectual exploration. One teacher said, "The Regents exams and the College Board[1] subject-matter exams should be designed to give a kid a chance to show how he can handle really challenging questions, but they don't always do this." Another teacher added: "I am all for having ways to maintain standards in schools. The Regents exams usually help us do that, but in some instances they may actually lower our standards of teaching when we feel that we are forced to make a course a memory ordeal to give our students adequate preparation for one of the exams."

MR. WHITE OR MR. GREEN?

Add to the Regents examinations' pressures the stress resulting from other tests and classroom grading in the "college admissions hassle" and you can understand the situation I found in an advanced biology class of seniors. We were talking about kinds of teaching. To summarize what had been said, I offered a quick description of the approaches to teaching which had been pictured in the discussion:

Take first *Mr. White:* he has a strong personality, he presents the material excitingly, and it is expertly, clearly organized. He offers the material to the class *as a group,* has little encounter with any individuals in the class as people. He selects the ques-

[1] *College Board:* a type of standard aptitude and achievement test required by most colleges for admission

tions and the grounds for discussion himself. He does a good deal of lively, vigorous lecturing.

Mr. Green is rather quiet, and you sometimes have difficulty seeing what is back of his questions. Most of his work is in organizing questions and activities which get the students into action on their own initiative. The members of the class have a good deal to do with how well an activity or a class period goes. He does not "run" the class, but he sets up plenty of challenge for any member who wants to take it.

I noticed responsive nods as I described each type of teaching, since my descriptions had come from what the students had been saying. After the two descriptions, I asked, "Which of these two kinds of teaching do you prefer?" There was a pause, some looking around, then one boy spoke out: "Which teacher would mark easier?"

In a burst of relief, as if "the real issue" had emerged, these advanced biology students plunged into talk about the fight for marks and scores. As the bell rang, they were beginning to agree on a conclusion which seemed to appall them. Yet they said it was realistic in relation to their own motives. Their conclusion was that their main concern would *have* to be, "Which one would give the highest marks?" because of "the terrific business of getting into college." Kinds of teaching dropped out of sight. The marks issue took over.

These students were impressively bright young men and women. Their acceptance of the marks-for-college drive was not perfunctory, but all-important. They regretted it, and they did not appear to be using it as an excuse for evading broad, explorative study, though this marks issue could be used that way. The teacher reinforced his students' comments after class when he told me:

You know, a lot of times I really think these students would like it best if they were given a perfectly worked-out, mimeographed course, with test questions mimeographed too, with blanks for the answers and a separate answer sheet from which to memorize the answers. And these are my brightest people! They ought to be searching deeply into the subject!

He didn't speak with any special bitterness, and he didn't seem critical of the students. He saw his students trapped in some kind of race, and he hated it.

"WHAT MARK DID YOU GET?"

I often heard a school's whole academic program discussed solely in terms of marks. Among some students who were talking about the emphasis on sports in their school, one said, "It's not just sports that are important. Marks count around here, too." Then the talk shifted to whether sports or marks were stressed more, and by which groups within the school. As these students went on, I saw clearly that they were using "marks" as a label for *the whole academic experience*. They were evidently making a distinction between the *experience* of sports and the *fact* of marks. They were not weighing the *experience* of sports against the *experience* of intellectual activity. Toward the end of the discussion, I pointed this out and one student retorted: "It *has* to be that way because of college." For him, "because of college" was an automatic, all-embracing explanation.

"THE STRIVER"

The terminology used in talking about people's behavior in the college admissions crush varied from one school to another. In one school, students talked about "the striver." Yet it appeared that often a student was divided within himself on the merits of "striving" in courses and in activities. As one boy said, "These 'strivers' join clubs and go out for activities just to get it on their high school record. Of course, I must say I have done this too, but I also join some things which I really care about and have real interest in."

Many college admissions officers have publicly decried the

idea of a huge list of activities as a "must" on a college application blank. Yet the "pad-the-activities" aspect of college admission appeared very strong in student thinking. "The
problem," one girl said, "is how to 'strive' and, at the same
time, maintain your integrity and even get something of an
education!" Some "strivers" tried to stay out of advanced
courses on the grounds that their marks might look better if
they led in the regular classes. Others are "in there pounding
to get the teacher to raise a mark from an 89 to a 90, or up
from a 94 to a 95." Still others are signing up for every club
and activity in the school, even those meeting at the same
time on the same afternoon. In one school in a high-powered
community, two tenth-grade boys sought me out to tell me
about "how the strivers work around here." One said, "Tomorrow at the 12:35 lunch period we'll bring you a real,
honest-to-goodness striver and you can see for yourself!"

The next day, at 12:35, the two boys escorted their Striver
Exhibit into the psychologist's office, where I had been sta-
tioned. "Here he is, a real striver. Talk to him!" one said,
and the two boys sat down to listen. The "Exhibit" stood
there in puzzled dismay. This was too much for me, and I
suggested we all go to lunch.

THE COLLEGE BOARDS

The College Board examinations still create an emotional
hurdle, even though they no longer have the curriculum-
limiting, restrictive quality of the subject examinations of
thirty years ago. The College Board aptitude tests are regarded with special awe. Refusing to accept the aptitude
evaluation obtained from the eleventh-grade trial run on
these tests, some students (with parental backing) press the
schools for cramming sessions for the senior-year aptitude
tests, seeking vocabulary-list drills and test-taking tricks.
Some amusing incidents result from these attempts to cram.
One girl reported: "I heard you could really raise your College Board aptitude scores by outside reading. I told a friend

of mine that. She was crazy to get her scores up, but she said, 'Isn't there some workbook or something? I *hate* to read!' "

I asked where her friend was applying for admission, and she gave the names of three of the most highly competitive women's colleges. The irony of her friend's hatred for reading in the light of her choices of colleges seemed to go unnoticed.

A BRAVE EFFORT TO BEAT THE SYSTEM

I met some students who fought this whole pressure as hard as they could. It was a brave fight, with "getting something that amounts to an education" right there in high school as the goal. But for most of these students the experience of one eleventh-grade boy would be very true-to-life:

In the summer session last year, I arranged to take a biology course that I really liked. I was determined that this summer course would be for learning, not for marks. Every now and then the mark would pop into my mind, but I could pretty well get rid of it. I succeeded pretty well during the summer. It was great! I was thinking about what was actually going on in biology. But this fall I can't seem to keep this attitude. I find that I'm constantly computing averages.

Questions and Comments

1. What basic conflict do students face in situations where parents are anxious about admission to "prestige" colleges?

2. How can learning be sacrificed for marks? Doesn't a high mark mean a student learned the subject thoroughly and well? Why or why not?

3. What dilemma faces the teachers who must prepare students for Regents? For College Boards?

4. What effect did the marks issue have upon the advanced biology students' attitude toward types of teachers?

5. One teacher saw these students as trapped "in some kind of race." What race was he referring to? Why was it a trap?

6. What happens to the meaning of the following quotation if you substitute the word *learning* for *marks*: "It's not just sports that are important. Marks count around here, too"?

7. What is a "striver"? Is a striver all good or all bad? What might be his good points? Bad points? Why might a student become a striver?

8. What big difference is there between learning "about what was actually going on in biology" and thinking about how to pass a test in biology with a high mark?

Word Study

1. The origin of *hassle* is uncertain, but the word may be a combination of *haggle* and *tussle*. How do you account for this derivation?

2. *Perfunctory* comes from the Latin *perfungor,* "to perform." In English, however, the word has more special meaning. What is it?

3. *Neurotic* contains the Greek root *neuron,* which means "nerve." Check your dictionary and notice all the other words which begin with *neuro.* It would also be a good idea to look up *psychotic* and contrast its meaning with *neurotic.* These two words are often confused in meaning.

4. *Integrity* is a word often used in speeches and sermons. The Latin word *integer* means "complete, whole, untouched." What does *integrity* mean as the author uses it on page 62?

Composition

1. In a brief essay describe what you would consider an intel-

ligent preparation for the College Boards.

2. Describe in some detail an experience in your own education when you literally "lost" yourself in learning something and momentarily forgot marks.

3. Using the title of this selection, write an article based on
your experiences in your own school.

Beneath the surface of everyday existence lies a seething, active world composed of cells, germs, and insects. Birth, life, death, survival, struggle, instinctive behavior and adaptability comprise that "other world" as much as they comprise ours. Whenever we turn a magnifying glass upon life other than human, surprises and insights are our inevitable rewards. Such are the rewards of reading Mr. Petrunkevitch's account of the death struggle between the tarantula spider and the digger wasp.

THE SPIDER
AND THE WASP

Alexander Petrunkevitch

To hold its own in the struggle for existence, every species of animal must have a regular source of food, and if it happens to live on other animals, its survival may be very delicately balanced. The hunter cannot exist without the hunted; if the latter should perish from the earth, the former would, too. When the hunted also prey on some of the hunters, the matter may become complicated.

This is nowhere better illustrated than in the insect world. Think of the complexity of a situation such as the following: There is a certain wasp, *Pimpla inquisitor,* whose larvae feed on the larvae of the tussock moth. *Pimpla* larvae in turn serve as food for the larvae of a second wasp, and the latter in their turn nourish still a third wasp. What subtle balance between fertility and mortality must exist in the case of each of these four species to prevent the extinction of all of them!

An excess of mortality over fertility in a single member of the group would ultimately wipe out all four.

This is not a unique case. The two great orders of insects, Hymenoptera[1] and Diptera,[2] are full of such examples of interrelationship. And the spiders (which are not insects but members of a separate order of arthropods) also are killers and victims of insects.

The picture is complicated by the fact that those species which are carnivorous in the larval stage have to be provided with animal food by a vegetarian mother. The survival of the young depends on the mother's correct choice of a food which she does not eat herself.

In the feeding and safeguarding of their progeny the insects and spiders exhibit some interesting analogies to reasoning and some crass examples of blind instinct. The case I propose to describe here is that of the tarantula spiders and their arch-enemy, the digger wasps of the genus Pepsis.[3] It is a classic example of what looks like intelligence pitted against instinct—a strange situation in which the victim, though fully able to defend itself, submits unwittingly to its destruction.

Most tarantulas live in the Tropics, but several species occur in the temperate zone and a few are common in the southern U. S. Some varieties are large and have powerful fangs with which they can inflict a deep wound. These formidable looking spiders do not, however, attack man; you can hold one in your hand, if you are gentle, without being bitten. Their bite is dangerous only to insects and small mammals such as mice; for a man it is no worse than a hornet's sting.

[1] *Hymenoptera:* order including bees, wasps, and ants

[2] *Diptera:* order including flies, mosquitoes, and gnats

[3] *genus Pepsis: Genus* (Latin) means "category" and *Pepsis* (Greek) means "digestion." This is an example of how science sometimes classifies species by means of Latin and Greek terms.

Tarantulas customarily live in deep cylindrical burrows, from which they emerge at dusk and into which they retire at dawn. Mature males wander about after dark in search of females and, occasionally stray into houses. After mating, the male dies in a few weeks, but a female lives much longer and can mate several years in succession. In a Paris museum is a tropical specimen which is said to have been living in captivity for 25 years.

A fertilized female tarantula lays from 200 to 400 eggs at a time; thus it is possible for a single tarantula to produce several thousand young. She takes no care of them beyond weaving a cocoon of silk to enclose the eggs. After they hatch, the young walk away, find convenient places in which to dig their burrows and spend the rest of their lives in solitude. Tarantulas feed mostly on insects and millepedes. Once their appetite is appeased, they digest the food for several days before eating again. Their sight is poor, being limited to sensing a change in the intensity of light and to the perception of moving objects. They apparently have little or no sense of hearing, for a hungry tarantula will pay no attention to a loudly chirping cricket placed in its cage unless the insect happens to touch one of its legs.

But all spiders, and especially hairy ones, have an extremely delicate sense of touch. Laboratory experiments prove that tarantulas can distinguish three types of touch: pressure against the body wall, stroking of the body hair and riffling of certain very fine hairs on the legs called trichobothria. Pressure against the body, by a finger or the end of a pencil, causes the tarantula to move off slowly for a short distance. The touch excites no defensive response unless the approach is from above where the spider can see the motion, in which case it rises on its hind legs, lifts its front legs, opens its fangs and holds this threatening posture as long as the object continues to move. When the motion stops, the spider drops back to the ground, remains quiet for a few seconds and then moves slowly away.

The entire body of a tarantula, especially its legs, is thickly clothed with hair. Some of it is short and woolly, some long and stiff. Touching this body hair produces one of two distinct reactions. When the spider is hungry, it responds with an immediate and swift attack. At the touch of a cricket's antennae the tarantula seizes the insect so swiftly that a motion picture taken at the rate of 64 frames per second shows only the result and not the process of capture. But when the spider is not hungry, the stimulation of its hairs merely causes it to shake the touched limb. An insect can walk under its hairy belly unharmed.

The trichobothria, very fine hairs growing from disk-like membranes on the legs, were once thought to be the spider's hearing organs, but we now know that they have nothing to do with sound. They are sensitive only to air movement. A light breeze makes them vibrate slowly without disturbing the common hair. When one blows gently on the trichobothria, the tarantula reacts with a quick jerk of its four front legs. If the front and hind legs are stimulated at the same time, the spider makes a sudden jump. This reaction is quite independent of the state of its appetite.

These three tactile responses—to pressure on the body wall, to moving of the common hair and to flexing of the trichobothria—are so different from one another that there is no possibility of confusing them. They serve the tarantula adequately for most of its needs and enable it to avoid most annoyances and dangers. But they fail the spider completely when it meets its deadly enemy, the digger wasp Pepsis.

These solitary wasps are beautiful and formidable creatures. Most species are either a deep shiny blue all over, or deep blue with rusty wings. The largest have a wing span of about four inches. They live on nectar. When excited, they give off a pungent odor—a warning that they are ready to attack. The sting is much worse than that of a bee or common wasp, and the pain and swelling last longer. In the adult stage the wasp lives only a few months. The female produces but a few eggs, one at a time at intervals of two or three days. For each egg the mother must provide one adult tarantula, alive but paralyzed. The tarantula must be of the correct species to nourish the larva. The mother wasp attaches the egg to the paralyzed spider's abdomen. Upon hatching from the egg, the larva is many hundreds of times smaller than its living but helpless victim. It eats no other food and drinks no water. By the time it has finished its single gargantuan meal and become ready for wasphood, nothing remains of the tarantula but its indigestible chitinous skeleton.

The mother wasp goes tarantula-hunting when the egg in her ovary is almost ready to be laid. Flying low over the ground late on a sunny afternoon, the wasp looks for its victim or for the mouth of a tarantula burrow, a round hole edged by a bit of silk. The sex of the spider makes no difference, but the mother is highly discriminating as to species. Each species of Pepsis requires a certain species of tarantula, and the wasp will not attack the wrong species. In a cage with a tarantula which is not its normal prey the wasp avoids the spider, and is usually killed by it in the night.

Yet when a wasp finds the correct species, it is the other way about. To identify the species the wasp apparently must explore the spider with her antennae. The tarantula shows an amazing tolerance to this exploration. The wasp crawls under it and walks over it without evoking any hostile response. The molestation is so great and so persistent that the tarantula often rises on all eight legs, as if it were on stilts. It may stand this way for several minutes. Meanwhile the wasp, having satisfied itself that the victim is of the right species, moves off a few inches to dig the spider's grave. Working vigorously with legs and jaws, it excavates a hole 8 to 10 inches deep with a diameter slightly larger than the spider's girth. Now and again the wasp pops out of the hole to make sure that the spider is still there.

When the grave is finished, the wasp returns to the tarantula to complete her ghastly enterprise. First she feels it all over once more with her antennae. Then her behavior becomes more aggressive. She bends her abdomen, protruding her sting, and searches for the soft membrane at the point where the spider's leg joins its body—the only spot where she can penetrate the horny skeleton. From time to time, as the exasperated spider slowly shifts ground, the wasp turns on her back and slides along with the aid of her wings, trying to get under the tarantula for a shot at the vital spot. During all this maneuvering, which can last for several minutes, the tarantula makes no move to save itself. Finally the wasp corners it against some obstruction and grasps one of its legs in her powerful jaws. Now at last the harassed spider tries a desperate but vain defense. The two contestants roll over. and over on the ground. It is a terrifying sight and the outcome is always the same. The wasp finally manages to thrust her sting into the soft spot and holds it there for a few seconds while she pumps in the poison. Almost immediately the tarantula falls paralyzed on its back. Its legs stop twitching; its heart stops beating. Yet it is not dead, as is shown by the fact that if taken from the wasp it can be restored to some sensitivity by being kept in a moist chamber for several months.

After paralyzing the tarantula, the wasp cleans herself by dragging her body along the ground and rubbing her feet, sucks the drop of blood oozing from the wound in the spider's abdomen, then grabs a leg of the flabby, helpless animal in her jaws and drags it down to the bottom of the grave. She stays there for many minutes, sometimes for several hours, and what she does all that time in the dark we do not know. Eventually she lays her egg and attaches it to the side of the spider's abdomen with a sticky secretion. Then she emerges, fills the grave with soil carried bit by bit in her jaws, and finally tramples the ground all around to hide any trace of the grave from prowlers. Then she flies away, leaving her descendant safely started in life.

In all this the behavior of the wasp evidently is qualitatively different from that of the spider. The wasp acts like an intelligent animal. This is not to say that instinct plays no part or that she reasons as man does. But her actions are to the point; they are not automatic and can be modified to fit the situation. We do not know for certain how she identifies the tarantula—probably it is by some olfactory or chemo-tactile sense—but she does it purposefully and does not blindly tackle a wrong species.

On the other hand, the tarantula's behavior shows only confusion. Evidently the wasp's pawing gives it no pleasure, for it tries to move away. That the wasp is not simulating sexual stimulation is certain, because male and female tarantulas react in the same way to its advances. That the spider is not anesthetized by some odorless secretion is easily shown by blowing lightly at the tarantula and making it jump suddenly. What, then, makes the tarantula behave as stupidly as it does?

No clear, simple answer is available. Possibly the stimulation by the wasp's antennae is masked by a heavier pressure on the spider's body, so that it reacts as when prodded by a pencil. But the explanation may be much more complex. Initiative in attack is not in the nature of tarantulas; most species fight only when cornered so that escape is impossible. Their inherited patterns of behavior apparently prompt them to avoid problems rather than attack them. For example, spiders always weave their webs in three dimensions, and when a spider finds that there is insufficient space to attach certain threads in the third dimension, it leaves the place and seeks another, instead of finishing the web in a single plane. This urge to escape seems to arise under all circumstances, in all phases of life and to take the place of reasoning. For a spider to change the pattern of its web is as impossible as for an inexperienced man to build a bridge across a chasm obstructing his way.

In a way the instinctive urge to escape is not only easier but often more efficient than reasoning. The tarantula does exactly what is most efficient in all cases except in an encounter with a ruthless and determined attacker dependent for the existence of her own species on killing as many tarantulas as she can lay eggs. Perhaps in this case the spider follows its usual pattern of trying to escape, instead of seizing and killing the wasp because it is not aware of its danger. In any case, the survival of the tarantula species as a whole is protected by the fact that the spider is much more fertile than the wasp.

Questions and Comments

1. What is the essay's central idea? In what paragraph do you think it is most clearly stated?

2. Of the spider's senses, which is the most sensitive? What are the spider's three responses to touch?

3. State the steps a wasp takes in killing a spider.

4. What explanations are given for the spider's strange behavior while the wasp kills it?

5. State one advantage of instinct over reason. State one of the disadvantages.

6. This piece has none of the ordinary devices of literature—elaborate metaphors, similes, poetic uses of language. What is its chief source of interest?

Word Study

1. Tell the meaning of the italicized words in the following sentence from the selection: "In the feeding and safeguarding of their *progeny* the insects and spiders exhibit some interesting *analogies* to reasoning and some *crass* examples of blind instinct."

2. Context provides clues to the meaning of the following words. Read again the sentences in which they appear and guess their meanings. Then check your guesses with the dictionary: *larvae* (page 66), *arthropods* (page 67), *carnivorous* (page 67), *riffling* (page 68), *tactile* (page 69), *pungent* (page 69), *gargantuan* (page 70), *chitinous* (page 70), *molestation* (page 70).

3. *Olfactory* comes from the Latin *olafacere* meaning "to smell." Check its dictionary meaning.

4. *Spider* comes from an Old English word *spinnan*, "to spin." *Wasp* is said to have come from *webh*, a pre-Teutonic word meaning "to weave," thus referring to the kind of nests some wasps construct. Look up the histories of other common insect names such as *fly, ant, caterpillar, ladybug, beetle, cricket.*

Composition

1. Write a composition treating the topic "Instinct vs. Reason" as it regards some human activity such as eating, defense, recreation.

2. Report the results from close observation of a pet, a fishtank, bird, an insect, or a rodent. Include an accurate description of the creature observed as well as a close account of its actions over an extended period of time.

3. Make a close analysis of the organization of "The Spider and the Wasp." How does the author move from paragraph to paragraph? (Hint: Outline the piece first.)

Annie Dillard, (1945—   ), was born in Pittsburgh, Pennsylvania. Her work has appeared in several magazines, including *Harpers, Sports Illustrated, Atlantic Monthly,* and *Cosmopolitan.* She has published a book of poems, *Tickets for a Prayer Wheel* (1974), and a book on her life in the woods, *Pilgrim at Tinker Creek* (1974), from which this selection was taken. A literary critic used a line from the famous English poet, William Blake (1757–1827), to describe the work of Ms. Dillard, "See a world in a grain of sand." The article which follows shows how the author can see the world in a common goldfish.

from INTRICACY

Annie Dillard

A ROSY, complex light fills my kitchen at the end of these lengthening June days. From an explosion on a nearby star eight minutes ago, the light zips through space, particle-wave, strikes the planet, angles on the continent, and filters through a mesh of land dust: clay bits, sod bits, tiny windborne insects, bacteria, shreds of wing and leg, gravel dust, grits of carbon, and dried cells of grass, bark, and leaves. Reddened, the light inclines into this valley over the green western mountains; it sifts between pine needles on northern slopes, and through all the mountain blackjack oak and haw, whose leaves are unclenching, one by one, and making an intricate, toothed and lobed haze. The light crosses the valley, threads through the screen on my open kitchen window, and gilds the painted wall. A plank of brightness bends from the wall and extends over the goldfish bowl on the table where I sit. The goldfish's side catches the light and bats it my way; I've an eyeful of fish-scale and star.

This Ellery cost me twenty-five cents. He is a deep red-orange, darker than most goldfish. He steers short distances mainly with his slender red lateral fins; they seem to provide impetus for going backward, up, or down. It took me a few days to discover his ventral[1] fins; they are completely transparent and all but invisible—dream fins. He also has a short anal fin, and a tail that is deeply notched and perfectly transparent at the two tapered tips. He can extend his mouth, so that it looks like a length of pipe; he can shift the angle of his eyes in his head so he can look before and behind himself, instead of simply out to his side. His belly, what there is of it, is white ventrally, and a patch of this white extends up his sides—the variegated Ellery. When he opens his gill slits he shows a thin crescent of silver where the flap overlapped—as though all his brightness were sunburn.

For this creature, as I said, I paid twenty-five cents. I had never bought an animal before. It was very simple; I went to a store in Roanoke[2] called "Wet Pets"; I handed the man a quarter, and he handed me a knotted plastic bag bouncing with water in which a green plant floated and the goldfish swam. This fish, two bits' worth, has a coiled gut, a spine radiating fine bones, and a brain. Just before I sprinkle his food flakes into his bowl, I rap three times on the bowl's edge; now he is conditioned, and swims to the surface when I rap. And, he has a heart.

Once, years ago, I saw red blood cells whip, one by one, through the capillaries in a goldfish's transparent tail. The goldfish was etherized. Its head lay in a wad of wet cotton wool; its tail lay on a tray under a dissecting microscope, one of those wonderful light-gathering microscopes with two eyepieces like a stereoscope in which the world's fragments—even the skin on my finger—look brilliant with

[1] *ventral:* situated on the abdominal side of the body

[2] *Roanoke:* a city in western Virginia

myriads of colored lights, and as deep as any alpine landscape. The red blood cells in the goldfish's tail streamed
and coursed through narrow channels invisible save for
glistening threads of thickness in the general translucency.
They never wavered or slowed or ceased flowing, like the
creek itself; they streamed redly around, up, and on, one
by one, more, and more, without end. (The energy of that
pulse reminds me of something about the human body: if
you sit absolutely perfectly balanced on the end of your
spine, with your legs either crossed tailor-fashion or drawn
up together, and your arms forward on your legs, then even
if you hold your breath, your body will rock with the energy
of your heartbeat, forward and back, effortlessly, for as long
as you want to remain balanced.) Those red blood cells are
coursing in Ellery's tail now, too, in just that way, and
through his mouth and eyes as well, and through mine. I've
never forgotten the sight of those cells; I think of it when
I see the fish in his bowl; I think of it lying in bed at
night, imagining that if I concentrate enough I might be
able to feel in my fingers' capillaries the small knockings
and flow of those circular dots, like a string of beads drawn
through my hand.

Something else is happening in the goldfish bowl. There
on the kitchen table, nourished by the simple plank of complex light, the plankton[1] is blooming. The water yellows
and clouds; a transparent slime coats the leaves of the
water plant, elodea; a blue-green film of single-celled algae[2]
clings to the glass. And I have to clean the doggone bowl.
I'll spare you the details: it's the plant I'm interested in.
While Ellery swims in the stoppered sink, I rinse the algae
down the drain of another sink, wash the gravel, and rub
the elodea's many ferny leaves under running water until
they feel clean.

The elodea is not considered much of a plant. Aquarists[3]

[1]*plankton:* the small animal and plant organisms that float or drift in the water
[2]*algae:* a form of fresh-water seaweed containing chlorophyll, hence very green
[3]*aquarists:* those who own or look after fish tanks (aquariums)

use it because it's available and it gives off oxygen completely submersed; laboratories use it because its leaves are only two cells thick. It's plentiful, easy to grow, and cheap —like the goldfish. And, like the goldfish, its cells have unwittingly performed for me on a microscope's stage.

I was in a laboratory, using a very expensive microscope. I peered through the deep twin eyepieces and saw again that color-charged, glistening world. A thin, oblong leaf of elodea, a quarter of an inch long, lay on a glass slide sopping wet and floodlighted brilliantly from below. In the circle of light formed by the two eyepieces trained at the translucent leaf, I saw a clean mosaic of almost colorless cells. The cells were large—eight or nine of them, magnified four hundred and fifty times, packed the circle—so that I could easily see what I had come to see: the streaming of chloroplasts.[1]

Chloroplasts bear chlorophyll; they give the green world its color, and they carry out the business of photosynthesis.[2] Around the inside perimeter of each gigantic cell trailed a continuous loop of these bright green dots. They spun like paramecia;[3] they pulsed, pressed, and thronged. A change of focus suddenly revealed the eddying currents of the river of transparent cytoplasm, a sort of "ether" to the chloroplasts, or "space-time," in which they have their tiny being. Back to the green dots: they shone, they swarmed in ever-shifting files around and around the edge of the cell; they wandered, they charged, they milled, raced, and ran at the edge of apparent nothingness, the empty-looking inner cell; they flowed and trooped greenly, up against the vegetative wall.

[1]*chloroplasts:* bodies containing chlorophyll—the substance which gives green color to leaves and plants

[2]*photosynthesis:* the process of a plant, using sunlight as a source of energy and chlorophyll as an aid, making its own food from carbon dioxide, water, and inorganic salts (*inorganic:* not having the characteristics of living things)

[3]*paramecia:* very common microscopic animals found in fresh water

All the green in the planted world consists of these whole, rounded chloroplasts wending their ways in water. If you analyze a molecule of chlorophyll itself, what you get is one hundred thirty-six atoms of hydrogen, carbon, oxygen, and nitrogen arranged in an exact and complex relationship around a central ring. At the ring's center is a single atom of magnesium. Now: If you remove the atom of magnesium and in its exact place put an atom of iron, you get a molecule of hemoglobin. The iron atom combines with all the other atoms to make red blood, the streaming red dots in the goldfish's tail.

It is, then, a small world there in the goldfish bowl, and a very large one. Say the nucleus of any atom in the bowl were the size of a cherry pit: its nearest electron would revolve around it one hundred seventy-five yards away. A whirling air in his swim bladder balances the goldfish's weight in the water; his scales overlap, his feathery gills pump and filter; his eyes work, his heart beats, his liver absorbs, his muscles contract in a wave of extending ripples. The daphnias[1] he eats have eyes and jointed legs. The algae the daphnias eat have green cells stacked like checkers or winding in narrow ribbons like spiral staircases up long columns of emptiness. And so on diminishingly down. We have not yet found the dot so small it is uncreated, as it were, like a metal blank, or merely roughed in—and we never shall. We go down landscape after mobile, sculpture after collage, down to molecular structures like a mob dance in Breughel,[2] down to atoms airy and balanced as a canvas by Klee,[3] down to atomic particles, the heart of the matter, as

[1]*daphnias:* so-called "water fleas" which can be seen as specks swimming with a jerky motion in ponds and other still water

[2]*Breughel:* Flemish aritst who often filled his paintings with people. Check library references for "The Wedding Dance" or "The Wedding Dance in Open Air" or "The Peasant Dance." (c. 1525-1569)

[3]*Klee:* Swiss artist. Check library references for sample plates of his work. (1879-1940)

spirited and wild as any El Greco[1] saints. And it all works. "Nature," said Thoreau[2] in his journal, "is mythical and mystical always, and spends her whole genius on the least work." The creator, I would add, churns out the intricate texture of least works that is the world with a spendthrift genius and an extravagance of care. This is the point.

Questions and Comments

1. Find the definition of *goldfish* in the dictionary and compare it with the description given on page 76. What are some of the essential differences between the dictionary goldfish and Dillard's goldfish?

2. If another goldfish the same size were put in the bowl with Dillard's, would she be able to tell which fish was her's? Why?

3. Ms. Dillard writes: "The goldfish's side catches the light and bats it my way. . . ." Why is "bats" a better word than "shines" or "reflects?"

4. This article is very factual and at times scientific. Yet you never see this kind of writing in textbooks. What makes this a non-textbook article?

5. Why does Ms. Dillard say, "It is, then, a small world there in the goldfish bowl, and a very large one"?

Word Study

1. *Lobe* is a word often associated with ears. On page 75 it is used as an adjective, *lobed*. What is its meaning? Check with the dictionary.

[1] *El Greco:* Greek artist who lived most of his life in Spain; El Greco means "The Greek" in Spanish. Check the library for samples of his work. (c. 1548-1614)
[2] *Thoreau:* Henry David Thoreau, American naturalist; famous for *Walden* and other works (1817-1862)

2. *Impetus* comes from the Latin *impetere* "to rush upon." Using that clue, what is the meaning of *impetus* on page 76? Check your definition with the dictionary's.

3. *Variegated* looks difficult. But there is a strong clue to its meaning in its beginning: *vari* or *vary*. What "varies" on the fish that the author is describing at that point? Check the meaning in the dictionary.

4. *Capillaries* comes from the Latin *capillus*, "hair." What might *capillaries* be in the blood systems of fish and animals? Check with the dictionary, and ask your science teacher to show you capillary glass tubes in the laboratory.

5. *Translucency*, on page 77, through the years has changed from its original Latin meaning, *translucens* "shining through." Look up its present meaning.

6. *Mosaic* and *collage* both have to do with design and the graphic arts, yet both are quite distinct and different in meaning. Look up each in a dictionary then find examples of each in references found in the library.

Composition

1. Using a magnifying glass, examine any common object you wish: a piece of string, a lemon, a stone, a piece of paper, a scratch on your desk, your own fingerprint. Then write a description of the object giving the specific details which make it unique and unlike any other object in the same category.

2. Using Thoreau's quotation at the end of the article, "Nature is mythical and mystical always," check first the meanings of *mythical* and *mystical;* then give your own reasons for agreeing or disagreeing with Thoreau.

3. If you have a pet fish, bird, or animal, examine it closely for an extended period of time—fifteen minutes or so. Report on details you discovered which you never noticed before, and on some of the thoughts you had which were triggered by your close observation.

4. Check with the librarian to see what other nature writers are represented in the library other than Dillard and Thoreau. Read an essay and compare another author's approach with Dillard's.

This essay appears in a collection entitled *Let Your Mind Alone* (1936) by James Thurber. Mr. Thurber established a very fine reputation for himself not only as a famous humorist but as a playwright and cartoonist as well. Perhaps one of his greatest talents was to take an ordinary situation—one which most people would scarcely notice—and suddenly make that situation very significant and alive with dramatic energy.

THE WOOD DUCK

James Thurber

Mr. Krepp, our vegetable man, had told us we might find some cider out the New Milford road a way—we would come to a sign saying "Morris Plains Farm" and that would be the place. So we got into the car and drove down the concrete New Milford road, which is black in the center with the dropped oil of a million cars. It's a main-trunk highway; you can go fifty miles an hour on it except where warning signs limit you to forty or, near towns, thirty-five, but nobody ever pays any attention to these signs. Even then, in November, dozens of cars flashed past us with a high, ominous whine, their tires roaring rubberly on the concrete. We found Morris Plains Farm without any trouble. There was a big white house to the left of the highway; only a few yards off the road a small barn had been made into a roadside stand, with a dirt driveway curving up to the front of it. A spare, red-cheeked man stood in the midst of baskets and barrels of red apples and glass jugs of red cider. He was waiting on a man and a woman. I turned into the driveway—and put the brakes on hard. I had seen, just in time, a duck.

It was a small, trim duck, and even I, who know nothing about wild fowl, knew that this was no barnyard duck, this was a wild duck. He was all alone. There was no other bird of any kind around, not even a chicken. He was immensely solitary. With none of the awkward waddling of a domestic duck, he kept walking busily around in the driveway, now and then billing up water from a dirty puddle in the middle of the drive. His obvious contentment, his apparently perfect adjustment to his surroundings, struck me as something of a marvel. I got out of the car and spoke about it to a man who had driven up behind me in a rattly sedan. He wore a leather jacket and high, hard boots, and I figured he would know what kind of duck this was. He did. "That's a wood duck," he said. "It dropped in here about two weeks ago, Len says, and's been here ever since."

The proprietor of the stand, in whose direction my informant had nodded as he spoke, helped his customers load a basket of apples into their car and walked over to us. The duck stepped, with a little flutter of its wings, into the dirty puddle, took a small, unconcerned swim, and got out again, ruffling its feathers. "It's rather an odd place for a wood duck, isn't it?" asked my wife. Len grinned and nodded; we all watched the duck. "He's a banded duck," said Len. "There's a band on his leg. The state game commission sends out a lot of 'em. This'n lighted here two weeks ago—it was on a Saturday—and he's been around ever since." "It's funny he wouldn't be frightened away, with all the cars going by and all the people driving in," I said. Len chuckled. "He seems to like it here," he said. The duck wandered over to some sparse grass at the edge of the road, aimlessly, but with an air of settled satisfaction. "He's tame as anything," said Len. "I guess they get tame when them fellows band 'em." The man in the leather jacket said, " 'Course they haven't let you shoot wood duck for a long while and that might make 'em tame, too." "Still," said my wife (we forgot about the cider for the moment), "it's strange he would stay here, right on the road almost." "Sometimes," said Len, reflectively, "he goes round back o' the barn. But mostly he's here in the drive." "But don't they," she asked, "let them loose in the woods after they're banded? I mean, aren't they supposed to stock up the forests?" "I guess they're supposed to," said Len, chuckling again. "But 'pears this'n didn't want to."

An old Ford truck lurched into the driveway and two men in the seat hailed the proprietor. They were hunters, big, warmly dressed, heavily shod men. In the back of the truck was a large bird dog. He was an old pointer and he wore an expression of remote disdain for the world of roadside commerce. He took no notice of the duck. The two hunters said something to Len about cider, and I was just about to chime in with my order when the accident happened. A car went by the stand at fifty miles an hour, leaving something scurrying in its wake. It was the duck, turning over and over on the concrete. He turned over and over swiftly, but lifelessly, like a thrown feather duster, and then he lay still. "My God," I cried, "they've killed your duck, Len!" The accident gave me a quick feeling of anguished intimacy with the bereaved man. "Oh, now," he wailed. "Now, that's awful!" None of us for a moment moved. Then the two hunters walked toward the road, slowly, self-conciously, a little embarrassed in the face of this quick incongruous ending of a wild fowl's life in the middle of a concrete highway. The pointer stood up, looked after the hunters, raised his ears briefly, and then lay down again.

It was the man in the leather jacket finally who walked out to the duck and tried to pick it up. As he did so, the duck stood up. He looked about him like a person who has been abruptly wakened and doesn't know where he is. He didn't ruffle his feathers. "Oh, he isn't quite *dead!*" said my wife. I knew how she felt. We were going to have to see the duck die; somebody would have to kill him, finish him off. Len stood beside us. My wife took hold of his arm. The man in the leather jacket knelt down, stretched out a hand and the duck moved slightly away. Just then, out from behind the barn, limped a setter dog, a lean white setter dog with black spots. His right back leg was useless and he kept it off the ground. He stopped when he saw the duck in the road and gave it a point, putting his head out, lifting his left front leg, maintaining a wavering, marvellous balance on two legs. He was like a drunken man drawing a bead with a gun. This new menace, this anticlimax, was too much. I think I yelled.

What happened next happened as fast as the automobile accident. The setter made his run, a limping, wobbly run, and he was in between the men and the bird before they saw him. The duck flew, got somehow off the ground a foot or two, and tumbled into the grass of the field across the road, the dog after him. It seemed crazy, but the duck could fly—a little, anyway. "Here, here," said Len, weakly. The hunters shouted, I shouted, my wife screamed, "He'll kill him! He'll *kill* him!" The duck flew a few yards again, the dog at his tail. The dog's third plunge brought his nose almost to the duck's tail, and then one of the hunters tackled the animal and pulled him down and knelt in the grass, holding him. We all breathed easier. My wife let go Len's arm.

Len started across the road after the duck, who was fluttering slowly, waveringly, but with a definite purpose, toward a wood that fringed the far side of the field. The bird was dazed, but a sure, atavistic urge was guiding him; he was going home. One of the hunters joined Len in his pursuit. The other came back across the road, dragging the indignant setter; the man in the leather jacket walked beside them. We all watched Len and his companion reach the edge of the wood and stand there, looking; they had followed the duck through the grass slowly, so as not to alarm him; he had been alarmed enough. "He'll never come back," said my wife. Len and the hunter finally turned and came back through the grass. The duck had got away from them. We walked out to meet them at the edge of the concrete. Cars began to whiz by in both directions. I realized, with wonder, that all the time the duck, and the hunters, and the setter were milling around in the road, not one had passed. It was as if traffic had been held up so that our little drama could go on. "He couldn't o' been much hurt," said Len. "Likely just grazed and pulled along in the wind of the car. Them fellows don't look out for anything. It's a sin." My wife had a question for him. "Does your dog always chase the duck?" she asked. "Oh, that ain't my dog," said Len. "He just comes around." The hunter who had been holding the setter now let him go, and he slunk away. The pointer, I noticed, lay with his eyes closed. "But doesn't the duck mind the dog?" persisted my wife. "Oh, he minds him," said Len. "But the dog's never really hurt him none yet. There's always somebody around."

We drove away with a great deal to talk about (I almost forgot the cider). I explained the irony, I think I explained the profound symbolism, of a wild duck's becoming attached to a roadside stand. My wife strove simply to understand the duck's viewpoint. She didn't get anywhere. I knew even then, in the back of my mind, what would happen. We decided, after a cocktail, to drive back to the place and find out if the duck had returned. My wife hoped it wouldn't be there, on account of the life it led in the driveway; I hoped it wouldn't because I felt that would be, somehow, too pat an ending. Night was falling when we started off again for Morris Plains Farm. It was a five-mile drive and I had to put my bright lights on before we got there. The barn door was closed for the night. We didn't see the duck anywhere. The only thing to do was to go up to the house and inquire. I knocked on the door and a young man opened it. "Is—is the proprietor here?" I asked. He said no, he had gone to Waterbury. "We wanted to know," my wife said, "whether the duck came back." "What?" he asked, a little startled, I thought. Then, "Oh, the duck. I saw him around the driveway when my father drove off." He stared at us, waiting. I thanked him and started back to the car. My wife lingered, explaining, for a moment. "He thinks we're crazy," she said, when she got into the car. We drove on a little distance. "Well," I said, "he's back." "I'm glad he is, in a way," said my wife. "I hated to think of him all alone out there in the woods."

Questions and Comments

1. The opening paragraph of this selection gives very definite details about automobiles, speed, traffic, and kind of highway. Why do these details become so important later?

2. Another point very clearly underlined is that the duck is wild. Why would a domestic duck be inappropriate as the subject of this essay?

3. Explain the difference in the two dogs' behavior. Why did they behave so differently?

4. The narrator is struck by "the profound symbolism of a wild duck's becoming attached to a roadside stand." He suggests it is ironic. Irony describes those situations in which the opposite to what is expected occurs. What might the author mean by "profound symbolism"? What is the irony that he speaks of? Name other ironies or events which go counter to expectations in this account.

5. Reader sympathy toward the duck is established swiftly and becomes at one or two points downright acute. At what point is your sympathy for the duck greatest? Why?

6. The narrator's wife in this essay reflects a popular attitude toward wild creatures. What is her attitude? How does it contrast with the narrator's?

Word Study

1. The author says an atavistic urge guided the duck toward the woods. The word *atavistic* holds a key to the meaning of this essay. What does it mean? Explain its importance toward a full understanding of the essay.

2. Taking the old words and giving them fresh and interesting use is one of the jobs of a truly fine writer. Which word in the sentence below suddenly becomes very effective and fresh in meaning as it is used by Mr. Thurber?

   "With none of the awkward waddling of a domestic duck, he kept walking busily around in the driveway, now and then billing up water from a dirty puddle in the middle of the drive." (page 84)

3. *Bereaved* comes from an Old English word which meant "to rob" or "to plunder." How is this meaning related to the meaning of the word as we use it today?

4. Guess at the meaning of *incongruous* in the context "Then the two hunters walked toward the road, slowly, self-consciously, a little embarrassed in the face of this quick incongruous ending of a wild fowl's life in the middle of a concrete highway."

Composition

1. In a brief composition discuss what you feel to be the central idea of this selection about a wild duck and its attempt to live in civilization.

2. Describe a personal experience in which you became deeply concerned with a wild creature. Be sure to include the reactions of family members and friends.

3. Recall the essay entitled "The Spider and the Wasp." What similarity do you see in the behavior of the spider and the wood duck? What human comparisons can you make?

Francis Parkman wrote *The Discovery of the Great West,* from which the following account comes. Prior to writing it, Parkman traveled the trails described by Marquette, Joliet, and La Salle, doing much of the traveling by foot and canoe just as they did, and doing so in spite of a nervous condition which made his whole body suffer extreme pain with every step. A true scholar, he practically memorized the old journals of La Salle. He once astounded farmers in New York State by describing the natural terrain in a particular region, including a rather large flat-topped rock near a river before he was given the chance to actually see the area he described. He told one farmer that there were probably lots of native American bones and articles in his cornfield and the farmer admitted finding such items every time he plowed. Parkman was elected to the American Hall of Fame in 1915.

THE DISCOVERY
OF THE MISSISSIPPI

Francis Parkman

IF Talon[1] had remained in the colony, Frontenac[2] would infallibly have quarrelled with him; but he was too clear-sighted not to approve his plans for the discovery and occupation of the interior. Before sailing for France, Talon recommended Joliet as a suitable agent for the discovery of the Mississippi, and the governor accepted his counsel.

[1] *Talon:* French manager of the Canadian Colony, sometimes referred to as "the intendant"

[2] *Frontenac:* French Governor of the Canadian Colony

Louis Joliet was the son of a wagon-maker in the service of the Company of the Hundred Associates,[1] then owners of Canada. He was born at Quebec in 1645, and was educated by the Jesuits.[2] When still very young, he resolved to be a priest. He received the tonsure and the minor orders at the age of seventeen. Four years after, he is mentioned with especial honor for the part he bore in the disputes in philosophy, at which the dignitaries of the colony were present, and in which the intendant[3] himself took part. Not long after, he renounced his clerical vocation, and turned fur-trader. Talon sent him, with one Péré, to explore the copper-mines of Lake Superior; and it was on his return from this expedition that he met La Salle and the Sulpitians[4] near the Head of Lake Ontario.

In what we know of Joliet, there is nothing that reveals any salient or distinctive trait of character, any especial breadth of view or boldness of design. He appears to have been simply a merchant, intelligent, well educated, courageous, hardy, and enterprising. Though he had renounced the priesthood, he retained his partiality for the Jesuits; and it is more than probable that their influence had aided not a little to determine Talon's choice. One of their number, Jacques Marquette, was chosen to accompany him.

He passed up the lakes to Michillimackinac,[5] and found his destined companion at Point St. Ignace, on the north side

---

[1] *Company of the Hundred Associates:* a company of 120 members formed under the aegis of Cardinal Richelieu. It was granted the whole St. Lawrence valley and had a monopoly of trade there and duty-free exports to France. In return, it was obliged to take 300 French Catholic colonists back to settle in Canada and had to provide three priests for them.

[2] *Jesuits:* members of a religious society for men founded by Ignatius Loyola in 1534

[3] *intendant:* an administrative officer next to the governor under Richelieu's centralized government

[4] *Sulpitians:* members of a Roman Catholic society of diocesan priests established in France in 1642 with the purpose of contributing teachers for ecclesiastical seminaries

[5] *Michillimackinac:* old name for Mackinac, presently a county in Michigan

of the strait, where, in his palisaded mission-house and chapel, he had labored for two years past to instruct the Huron refugees from St. Esprit, and a band of Ottawas who had joined them. Marquette was born in 1637, of an old and honorable family at Laon, in the north of France, and was now thirty-five years of age. When about seventeen, he had joined the Jesuits, evidently from motives purely religious; and in 1666 he was sent to the missions of Canada. At first, he was destined to the station of Tadoussac; and, to prepare himself for it, he studied the Montagnais[1] language under Gabriel Druilletes. But his destination was changed, and he was sent to the Upper Lakes in 1668, where he had since remained. His talents as a linguist must have been great; for, within a few years, he learned to speak with ease six Indian languages. The traits of his character are unmistakable. He was of the brotherhood of the early Canadian missionaries, and the true counterpart of Garnier or Jogues.[2] He was a devout votary of the Virgin Mary, who, imaged to his mind in shapes of the most transcendent loveliness with which the pencil of human genius has ever informed the canvas, was to him the object of an adoration not unmingled with a sentiment of chivalrous devotion. The longings of a sensitive heart, divorced from earth, sought solace in the skies. A subtile element of romance was blended with the fervor of his worship, and hung like an illumined cloud over the harsh and hard realities of his daily lot. Kindled by the smile of his celestial mistress, his gentle and noble nature knew no fear. For her he burned to dare and to suffer, discover new lands and conquer new realms to her sway.

He begins the journal of his voyage thus: "The day of the Immaculate Conception of the Holy Virgin; whom I had continually invoked, since I came to this country of the Ottawas, to obtain from God the favor of being enabled to visit

[1] *Montagnais:* name of an Indian tribe

[2] *Garnier and Jogues:* Jesuit missionaries and explorers who had earlier arrived in Canada. They were both killed by Indians on separate occasions.

the nations on the river Mississippi,—this very day was precisely that on which M. Joliet arrived with orders from Count Frontenac, our governor, and from M. Talon, our intendant,[1] to go with me on this discovery. I was all the more delighted at this good news, because I saw my plans about to be accomplished, and found myself in the happy necessity of exposing my life for the salvation of all these tribes; and especially of the Illinois, who, when I was at Point St. Esprit, had begged me very earnestly to bring the word of God among them."

The outfit of the travellers was very simple. They provided themselves with two birch canoes, and a supply of smoked meat and Indian corn; embarked with five men; and began their voyage on the seventeenth of May. They had obtained all possible information from the Indians, and had made, by means of it, a species of map of their intended route. "Above all," writes Marquette, "I placed our voyage under the protection of the Holy Virgin Immaculate, promising that, if she granted us the favor of discovering the great river, I would give it the name of the Conception." Their course was westward; and, plying their paddles, they passed the Straits of Michillimackinac, and coasted the northern shores of Lake Michigan; landing at evening to build their camp-fire at the edge of the forest, and draw up their canoes on the strand. They soon reached the river Menomonie, and ascended it to the village of the Menomonies, or Wild-rice Indians. When they told them the object of their voyage, they were filled with astonishment, and used their best ingenuity to dissuade them. The banks of the Mississippi, they said, were inhabited by ferocious tribes, who put every stranger to death, tomahawking all newcomers without cause or provocation. They added that there was a demon in a certain part of the river, whose roar could be heard at a great distance, and who would engulf them in the abyss where he dwelt; that its waters were full of frightful monsters, who would de-

[1] *intendant:* an administrative officer next to the governor under Richelieu's centralized government

vour them and their canoe; and, finally, that the heat was so great that they would perish inevitably. Marquette set their counsel at naught, gave them a few words of instruction in the mysteries of the Faith, taught them a prayer, and bade them farewell.

The travellers next reached the mission at the head of Green Bay; entered Fox River; with difficulty and labor dragged their canoes up the long and tumultuous rapids; crossed Lake Winnebago; and followed the quiet windings of the river beyond, where they glided through an endless growth of wild rice, and scared the innumerable birds that fed upon it. On either hand rolled the prairie, dotted with groves and trees, browsing elk and deer. On the seventh of June, they reached the Mascoutins and Miamis, who, since the visit of Dablon and Allouez,[1] had been joined by the Kickapoos. Marquette, who had an eye for natural beauty, was delighted with the situation of the town, which he describes as standing on the crown of a hill; while, all around, the prairie stretched beyond the sight, interspersed with groves and belts of tall forest. But he was still more delighted when he saw a cross planted in the midst of the place. The Indians had decorated it with a number of dressed deer-skins, red girdles, and bows and arrows, which they had hung upon it as an offering to the Great Manitou[2] of the French; a sight by which Marquette says he was "extremely consoled."

The travellers had no sooner reached the town than they called the chiefs and elders to a council. Joliet told them that the governor of Canada had sent him to discover new countries, and that God had sent his companion to teach the true faith to the inhabitants; and he prayed for guides to show them the way to the waters of the Wisconsin. The council readily consented; and on the tenth of June the Frenchmen embarked again, with two Indians to conduct them. All the town came down to the shore to see their departure. Here were the Miamis, with long locks of hair dangling over each

[1] *Dablon and Allouez:* missionaries who preceded Marquette
[2] *Great Manitou:* Manitou is an Indian word for spirit.

ear, after a fashion which Marquette thought very becoming; and here, too, the Mascoutins and the Kickapoos, whom he describes as mere boors in comparison with their Miami townsmen. All stared alike at the seven adventurers, marvelling that men could be found to risk an enterprise so hazardous.

The river twisted among lakes and marshes choked with wild rice; and, but for their guides, they could scarcely have followed the perplexed and narrow channel. It brought them at last to the portage, where, after carrying their canoes a mile and a half over prairie and through the marsh, they launched them on the Wisconsin, bade farewell to the waters that flowed to the St. Lawrence, and committed themselves to the current that was to bear them they knew not whither,—perhaps to the Gulf of Mexico, perhaps to the South Sea or the Gulf of California. They glided calmly down the tranquil stream, by islands choked with trees and matted with entangling grape-vines; by forests, groves, and prairies, the parks and pleasure-grounds of a prodigal nature; by thickets and marshes and broad bare sand-bars; under the shadowing trees, between whose tops looked down from afar the bold brow of some woody bluff. At night, the bivouac,—the canoes inverted on the bank, the flickering fire, the meal of bison-flesh or venison, the evening pipes, and slumber beneath the stars; and when in the morning they embarked again, the mist hung on the river like a bridal veil; then melted before the sun, till the glassy water and the languid woods basked breathless in the sultry glare.

On the 17th of June, they saw on their right the broad meadows, bounded in the distance by rugged hills, where now stand the town and fort of Prairie du Chien. Before them a wide and rapid current coursed athwart their way, by the foot of lofty heights wrapped thick in forests. They had found what they sought, and "with a joy," writes Marquette, "which I cannot express," they steered forth their canoes on the eddies of the Mississippi.

Turning southward, they paddled down the stream, through a solitude unrelieved by the faintest trace of man. A large fish, apparently one of the huge cat-fish of the Mississippi, blundered against Marquette's canoe, with a force which seems to have startled him; and once, as they drew in their net, they caught a "spade-fish,"[1] whose eccentric appearance greatly astonished them. At length, the buffalo began to appear, grazing in herds on the great prairies which then bordered the river; and Marquette describes the fierce and stupid look of the old bulls, as they stared at the intruders through the tangled mane which nearly blinded them.

They advanced with extreme caution, landed at night, and made a fire to cook their evening meal; then extinguished it, embarked again, paddled some way farther, and anchored in the stream, keeping a man on the watch till morning. They had journeyed more than a fortnight without meeting a human being, when, on the twenty-fifth, they discovered footprints of men in the mud of the western bank, and a well-trodden path that led to the adjacent prairie. Joliet and Marquette resolved to follow it; and, leaving the canoes in charge of their men, they set out on their hazardous adventure. The day was fair, and they walked two leagues[2] in silence, following the path through the forest and across the sunny prairie, till they discovered an Indian village on the banks of a river, and two others on a hill half a league distant.[3] Now, with beating hearts, they invoked the aid of Heaven, and, again advancing, came so near, without being seen, that they could hear the voices of the Indians among the wigwams. Then they stood forth in full view, and shouted to attract attention. There was great commotion in the

[1] "spade-fish": probably a garfish, which has long jaws resembling a spade
[2] leagues: A league is approximately three miles.
[3] Author's note: The Indian villages, under the names of Peouaria (Peoria) and Moingouena, are represented in Marquette's map upon a river corresponding in position with the Des Moines; though the distance from the Wisconsin, as given by him, would indicate a river farther north.

village. The inmates swarmed out of their huts, and four of their chief men presently came forward to meet the strangers, advancing very deliberately, and holding up toward the sun two calumets, or peace-pipes, decorated with feathers. They stopped abruptly before the two Frenchmen, and stood gazing at them without speaking a word. Marquette was much relieved on seeing that they wore French cloth, whence he judged that they must be friends and allies. He broke the silence, and asked them who they were; whereupon they answered that they were Illinois, and offered the pipe; which having been duly smoked, they all went together to the village. Here the chief received the travellers after a singular fashion, meant to do them honor. He stood stark naked at the door of a large wigwam, holding up both hands as if to shield his eyes. "Frenchmen, how bright the sun shines when you come to visit us! All our village awaits you; and you shall enter our wigwams in peace." So saying, he led them into his own, which was crowded to suffocation with savages, staring at their guests in silence. Having smoked with the chiefs and old men, they were invited to visit the great chief of all the Illinois, at one of the villages they had seen in the distance; and thither they proceeded, followed by a throng of warriors, squaws, and children. On arriving, they were forced to smoke again, and listen to a speech of welcome from the great chief, who delivered it standing between two old men, naked like himself. His lodge was crowded with the dignitaries of the tribe, whom Marquette addressed in Algonquin, announcing himself as a messenger sent by the God who had made them, and whom it behooves them to recognize and obey. He added a few words touching the power and glory of Count Frontenac, and concluded by asking information concerning the Mississippi, and the tribes along its banks, whom he was on his way to visit. The chief replied with a speech of compliment; assuring his guests that their presence added flavor to his tobacco, made the river more calm, the sky more serene, and the earth more beautiful. In conclusion, he gave them a young slave and a calumet, begging them at the same time to abandon their purpose of descending the Mississippi.

A feast of four courses now followed. First, a wooden bowl full of a porridge of Indian meal boiled with grease was set before the guests; and the master of ceremonies fed them in turn, like infants, with a large spoon. Then appeared a platter of fish; and the same functionary, carefully removing the bones with his fingers, and blowing on the morsels to cool them, placed them in the mouths of the two Frenchmen. A large dog, killed and cooked for the occasion, was next placed before them; but, failing to tempt their fastidious appetites, was supplanted by a dish of fat buffalo-meat, which concluded the entertainment. The crowd having dispersed, buffalo-robes were spread on the ground, and Marquette and Joliet spent the night on the scene of the late festivity. In the morning, the chief, with some six hundred of his tribesmen, escorted them to their canoes, and bade them, after their stolid fashion, a friendly farewell.

Again they were on their way, slowly drifting down the great river. They passed the mouth of the Illinois, and glided beneath that line of rocks on the eastern side, cut into fantastic forms by the elements, and marked as "The Ruined Castles" on some of the early French maps. Presently they beheld a sight which reminded them that the Devil was still lord paramount of this wilderness. On the flat face of a high rock were painted, in red, black, and green, a pair of monsters, each "as large as a calf, with horns like a deer, red eyes, a beard like a tiger, and a frightful expression of countenance. The face is something like that of a man, the body covered with scales; and the tail so long that it passes entirely round the body, over the head and between the legs, ending like that of a fish." Such is the account which the worthy Jesuit gives of these manitous, or Indian gods. He confesses that at first they frightened him; and his imagination and that of his credulous companions were so wrought upon by these unhallowed efforts of Indian art, that they continued for a long time to talk of them as they plied their paddles. They were thus engaged, when they were suddenly aroused by a real danger. A torrent of yellow mud rushed furiously athwart the calm blue current of the Mississippi; boiling and surging, and sweeping in its course logs, branches, and uprooted trees. They had reached the mouth of the Missouri, where that savage river, descending from its mad career through a vast unknown of barbarism, poured its turbid floods into the bosom of its gentler sister. Their light canoes whirled on the miry vortex like dry leaves on an angry brook. "I never," writes Marquette, "saw any thing more terrific;" but they escaped with their fright, and held their way down the turbulent and swollen current of the now united rivers. They passed the lonely forest that covered the site of the destined city of St. Louis, and, a few days later, saw on their left the mouth of the stream to which the Iroquois had given the well-merited name of Ohio, or the Beautiful River.[1] Soon they began to see the marshy shores buried in a dense growth of the cane, with its tall straight stems and feathery light-green foliage. The sun glowed through the hazy air with a languid stifling heat, and by day and night mosquitoes in myriads left them no peace. They floated slowly down the current, crouched in the shade of the sails which they had spread as awnings, when suddenly they saw Indians on the east bank. The surprise was mutual, and each party was as much frightened as the other. Marquette hastened to display the calumet which the Illinois had given him by way of passport; and the Indians, recognizing the pacific symbol, replied with an invitation to land. Evidently, they were in communication with Europeans, for they were armed with

---

[1] *Author's note:* called, on Marquette's map, Ouabouskiaou. On some of the earliest maps, it is called Ouabache (Wabash).

guns, knives, and hatchets, wore garments of cloth, and carried their gunpowder in small bottles of thick glass. They feasted the Frenchmen with buffalo-meat, bear's oil, and white plums; and gave them a variety of doubtful information, including the agreeable but delusive assurance that they would reach the mouth of the river in ten days. It was, in fact, more than a thousand miles distant.

They resumed their course, and again floated down the interminable monotony of river, marsh, and forest. Day after day passed on in solitude, and they had paddled some three hundred miles since their meeting with the Indians, when, as they neared the mouth of the Arkansas, they saw a cluster of wigwams on the west bank. Their inmates were all astir, yelling the war-whoop, snatching their weapons, and running to the shore to meet the strangers, who, on their part, called for succor to the Virgin. In truth, they had need of her aid; for several large wooden canoes, filled with savages, were putting out from the shore, above and below them, to cut off their retreat, while a swarm of headlong young warriors waded into the water to attack them. The current proved too strong; and, failing to reach the canoes of the Frenchmen, one of them threw his war-club, which flew over the heads of the startled travellers. Meanwhile, Marquette had not ceased to hold up his calumet, to which the excited crowd gave no heed, but strung their bows and notched their arrows for immediate action; when at length the elders of the village arrived, saw the peace-pipe, restrained the ardor of the youth, and urged the Frenchmen to come ashore. Marquette and his companions complied, trembling, and found a better reception than they had reason to expect. One of the Indians spoke a little Illinois, and served as interpreter; a friendly conference was followed by a feast of sagamite[1] and fish; and the travellers, not without sore misgivings, spent the night in the lodges of their entertainers.

Early in the morning, they embarked again, and pro-

[1] *sagamite:* a thin porridge of hulled corn

ceeded to a village of the Arkansas tribe, about eight leagues below. Notice of their coming was sent before them by their late hosts; and, as they drew near, they were met by a canoe, in the prow of which stood a naked personage, holding a calumet, singing, and making gestures of friendship. On reaching the village, which was on the east side,[1] opposite the mouth of the river Arkansas, they were conducted to a sort of scaffold, before the lodge of the war-chief. The space beneath had been prepared for their reception, the ground being neatly covered with rush mats. On these they were seated; the warriors sat around them in a semi-circle; then the elders of the tribe; and then the promiscuous crowd of villagers, standing, and staring over the heads of the more dignified members of the assembly. All the men were naked; but, to compensate for the lack of clothing, they wore strings of beads in their noses and ears. The women were clothed in shabby skins, and wore their hair clumped in a mass behind each ear. By good luck, there was a young Indian in the village, who had an excellent knowledge of Illinois; and throught him Marquette endeavored to explain the mysteries of Christianity, and to gain information concerning the river below. To this end he gave his auditors the presents indispensable on such occasions, but received very little in return. They told him that the Mississippi was infested by hostile Indians, armed with guns procured from white men; and that they, the Arkansas, stood in such fear of them that they dared not hunt the buffalo, but were forced to live on Indian corn, of which they raised three crops a year.

During the speeches on either side, food was brought in without ceasing: sometimes a platter of sagamite or mush; sometimes of corn boiled whole; sometimes a roasted dog. The villagers had large earthen pots and platters, made by themselves with tolerable skill, as well as hatchets, knives, and beads, gained by traffic with the Illinois and other tribes in contact with the French or Spaniards. All day there was

[1] *Author's note:* A few years later, the Arkansas were all on the west side.

feasting without respite, after the merciless practice of Indian hospitality; but at night some of their entertainers proposed to kill and plunder them, a scheme which was defeated by the vigilance of the chief, who visited their quarters, and danced the calumet dance to reassure his guests.

The travellers now held counsel as to what course they should take. They had gone far enough, as they thought, to establish one important point: that the Mississippi discharged its waters, not into the Atlantic or sea of Virginia, nor into the Gulf of California, or Vermilion Sea, but into the Gulf of Mexico. They thought themselves nearer to its mouth than they actually were, the distance being still about seven hundred miles; and they feared that, if they went farther, they might be killed by Indians or captured by Spaniards, whereby the results of their discovery would be lost. Therefore they resolved to return to Canada, and report what they had seen.

They left the Arkansas village, and began their homeward voyage on the seventeenth of July. It was no easy task to urge their way upward, in the heat of midsummer, against the current of the dark and gloomy stream, toiling all day under the parching sun, and sleeping at night in the exhalations of the unwholesome shore, or in the narrow confines of their birchen vessels, anchored on the river. Marquette was attacked with dysentery. Languid and well-nigh spent, he invoked his celestial mistress, as day after day, and week after week, they won their slow way northward. At length, they reached the Illinois, and, entering its mouth, followed its course, charmed, as they went, with its placid waters, its shady forests, and its rich plains, grazed by the bison and the deer. They stopped at a spot soon to be made famous in the annals of western discovery. This was a village of the Illinois, then called Kaskaskia; a name afterwards transferred to another locality.[1] A chief, with a band of young warriors,

---

[1] *Author's note:* Marquette says that it consisted at this time of seventy-four lodges. This village was about seven miles below the site of the present town of Ottawa.

offered to guide them to the Lake of the Illinois; that is to say, Lake Michigan. Thither they repaired; and, coasting its shores, reached Green Bay at the end of September, after an absence of about four months, during which they had paddled their canoes somewhat more than two thousand five hundred miles.

Marquette remained to recruit his exhausted strength; but Joliet descended to Quebec, to bear the report of his discovery to Count Frontenac. Fortune had wonderfully favored him on his long and perilous journey; but now she abandoned him on the very threshold of home. At the foot of the rapids of La Chine, and immediately above Montreal, his canoe was overset, two of his men and an Indian boy were drowned, all his papers were lost, and he himself narrowly escaped. In a letter to Frontenac, he speaks of the accident as follows: "I had escaped every peril from the Indians; I had passed forty-two rapids; and was on the point of disembarking, full of joy at the success of so long and difficult an enterprise, when my canoe capsized, after all the danger seemed over. I lost two men, and my box of papers, within sight of the first French settlements, which I had left almost two years before. Nothing remains to me but my life, and the ardent desire to employ it on any service which you may please to direct."

Marquette spent the winter and the following summer at the mission of Green Bay, still suffering from his malady. In the autumn, however, it abated; and he was permitted by his Superior to attempt the execution of a plan to which he was devotedly attached,—the founding, at the principal town of the Illinois, of a mission to be called the Immaculate Conception, a name which he had already given to the river Mississippi. He set out on this errand on the twenty-fifth of October, accompanied by two men, named Pierre and Jacques, one of whom had been with him on his great journey of discovery. A band of Pottawattamies and another band of Illinois also joined him. The united parties—ten canoes in all —followed the east shore of Green Bay as far as the inlet then called Sturgeon Cove, from the head of which they crossed by a difficult portage through the forest to the shore of Lake Michigan. November had come. The bright hues of the autumn foliage were changed to rusty brown. The shore was desolate, and the lake was stormy. They were more than a month in coasting its western border, when at length they reached the river Chicago, entered it, and ascended about two leagues. Marquette's disease had lately returned, and hemorrhage now ensued. He told his two companions that this journey would be his last. In the condition in which he was, it was impossible to go farther. The two men built a log hut by the river, and here they prepared to spend the winter; while Marquette, feeble as he was, began the spiritual exercises of Saint Ignatius, and confessed his two companions twice a week.

Meadow, marsh, and forest were sheeted with snow, but game was abundant. Pierre and Jacques killed buffalo and deer and shot wild turkeys close to their hut. There was an encampment of Illinois within two days' journey; and other Indians, passing by this well-known thoroughfare, occasionally visited them, treating the exiles kindly, and sometimes bringing them game and Indian corn. Eighteen leagues distant was the camp of two adventurous French traders: one of them, a noted *coureur de bois*,[1] nicknamed La Taupine; and the other, a self-styled surgeon. They also visited Marquette, and befriended him to the best of their power.

Urged by a burning desire to lay, before he died, the foundation of his new mission of the Immaculate Conception, Marquette begged his two followers to join him in a *novena,* or nine days' devotion to the Virgin. In consequence of this as he believed, his disease relented; he began to regain strength, and in March was able to resume the journey. On the thirtieth of the month, they left their hut, which had been inundated by a sudden rise of the river, and carried their canoe through mud and water over the portage

---

[1] *coureur de bois:* a trapper

which led to the Des Plaines. Marquette knew the way, for he had passed by this route on his return from the Mississippi. Amid the rains of opening spring, they floated down the swollen current of the Des Plaines, by naked woods and spongy, saturated prairies, till they reached its junction with the main stream of the Illinois, which they descended to their destination, the Indian town which Marquette calls Kaskaskia. Here, as we are told, he was received "like an angel from Heaven." He passed from wigwam to wigwam, telling the listening crowds of God and the Virgin, Paradise and Hell, angels and demons; and, when he thought their minds prepared, he summoned them all to a grand council.

It took place near the town, on the great meadow which lies between the river and the modern village of Utica. Here five hundred chiefs and old men were seated in a ring; behind stood fifteen hundred youths and warriors, and behind these again all the women and children of the village. Marquette, standing in the midst, displayed four large pictures of the Virgin; harangued the assembly on the mysteries of the Faith, and exhorted them to adopt it. The temper of his auditory met his utmost wishes. They begged him to stay among them and continue his instructions; but his life was fast ebbing away, and it behooved him to depart.

A few days after Easter he left the village, escorted by a crowd of Indians, who followed him as far as Lake Michigan. Here he embarked with his two companions. Their destination was Michillimackinac, and their course lay along the eastern borders of the lake. As, in the freshness of advancing spring, Pierre and Jacques urged their canoe along that lonely and savage shore, the priest lay with dimmed sight and prostrated strength, communing with the Virgin and the angels. On the nineteenth of May, he felt that his hour was near; and, as they passed the mouth of a small river, he requested his companions to land. They complied, built a shed of bark on a rising ground near the bank, and carried thither the dying Jesuit. With perfect cheerfulness and composure, he gave directions for his burial, asked their forgiveness for the trouble he had caused them, administered to them the sacrament of penitence, and thanked God that he was permitted to die in the wilderness, a missionary of the Faith and a member of the Jesuit brotherhood. At night, seeing that they were fatigued, he told them to take rest, saying that he would call them when he felt his time approaching. Two or three hours after, they heard a feeble voice, and, hastening to his side, found him at the point of death. He expired calmly, murmuring the names of Jesus and Mary, with his eyes fixed on the crucifix which one of his followers held before him. They dug a grave beside the hut, and here they buried him according to the directions which he had given them; then, re-embarking, they made their way to Michillimackinac, to bear the tidings to the priests at the mission of St. Ignace.

In the winter of 1676, a party of Kiskakon Ottawas were hunting on Lake Michigan; and when, in the following spring, they prepared to return home, they bethought them, in accordance with an Indian custom, of taking with them the bones of Marquette, who had been their instructor at the mission of St. Esprit. They repaired to the spot, found the grave, opened it, washed and dried the bones and placed them carefully in a box of birch-bark. Then, in a procession of thirty canoes, they bore it, singing their funeral songs, to St. Ignace of Michillimackinac. As the approached, priests, Indians, and traders all thronged to the shore. The relics of Marquette were received with solemn ceremony, and buried beneath the floor of the little chapel of the mission.

Questions and Comments

1. What were the chief character traits of Joliet and Marquette? What single aspect of their characters probably helped them most in their journey of exploration?

2. At what point in the narrative do Marquette and Joliet display the most courage?

3. The Menomonies predicted that terrible things would happen to Marquette and Joliet on the Mississippi River. Did any of their predictions have basis in fact? What might this show about rumors concerning the unknown?

4. What are four or five clues which prove that earlier white explorers had contact with the tribes along the Mississippi River?

5. The motives for exploration often vary with different ex-explorers. What was the motive of Marquette and Joliet?

6. What details from the account did Parkman probably have to supply for himself because it would be unlikely that they were mentioned in a journal or diary?

7. In what passage of the selection do you think that Parkman achieves a very peaceful or restful mood? Where in the selection does he achieve a very threatening mood?

Word Study

1. Joliet "received the *tonsure* and the *minor orders* at the age of seventeen." What is the *tonsure* and the *minor orders?* Check with a dictionary.

2. *Boor,* from the Dutch *boer,* originally referred to a peasant, a rustic, or a clownish person from the countryside. Its meaning has become more general, for it now may refer to anyone, whether the person is from the country or not. What does *boor* mean today?

3. Give the meaning of the following words using clues from the context wherever possible.

"He was a devout *votary* of the Virgin Mary. . . . . (page 92)

". . . they passed the Straits of Michillimackinac, and coasted the northern shores of Lake Michigan; landing at evening to build their camp-fire at the edge of the forest, and draw up their canoes on the *strand*." (page 93)

"... that savage river poured its *turbid* floods into the bosom of its gentler sister." (page 99)

"Their light canoes whirled on the miry *vortex* like dry leaves on an angry brook." (page 99)

4. Show how the derivation of the following words helps to reveal their meaning. Check your guesses with a dictionary.

   interspersed from the Latin *inter* meaning "between" and *spargere* meaning "to scatter"

   paramount from the Old French *par* meaning "through" and *amont* meaning "above"

   promiscuous from the Latin *promiscuus* meaning "mixed"

   delusive from the Latin *delude* meaning "to play false" or "to deceive"

   fastidious from the Latin *fastidium* meaning "a loathing" or "an aversion"

   palisaded from the Latin *palus* meaning "a stake"

5. Here are some other words which should be looked up if you do not know them: *infallibly* (page 90), *bivouac* (page 95), *languid* (page 99), *exhorted* (page 105)

Composition

1. Recount in a composition some of the adventures encountered by Marquette and Joliet on their search for and discovery of the Mississippi. Tell which adventure remains most unforgettable for you, and why.

2. There are still many areas of the world which remain largely unexplored. Use an encyclopedia to find out where these areas are. In a composition discuss whatever is known about them and offer reasons why in this day and age they still remain unknown and uncharted.

A tragic marriage, selling out his talent to slick magazines, and succumbing to the movies' "big money" were all a part of F. Scott Fitzgerald's failure. But none of these can cast even a pale shadow upon the brilliance of his lasting literary successes. He said himself, "I never blame failure—there are too many complicated situations in life—but I am absolutely merciless toward lack of effort." Perhaps because of his own realization of personal failings, he could write very movingly to his daughter about her own personal problems while attending college. The letters to his daughter which are a part of *The Crack-Up,* a collection of Fitzgerald's essays, letters, and comments, urge over and over that she accept her duties and responsibilities, that she work hard in developing her talents. But the letters are more than sermons; they reflect a warm love, a respect for her individuality, a father's concern, and a very deep sympathy.

LETTERS TO FRANCES SCOTT FITZGERALD

F. Scott Fitzgerald

August 8, 1933
La Paix, Rodgers' Forge
Towson, Maryland

DEAR PIE:

I feel very strongly about you doing duty. Would you give me a little more documentation about your reading in French? I am glad you are happy—but I never believe much in happiness. I never believe in misery either. Those are things you see on the stage or the screen or the printed page, they never really happen to you in life.

All I believe in in life is the rewards for virtue (according to your talents) and the *punishments* for not fulfilling your duties, which are doubly costly. If there is such a volume in the camp library, will you ask Mrs. Tyson to let you look up a sonnet of Shakespeare's in which the line occurs *Lilies that fester smell far worse than weeds*.[1]

Have had no thoughts today, life seems composed of getting up a *Saturday Evening Post* story. I think of you, and always pleasantly; but if you call me "Pappy" again I am going to take the White Cat out and beat his bottom *hard, six times for every time you are impertinent*. Do you react to that?

I will arrange the camp bill.

Half-wit, I will conclude. Things to worry about:

    Worry about courage
    Worry about cleanliness
    Worry about efficiency
    Worry about horsemanship . . .

Things not to worry about:

    Don't worry about popular opinion
    Don't worry about dolls
    Don't worry about the past
    Don't worry about the future
    Don't worry about growing up
    Don't worry about anybody getting ahead of you
    Don't worry about triumph
    Don't worry about failure unless it comes through your
       own fault
    Don't worry about mosquitoes
    Don't worry about flies
    Don't worry about insects in general
    Don't worry about parents
    Don't worry about boys
    Don't worry about disappointments
    Don't worry about pleasures
    Don't worry about satisfactions

---

[1] *Lilies . . . weeds:* Shakespeare's "Sonnet XCIV"

Things to think about:

What am I really aiming at?

How good am I really in comparison to my contemporaries in regard to:

(a) Scholarship

(b) Do I really understand about people and am I able to get along with them?

(c) Am I trying to make my body a useful instrument or am I neglecting it?

With dearest love,

Spring, 1940

Spring was always an awful time for me about work. I always felt that in the long boredom of winter there was nothing else to do but study. But I lost the feeling in the long, dreamy spring days and managed to be in scholastic hot water by June. I can't tell you what to do about it—all my suggestions seem to be very remote and academic. But if I were with you and we could talk again like we used to, I might lift you out of your trouble about concentration. It really isn't so hard, even with dreamy people like you and me—it's just that we feel so damned secure at times as long as there's enough in the bank to buy the next meal, and enough moral stuff in reserve to take us through the next ordeal. Our danger is imagining we have resources—material and moral—which we haven't got. One of the reasons I find myself so consistently in valleys of depression is that every few years I seem to be climbing uphill to recover from some bankruptcy. Do you know what bankruptcy exactly means? It means drawing on resources which one does not possess. I thought I was so strong that I never would be ill and suddenly I was ill for three years, and faced with a long, slow uphill climb. Wiser people seem to manage to pile up a reserve—so that if on a night you had set aside to study for a philosophy test, you learned that your best friend was in trouble and needed your help, you could skip that night and find you had a reserve of one or two days preparation to draw on. But I think that, like me, you will be something of a fool in that regard all your life, so I am wasting my words.

June 12, 1940

I could agree with you as opposed to Dean Thompson if you were getting "B's." Then I would say: As you're not going to be a teacher or a professional scholar, don't try for "A's"— don't take the things in which you can get "A," for you can learn them yourself. Try something hard and new, and try it hard, and take what marks you can get. But you have no such margin of respectability, and this borderline business is a fret to you. Doubt and worry—you are as crippled by them as I am by my inability to handle money or my self-indulgences of the past. It is your Achilles' heel—and no Achilles' heel ever toughened by itself. It just gets more and more vulnerable. What little I've accomplished has been by the most laborious and uphill work, and I wish now I'd *never* relaxed or looked back—but said at the end of *The Great Gatsby:* "I've found my line—from now on this comes first. This is my immediate duty—without this I am nothing."

August 3, 1940

It isn't something easy to get started on by yourself. You need, at the beginning, some enthusiast who also knows his way around—John Peale Bishop performed that office for me at Princeton. I had always dabbled in "verse," but he made me see, in the course of a couple of months, the difference between poetry and non-poetry. After that, one of my first discoveries was that some of the professors who were teaching poetry really hated it and didn't know what it was about. I got in a series of endless scraps with them, so that finally I dropped English altogether. . . .

Poetry is either something that lives like fire inside you— like music to the musician or Marxism to the Communist—

or else it is nothing, an empty, formalized bore, around which pendants can endlessly drone their notes and explanations. *The Grecian Urn*[1] is unbearably beautiful, with every syllable as inevitable as the notes in Beethoven's *Ninth Symphony,* or it's just something you don't understand. It is what it is because an extraordinary genius paused at that point in history and touched it. I suppose I've read it a hundred times. About the tenth time I began to know what it was about, and caught the chime in it and the exquisite inner mechanics. Likewise with the *Nightingale,*[2] which I can never read through without tears in my eyes; likewise the *Pot of Basil*[3] with its great stanzas about the two brothers: "Why were they proud, etc."; and *The Eve of Saint Agnes,* which has the richest, most sensuous imagery in English, not excepting Shakespeare. And finally his three or four great sonnets: *Bright Star*[4] and the others....

Knowing those things very young and granted an ear one could scarely ever afterwards be unable to distinguish between gold and dross in what one read. In themselves those eight poems are a scale of workmanship for anybody who wants to know truly about words, their must utter value for evocation, persuasion or charm. For awhile after you quit Keats all other poetry seems to be only whistling or humming.

August 12, 1940

Working among the poor has differing effects on people. If you're poor yourself, you get their psychology and it's broadening—for example, when a boy of the bourgeoisie ships before the mast on a tramp schooner where he has to endure the same privations as the seamen, undoubtedly he achieves

[1] *The Grecian Urn:* "Ode on a Grecian Urn" is by John Keats, as are the other poems mentioned in this paragraph.
[2] *Nightingale:* "Ode to a Nightingale"
[3] *Pot of Basil:* "Isabella, or The Pot of Basil"
[4] *Bright Star:* a sonnet also known as "The Last Sonnet"

something of their point of view forever. On the contrary, a Bennington[1] girl spending a month in slum work and passing the weekend at her father's mansion in Long Island gets nothing at all except a smug feeling that she is Lady Bountiful.

Questions and Comments

Some books by F. Scott Fitzgerald are *Tender is the Night*, *The Great Gatsby*, and *This Side of Paradise*.

1. In the August 8th letter Fitzgerald asks his daughter to worry about four things but not to worry about sixteen things. Which items seem most important to you in each list? Why? Is such a list an effective way to give advice? Why or why not?

2. What is Fitzgerald's advice to his daughter concerning concentration in the letter dated Spring, 1940?

3. What facts does Fitzgerald state about himself which reveal his frankness and his habit of close self-examination?

4. What does *It* probably refer to as the first word of the first sentence in the August 3, 1940, letter?

5. A considerable amount of Fitzgerald's advice concerns his daughter's progress in school. What are at least four pieces of advice you consider valuable or worth remembering?

6. Which sentences or phrases in the letters do you think reveal most clearly that Fitzgerald was a professional writer who could really use the language?

Word Study

1. The word *impertinent* should be self-explanatory when

[1] *Bennington:* a private college in Vermont, formerly for women only

you examine the context in the first letter. What is its meaning?

2. Find out from a dictionary why *Achilles' heel* and *vulnerable* are so closely associated.

3. *Dross* in the August 3rd letter is an interesting word which comes from the Old English *dros,* which meant "to drip." *Dross* at first had a rather special meaning, "the waste or slag material which came from smelting or purifying metals." Today this word has become more general in its meaning. In what sense does Fitzgerald use it?

4. Fitzgerald says that eight poems by Keats "are a scale of workmanship for anybody who wants to know truly about words, their most utter value for evocation, persuasion or charm." *Evocation* is a word which can be terribly important to any discussion of poetry. Look it up and be sure of its use.

5. Give the meaning of the italicized words using clues from the context:

"Lilies that *fester* smell far worse than weeds." (page 110)
". . . a boy of the *bourgeoisie* . . . has to endure the same *privations* as the seaman . . ." (page 113)

Composition

1. Fitzgerald is a philosopher in that he is constantly making observations about people in general which seem both valid and profound. He has insight concerning humanity. Tell why you agree or disagree with this in a short essay dealing with the letters to his daughter.

2. Write a short critical essay in which you evaluate some of the advice Fitzgerald gives to his daughter.

3. Look up one of the literary pieces which Fitzgerald mentions in the letters and discuss its content in terms of what Fitzgerald says about it and why he wants his daughter to read it.

From the time James Agee was ten until his death in 1955 at the age of forty-five, he kept a close relationship with Father Flye, a teacher in St. Andrew's, a school for boys in Tennessee. Agee's father died shortly before James entered St. Andrew's. His friendship with Father Flye helped him over a difficult period and healed a wound in Agee's life which might otherwise have permanently hurt him. The friendship lasted for thirty years.

James Agee's interests ranged widely: he loved films and wrote what experts consider to be one of the most important bodies of film criticism. Not content to merely write about films, he had to actually write films himself. He wrote the scenarios for such distinguished films as *The Bride Comes to Yellow Sky, Night of the Hunter,* and the widely acclaimed *The African Queen.* In addition to his film work, he wrote articles for *Fortune* and *Time,* many of them masterpieces, and a fine novel, *A Death in the Family.*

from LETTERS OF JAMES AGEE TO FATHER FLYE

James Agee

Cambridge, Mass.
November 19th, 1930

DEAR FATHER FLYE:

Last summer, and more this fall, I've thought of you often, and wished I could see you, and intended to write you. Until now I haven't even begun and lost a letter to you—as I did several times last spring. I'd like to make this a long letter, and a good one; but as is usual these days I feel fairly tongue-tied the minute I have a sheet of paper before me. If I could see you for any decent length of time, I'd without effort say what here I can't write. But I haven't seen you or even written you in a very long time—and would like if possible to give some sort of account of myself in the interim. That's a difficult job for me, and I don't know just how to go about it.

I suppose the two chief things that have happened to me, and that after a fashion include the others, have to do with what I want to do with my life, and with the nasty process of growing up, or developing, or whatever it may best be called.

So far as I can tell, I definitely want to write—probably poetry in the main. At any rate, nothing else holds me in the same way. As you know, I had two other interests just as strong a few years ago—music and directing movies of my own authorship. These have slowly been killed off, partly by brute and voluntary force on my part, chiefly by the overcrowding of my wish to write. Each of them occasionally flares up; last spring I was all but ready to quit college and bum to California and trust to luck for the rest. And more often, I feel I'd give anything to have forgotten everything but music, because I want so to compose. I really think I could have done it—possibly better than writing. I suppose a native inertia has as much to do with my keeping on with writing instead, as has an instinct (which I over-credit) for knowing that writing is my one even moderate talent.

Up to 6 or 8 months ago, I took this with only sporadic seriousness. But as I read more and wrote somewhat more carefully, it took hold of me more. Last spring I finished a fairly longish poem that finally finished the business. For one thing, I worked harder on it than ever before. And, when it was finished, various people thought it was very good, and encouraged me a good deal. I don't know what I think of the poem itself—but I'm from now on committed to writing with a horrible definiteness.

In fact it amounts to a rather unhealthy obsession. I'm thinking about it every waking minute, in one way or another; and my head is spinning and often—as now—dull with the continuous overwork. The sad part of it—but necessary—is that, most of the time, I'm absorbed in no tangible subject that can be thought through and put aside. The thing I'm trying hardest to do is, to decide what I want to write, and in exactly what way. After a fashion, I know, but it will take a lot more time before I'm able to do it. The great trouble is, I'm terribly anxious to do as well as I possibly can. It sounds conceited; whether it is or not: I'd do anything on earth to become a really great writer. That's as sincere a thing as I've ever said. Do you see, though, where it leads me? In the first place I have no faith to speak of in my native ability to become more than a very minor writer. My intellectual pelvic girdle simply is not Miltonically wide.[1] So, I have, pretty much, to keep same on a stretcher, or more properly a rack,[2] day and night. I've got to make my mind as broad and deep and rich as possible, as quick and fluent as possible; abnormally sympathetic and yet perfectly balanced. At the same time, I've got to strengthen those segments of my talent which are naturally weak; and must work out for myself a way of expressing what I want to write. You see, I should like to parallel, foolish as it sounds, what Shakespeare did. That is, in general—to write primarily about people—giving their emotions and dramas the expression that, because of its beauty and power, will be most likely to last. But —worse than that: I'd like, in a sense, to combine what Chekhov did with what Shakespeare did—that is, to move from the dim, rather eventless beauty of C.[3] to huge geometric plots such as Lear.[4] And to make this transition without

[1] *My . . . wide:* The pelvic bones support the body's whole upper skeleton; Milton is a noted 17th-century poet whose education and reading was extensive and vast. Thus Agee is simply admitting his own intellectual background to be inadequate.

[2] *rack:* an instrument of torture by stretching the body

[3] *C.:* Anton Chekhov, Russian writer and playwright (1860-1904)

[4] *Lear: King Lear,* a tragedy by Shakespeare

its seeming ridiculous. And to do the whole so that it flows naturally, and yet, so that the whole—words, emotion, characters, situation, etc.—has a discernible symmetry and a very definite *musical* quality—inaccurately speaking—I want to *write symphonies.* That is, characters introduced quietly (as are themes in a symphony, say) will recur in new lights, with new verbal orchestration, will work into counterpoint[1] and get a sort of monstrous grinding beauty—and so on. By now you probably see what I mean at least as well as I do.

Well—this can't be done to best advantage in a novel. Prose holds you down from the possibility of such music. And put into poetic drama, it would certainly be stillborn or worse; besides, much of what I want to get can't well be expressed in dialogue. It's got to be narrative poetry, but of a sort that so far as I know has never been tried. In the sort I've read, the medium is too stiff to allow you to get exactly a finely shaded atmosphere, for instance—in brief, to get the effects that *can* be got in a short story or novel. I've thought of inventing a sort of amphibious style—prose that would run into poetry when the occasion demanded poetic expression. That may be the solution; but I don't entirely like the idea. What I want to do is, to devise a poetic diction that will cover the whole range of events as perfectly and evenly as skin covers every organ, vital as well as trivial, of the human body. And this style can't, of course, be incongruous, no matter what I'm writing about. For instance, I'm quite determined to include comedy in it—of a sort that would demand realistic slangy dialogue and description.

That leads to another thing—the use of words in general. I'm very anxious not to fall into archaism or "literary" diction. I want my vocabulary to have a very large range, but the words *must* be alive.

Well, that's one thing that keeps me busy: you can see what it leads to. For instance, what sort of characters to use? I want them to be of the present day—at least superficially.

[1] *counterpoint:* a combination of two or more independent melodies into a single harmonic texture

Well, present-day characters are obviously good for novels, but not so obviously material for high poetry. Further, just how shall they speak? At the climaxes they certainly can't speak realistically: and in the calmer stretches it would be just as silly for them to speak idealized blank verse.[1]

Life is too short to try to go further into details about this. But it's part of what serves to keep me busy; and unhappy. The whole thing still seems just within the bounds of possible achievement; but highly improbable. There are too many other things crowding in to ruin it: the whole course of everyday life. And yet, of course, it's absolutely necessary for me to live as easily and calmly and fully as I can; and to be and feel human rather than coldblooded about the whole thing. It's only too easy, I find, to be "Human." I care as much as I ever did about other people's feelings, and worry much more when I hurt them. Of course I should be and am thankful for this, but it certainly helps complicate matters. For one thing, with most of my best friends, I feel rather dumb. I don't like to be unhappy or introspective to any noticeable extent in their presence; the result is that I'm pretty dull. Also, most of them are graduated or otherwise removed from the neighborhood, so that I'm pretty awfully lonely a good deal of the time. I'm too preoccupied with the whole business sketched in above to give my courses constant or thorough attention; I don't do much actual work; yet I feel exhausted most of the time. There are a few ways of relaxing, to a certain extent; I like to walk—especially at night; but frequently am too tired. I love to listen to music; but that involves being parasitic around music stores, or cutting classes to get rush seat at Friday symphony. At times, I like to play the piano. Just now, I'm cracked about it, having got a lovely thing by Cesar Franck:[2] Prelude, Fugue and Variation. I played it for three hours tonight. I've been to a half-a-dozen movies, one play, and three concerts. Once a week or

---

[1] *blank verse:* unrhymed verse with a definite meter

[2] *Cesar Franck:* Belgian (naturalized French) composer (1822–1890)

so Franklin Miner comes in from the suburbs and we take a
walk and eat together. I see a young tutor named Ted
Spencer[1] when I can . . .

I've got to stop, and get to bed soon. This isn't as full a letter as I'd like to have written, but I'm deadly tired. I hope
you'll write soon—and I shall, too. Will you tell me about
any further plans for your school? And about yourself and
Mrs. Flye? I wish I could see you both again. Are you by any
chance coming north this Christmas? Maybe I could see you
then. I hope you are.

Much love to you both,

Rufus.

New York City
Oct. 30, 1934

Dear Father Flye:

Pardon this morning's letter. But the present note is for
more than to ask pardon. The idea fell into my head this
noon, after absence of some months, of what possibilities
there might be of teaching at St. Andrew's. For some time,
and very much so lately, I have been sure I wanted, sooner
or later and by preference sooner, to quit this job and all
others that take much time, and definitely to concentrate on
writing and on the amount of reading, talking, seeing and
free time which are best needed to go into writing. An exceedingly hard problem, practically, because we have no
money and must live and must even, before much more time
has gone, figure in what it would take to support a family.
(Not that it's at all pressing.) In other words I must find ways
to support life which will also be ways that will allow me a
maximum amount of freedom. Hard combination. That is
where the idea of St. Andrew's comes in. I would like to quit

[1] *Ted Spencer:* Theodore Spencer, later a professor at Harvard and respected
poet

here, if I could, within a year, but can't be sure. In the first place do you think there would be a chance of my getting a job there? But that is at present less important to me than everything else about it. Here is the way it is to me: 1. I am attracted to teaching almost enough to dread it, but would in all ways predispose myself in coldness toward it: would use it only as a job which I would try to do well but would make no effort to break my heart over. 2. Would you guess, from your experience, that teaching at St. Andrew's would give me much and uninterrupted leisure? 3. Would you guess that I could do that sort of teaching (a) decently enough not to be shameful and (b) without cracking up nervously? I think I could but I know my weaknesses are many. 4. Especially important: how well do you think Via[1] could manage? The whole thing would be as alien to her as anything that can be imagined, and though such changes for a harder life may be "good" for people, it depends on the people. She is an unusually gentle, sensitive and complicated person, by no means free of all the potentialities of melancholia and what have you, and it very seriously occurs to me that the life there might do her a great deal of harm. A heavy lot of questions to impose upon you, but for any answers whatever, I would be grateful.

Do you ever happen to see any of the Silly Symphonies by Walt Disney?[2] On the whole they are very beautiful. A sort of combination of Mozart,[3] super-ballet, and La Fontaine[4] . . . Another thing to see, I hear, is *Men of Aran.*[5]

Much love,
Rufus

[1] *Via:* Agee's wife
[2] *Walt Disney:* famous producer of animated cartoons (1901–1966)
[3] *Mozart:* Wolfgang A. Mozart, Austrian composer (1756–1791)
[4] *La Fontaine:* French writer of fables (1621–1695)
[5] *Men of Aran:* a documentary movie by Robert Flaherty about the Aran Islands off the west coast of Ireland

Questions and Comments

1. What reasons does Agee give for wanting to become a writer?

2. What does Agee say is his most pressing problem in regard to writing?

3. What two authors does Agee wish to combine in himself?

4. What does James Agee mean when he says, "I want to *write symphonies*"?

5. The kind of writing Agee is determined to do poses several problems. What are at least four of these problems?

6. What conflict does Agee see between being "Human" and being an "artist"? In what way does this conflict present itself in the 1934 letter?

7. What reasons does Agee give for wanting to become a teacher? From what he says, do you think he shows the proper temperament for teaching? Why?

Word Study

1. Explain how the context helps to reveal the meaning of the italicized words:

   "But I haven't seen you or even written you in a very long time—and would like if possible to give some sort of account of myself in the *interim*." (page 117)

   "I suppose a native *inertia* has as much to do with my keeping on with writing instead. . . ." (page 117)

   "I've thought of inventing a sort of *amphibious* style—prose that would run into poetry when the occasion demanded poetic expression." (page 119)

   "I am attracted to teaching almost enough to dread it, but would in all ways *predispose* myself in coldness toward it. . . ." (page 122)

2. The word *sporadic* as in "Up to 6 or 8 months ago, I took this with only sporadic seriousness" comes from the Greek word *sporadikos,* "scattered." How does its derivation help to reveal the meaning of *sporadic?*

3. The word *archaism* as in "I'm very anxious not to fall into archaism or 'literary' diction" comes from the Greek word *arché,* "beginning" or "origin." What does *archaism* mean? What other English words beginning with *arch* do you know?

4. Is *introspective* (page 120) a good adjective for James Agee? Why?

Composition

1. Write an essay in which you describe and analyze the character of James Agee as revealed in the two letters.

2. Write a letter to an adult friend you respect, explaining your future plans.

John Keats (1920–   ) is a free-lance writer who has contributed hundreds of articles to newspapers and magazines such as *Esquire, Harpers,* and *Holiday,* from which this selection is taken. Among the recent books he was written are biographies of Howard Hughes, the recluse billionaire who died in 1976, and Dorothy Parker, the popular American writer and humorist. Other recent books are *What Ever Happened to Mom's Apple Pie* and *Eminent Domain.*

ON RUNNING AWAY

John Keats

Ralph and I considered the possibility of police pursuit. We briefly debated the advisability of disguises. We decided that the wisest course was to try to postpone pursuit. To that end, we would tell our parents that we had each been invited by the other boy's family to spend the summer in Michigan. We made our secret plans, and one afternoon, shortly after high school graduation, we uttered our little lies and headed for the railroad yards. That evening, while our families were no doubt discovering that neither owned a summer camp in Michigan, we were already far from our comfortable New Jersey suburb, rattling west across America. Our object was to get to China to join the American Volunteer Group in its aerial combat against the Japanese.

Two weeks later America was still rattling past, but now there was not a tree or house in sight. We slid the boxcar door wide open at dawn to see a vast prairie, pale gold in the east, dark in the west. Mountaintops shone above the shadows as they caught the first light. We were lonely, stiff from sleeping on a jittering wooden floor, cold, and tired of eating canned dog food. I have a clear memory of that morning in the morning of my life, now more than a quarter century ago. I can see in mind's eye those empty distances, and feel again that emptiness inside me. I am certain that Ralph was as fearful as I that day, but we did not admit our misgivings to each other. That would have been as much an admission of failure as returning home.

As we sat in the open doorway, watching the day brighten and the Rockies draw slowly nearer, I reflected on the recent past. No small part of the charm of running away from home lay in the presumption that the world was full of dangers. Naturally, we were eager to encounter them. Nothing was more pleasant than to imagine returning home as bronzed soldiers of fortune, bearing interesting scars and laden with the gifts of a grateful Chinese government. En route to the wars we would, of course, slay the usual number of local dragons. We were not running away from life but into it. We were sure that what we had left behind was lifeless. Our New Jersey suburb was pudgy with Buicks and Packards; a thing of clean linen, toothbrushes, electric razors, the once-a-week sound of the maid running the vacuum cleaner, and the empty conversations of soft-bellied people who worked in offices and played bridge and went to Bermuda in the spring.

Our view of ourselves, now that we rode boxcars and rolled our own cigarettes, was that we were tough. We wore blue denims, and soot from the coal-burning trains was ground into our clothing and our skin. Our adolescent stubble always seemed to be three days old. The men we now met were, for the most part, illiterates. Two of the men in the gondola ahead of us looked to be thieves. There was no question about it: we were seeing Life. Unfortunately, it only too closely resembled the one we had left.

I could not help thinking, as we clacked along, that we

knew of two thieves at home. One was a member of Rotary; the other, a minister's son. I have said that Ralph and I were inwardly fearful, but I should make clear that what we secretly feared was that life would not prove challenging but merely dull. In fact, we were finding it not only dull but dirty.

There were perils, but they were largely mechanical. For instance, one of our fellow passengers, an elderly nondescript, had made the mistake of dozing in the sunlight near the forward edge of a boxcar roof. When the cars banged together as the fast freight trains began to break, clattering down the long hill into Cheyenne, the first sudden lurch tossed him forward, off the roof and under the wheels, which instantly bisected him. One night when Ralph and I sheltered from the rain in a sort of cave formed by overhanging boards piled on a flatcar, we narrowly escaped a similar fate when the load shifted as we rounded a curve. Stupidity, we realized, was lethal. But where were the unknown dangers with which the world was supposedly replete? Specifically, where were the toughs and murderers who, in the public mind, so thickly populated the hobo jungles and the Hoovervilles?[1]

We met none. The well-fed burghers[2] of our hometown, to whom the Depression was more of a nuisance than a catastrophe, regarded the scarecrows of the Hoovervilles as dubiously as a French marquis[3] might have looked on a Parisian mob in 1790, but they were wrong. At least in the West, the hobo jungles were merely unofficial public campsites tenanted by a slowly changing population of migrants down on their luck. Feeling a need for government, these men formed their own. Many were veterans of World War I, and in camp after camp a former sergeant was elected or appointed leader. He greeted new arrivals, assigned them

---

[1]*Hoovervilles:* a collection of shacks at the edge of a city, housing the unemployed during the 1930s; named after President Herbert Hoover (1929-33)

[2]*burghers:* citizens

[3]*French marquis:* French aristocrat, hence an enemy of the French revolutionists

huts or sleeping space and explained the rules: *No fighting, thieves get beat up, you keep your place clean. And remember, try to bring back something for chow. Everybody brings something for chow.*

In the America of those days everyone understood everyone else's problem, because it was also his own. If a man could not find work in one town, he tried another. Having no money to spend for transportation, he thumbed rides (which those who had cars were glad to offer), or he hopped a freight (while the brakemen looked the other way). The people on the road were not derelicts. The derelicts, then as now, lived in the Skid Rows[1] of our cities. All the men and boys on the road, however modest their abilities and backgrounds, were looking for work. Some were bindle stiffs[2] who had known nothing all their lives except stoop labor, moving forever from harvest to harvest. Others were genuine hobos—men who could work at nearly any trade, but whose free choice it was to hold no job long. All hobos said they intended to settle down someday, but not just yet. There was still a lot of country they wanted to see first. With rare exceptions, we met none but friends. Perhaps it is true that in good times no one takes to the road but the bad, but in our bad times we met virtually none but the good.

Ralph and I had looked for jobs wherever the trains stopped on our way through the Midwest, and while we found none, there were always housewives who would put their cares aside to consider ours. They would give us makework so that we should not seem beggars. We would wash the windows, or whitewash the henhouse, or clean the yard or the rain gutters, and while we puttered, the woman would prepare us a meal. Often as not they would also give us a package of food to take to the train. In small towns everyone

[1]*Skid Rows:* that part of a city where derelicts congregate
[2]*bindle stiffs:* (slang) hoboes

knew the train schedules, and sometimes we would be told, "Gracious, there *is* some work I do want done, but you boys won't have time for it before the train leaves, so why don't you just sit down and I'll try to find something in the icebox."

It was disappointing to be welcomed everywhere, when it was so important for us to learn whether we could make our unaided way through a violent world. Of course, we heard that the railroad detectives were the sadistic enemies of the tramp. We heard they loved nothing more than to beat a defenseless man insensible and toss his body on an outbound freight. The most famous of these detectives was one Green River Slim. Alas, we never saw a yard detective, and Green River Slim turned out to be just as imaginary, and as ubiquitous, as that other great American whose name was also found chalked upon a thousand boxcars (and who later would go to war)—Kilroy.[1]

In retrospect it is clear to me that Ralph and I were the only people of our acquaintance on the road who were dangerous. We were looking for trouble; everyone else was looking for work. Our ambition was to kill Japanese for fun and money, and meanwhile prove to the world how tough we were. Nobody seemed to view us in just this light except, perhaps, a toothless old wreck, with breath like a vulture's, who accosted us outside a Skid Row bar in Chicago.

"Want to see how hard you can hit?" he asked us. "Gimme a quarter, I'll let you hit me. See can you knock me out."

He followed us for nearly a block, pleading, promising not to hit back, flattering us, and finally, when he saw it was no use, cursing. Looking back on it, I think we fled from him.

---

[1]*Kilroy:* During World War II, GIs made a fad of writing "Kilroy was here" on walls, fences, trees, etc. The name "Kilroy" has no known meaning beyond its use by GIs.

Novelty, rather than true discovery, entertained us to the
foothills of the Rockies. It would be years before we learned
the truth of Montaigne's[1] remark that the traveler must
take himself wherever he goes. Yet I do remember that our
first sight of those mountains seemed a mockery; I remember the feeling of emptiness they created inside me. In themselves they were an enormous fact, and consideration of
one fact led to a consideration of others. One was that no
one wanted us to do anything for him except leave town;
people were glad to help us on our way. Another was that
we had nothing to offer anyone except manual labor, which
was not in demand, or our money, which was. We had left
home with two hundred dollars between us, all saved from
the unearned money our families had allowed us. It had
cost us thirty dollars to purchase blankets, denims, work
shoes and sufficient dog food to carry us to South Dakota.
Canned dog food recommended itself to us as the cheapest
comestible to be had. It constituted a balanced diet, and was
rather tasty—at first. The meals donated by housewives were
occasional banquets, but as the trains rolled farther west
and the towns thinned out, dog food became our staple,
and it seemed that we might have to consume another one
hundred and seventy dollars' worth of it if we could not
immediately find a ship for China. I now suspect that what
caused my feeling of emptiness was a premonition that
one could not live without money, but that no one could
earn money save at the loss of one's freedom. The world
seemed a jail.

   In the high Rockies, two boys our age boarded the train.
They were Louis Wang, a Chinese-American of Fresno,
and Phillip Benoff, a Russian-American from Los Angeles.
They had gone adventuring to the East Coast and now
were returning to California; Phil to join the Army and
Louis to join a gambling house where he would run a dice
table. We told them of our plans, and they decided to come

[1]*Montaigne:* Michel Montaigne,French philosopher and moralist (1533–1592)

along with us instead. In that moment we became an army, and the world brightened considerably. Changed by the alchemy of a dream, the mountains' vast sterility was transformed into magnificence. We would sort the facts of life to suit ourselves. Crossing the Pacific would be no problem. Everyone knew that boys could get jobs as wipers[1] to work a passage. Boys had been running away to sea for centuries. We had only to find a ship that needed four wipers.

Before it was over, we must have walked the docks of every port on the West Coast—including those of minor fishing towns. *Were we members of the union?* No. *Let's see your identification papers.* We had none.

Do you have passports? Passports?

We went to the union offices. *Buddy, we got 3,000 guys on the beach, and every single one of them is an Able Seaman.*

Ralph and I, blue-eyed and blond, went to Scandinavian shipping companies, saying, "Ay ban Swade. Ay yust want ship home." And they laughed and said they were sorry.

We persisted until someone finally told us the truth about the American Volunteer Group. It seemed that the volunteers had been carefully selected by the United States Government from its ranks of Army, Navy and Marine Corps pilots. We went to the recruiting offices, only to be told that we would need at least two years of college credits to qualify for the aviation-cadet programs. At this point, we all went to Fresno with Louis to think things over.

College was out of the question for Louis and Phil, but Ralph and I had only to ask to go, and our parents would send us. In Fresno I began to see the fallacy of our position: our confidence in ourselves had all along been based on the assumption that we were different from all other men; not on the slightest feeling of identity with mankind. This could not be helped; we were what our first eighteen years had made us. At any moment we could have walked out of

[1]*wiper:* lowest rank aboard a commercial vessel; one who does all the dirty work

the shacks of the hobo jungle to the nearest Western Union office, and hours later been dressed in decent clothes, sitting down to the best dinner in the best hotel of whatever town it was, while a hotel clerk booked reservations for us on the next Pullman headed for Newark, New Jersey. The difference between us and all others was, as Smollett would say, wholly matter-money. In the back of our minds we had always known this, and it was the source of our strength and the source of our great weakness; it made us hold something back in our relationships with others; we were never identifying with them; thus a barrier, built of dollars, shut us off from the kindness of Midwestern housewives, and from Louis and Phil. We and the other people on the road were of different tribes.

I do not mean to say that I worked all this out in so many words at age eighteen, sitting at the bar of a tacky one-story gambling house in Fresno, watching Chinese playing fan-tan and Americans shooting craps. I simply mean that I was then dimly but uneasily aware of what I am now saying. I remember that we did wonder aloud whether going back home to college would not be an admission of defeat, but that we rationalized our way to the view that the *only* path to war in the Chinese skies led through two years of college followed by an aviation-cadet program. This decided, we broke what had been a summer-long silence and wrote our first letters home.

The immediate answer was a large check, which we expected, and the utterly demoralizing news—which we had not expected at all—that our parents, confident that we would get over our silliness, had already entered us in college for the fall term. In those days not many colleges demanded College Entrance Examination Board test scores, but all of them had vacancies and most were willing to pretend that the customer was always bright.

Our parents' casual certainty about us was infuriating. We therefore determined upon one final gesture that would restore to us something of our romantic view of ourselves as hard, tough men. Louis Wang had a motorcycle. If he would let us borrow it, we would ride it east and send it back to him. Ralph's father owned a manufacturing concern (Ralph showed Louis the company letterhead) and Ralph would have the shipping department crate the motorcycle and send it back.

Oddly enough, Louis agreed. Perhaps he was intrigued by our idea of trying to drive across the continent without stopping except for gasoline. We all wondered if anyone had done this before; if it really could be done; if so, in how little time. So Louis showed us how to start and stop the thing, and we brought a pillow in a five-and-ten-cent store to wire onto the back fender to form a seat for the one who would not be driving. It would not take us long to learn how to drive it, Louis said. We shook hands and went blasting out of Fresno forever.

We raced furiously to Sacramento; scuttered over the mountains and into Reno with our backsides beginning to turn black and blue. We sped across the salt flats; paused for gasoline, coffee and a bottle of whiskey at a Wyoming town where all three were sold at the town's one store. Our headlights, at ninety miles an hour, suddenly illuminated white-faced Herefords wandering across an open range in Montana, and we went off the road to avoid them, shouting and scattering gravel and cattle; somehow wobbled back onto the road again and out of the herd. We gradually drew closer to what we believed to be the lights of a town, shining far ahead in the clear Western distances, only to realize at last that, in our grogginess, we were creeping nearer and nearer to the tailgate of an enormous, brightly lighted trailer truck. We drank black coffee at the next gas pump; coffee laced with whiskey. We also fell asleep while rounding a curve in Iowa. I remember seeing a shower of sparks, and eventually realizing they were caused by the foot peg grinding along the pavement while centrifugal force and an unbanked curve were keeping us alive. I shouted to Ralph to stop trying to show off, and he woke up suddenly, caught himself, and swerved back to our own side of the road.

Eighty hours after leaving Fresno we were streaking along the new Pennsylvania Turnpike at night, chased by police. They did not arrest us. They merely wanted to tell us the road was not yet open; that a thousand yards ahead was a place where the first bridge would be, when it was built. When we reached New Jersey we slept for two days, and it was some days later before the swelling left our hands and arms and the bruises faded from our buttocks.

Then, having nothing better to do, we went to college. We hated that. The boys and girls who went to college were nothing but tame kids who would unquestioningly evolve into the bridge players who made non-conversation. They joined fraternities, cheered at the games, did their homework, earned their grades, went to the dances and swung and swayed with Sammy Kaye,[1] while we, in our arrogant innocence, looked derisively upon all this from an outside world. We were different. We were 6,000 miles by boxcar and motorcycle apart from them. We knew it, and they did too. Just to be sure they knew, we always rolled our own cigarettes on campus and dressed in our sooty denim pants.

Looking back on it now, it seems odd to say we felt such a difference between ourselves and the college children, particularly when I have already said that we, in a formless way, had begun to suspect that the artificial differences between one man and another are inconsequential when compared to the real similarities that unite them. Moreover, Ralph and I were now back among our own kind. Why, then, the studied insolence of the Bull Durham[2] and the dirty Levi's?

[1]*Sammy Kaye:* popular big-band leader of the 30's and 40's
[2]*Bull Durham:* popular tobacco used in rolling one's own cigarettes

I suppose, now, that the pose and the costume was our way of saying to other collegians, *You know nothing about it.* We would sit in economics class, and the others would brightly chatter with the young doctoral student who was our instructor, and I would slump back in my chair with my hands in my pockets, angry and silent, hearing nothing of this footless patter of cyclical depressions. Instead, I would see in my mind's eye a filling-station door open, and the woman in the man's coat and hat emerge, a scarf wrapped around her nose and mouth to keep out the driving dust; she would wad another protective rag around the nozzle of the hose and the opening of the gas tank to put two dollars' worth of gasoline into a wretched jalopy crowded with an empty-faced family of spindly children and bearing on its roof rug-wrapped bundles and the flat steel web of a cheap double bed, and hear the man ask whether, instead of paying the money, he could stay and work for two days.

An *ad hominem*[1] approach to Economics 201A was not a certain path to success in the subject, but I cared nothing for the course and less for the grade. The feeling grew on me that no one in college, including the smug young instructors with the Phi Beta Kappa[2] keys, knew what the devil he was talking about; that they were all playing at an intellectual game that insulted the dignity of experience.

This was not a feeling I could put into words at that time. I had only the unexpressed knowledge, sitting silent inside me, that there was no place for me then, or perhaps ever, in any world I did not make for myself. Indeed, in retrospect, this seems to have been the cardinal lesson of our summer's trip. It will be seen that Ralph and I failed to make our dream come true; that our first young search for the stuff of life proved only that we were not at home in

---

[1] *ad hominem:* personal as opposed to objective and open-minded
[2] *Phi Beta Kappa:* honorary collegiate society; membership based on high scholarship records

either the suburban or the proletarian[1] worlds. Nor were we at home in the academic world. In fact, we would never be at home in any patterned world. No one ever is. No matter how much we share with all mankind, each of us is bitterly alone. Our true distance from our neighbor begins to yawn when we at length discover the unexplored darkness within ourselves, and begin to understand that he who travels farthest and fastest into this darkness must travel alone; and that the ultimate destination of every traveler is always himself.

It was just this sense of the void within us that our trip had given us; it was our first, urgent command to get to work and fill the void; our summer trip provided us with our first inkling that our claims to identity would be entirely determined by our experience of ourselves.

In this sense, I can say that some part of me, now and forever, answers to the sounds of a train whistling lonely in the night, and to the deep tones of foghorns in the mists of the Northwestern coast. Some part of me is still a boy sweating at unloading watermelons from a truck in Portland; I am still shivering atop a cattle car in the winds driving through the snow-covered high passes. There is still in whoever I am the wink of campfires and the sight of the drunken man jumping across a fire and someone hitting him with a railroad spike and him falling into the fire. I can still see the lights of San Francisco and of Alcatraz from Coit Tower, and the delicate faces of the Chinese girls that Louis found for us. I have a memory of walking the docks in the rain in Seattle, and of sleepless nights in the fumigated cots of flophouses run by the Gospel Mission; of the Western wastelands creeping past and a hawk swooping on a gopher. Most clearly, I can see the faces of hopeful men who would never know anything other than disap-

---

[1] *proletarian:* belonging to the lowest or poorest class of the people

pointment, and the burst of spray against the rocks and among the tidal pools of Monterey. I remember lying on rattling floorboards at night, wondering whether I would wind up in jail, or whether any girl would ever want to marry me, and if I would ever see my family again. I have many memories, and if I am not sure yet what all of them mean, I am nonetheless certain that whoever I am is whatever my memories have made me; that I am becoming whatever I can find out about myself.

Nagging at my mind is Churchill's[1] remark that "Without a measureless and perpetual uncertainty, the drama of human life would be destroyed." I suppose that each of us, in his own way and at his own time, ventures as far as he chooses to dare in search of himself. Amy Lowell[2] wondered, "Christ! What are patterns for?" They are largely for the timid; for those who find them comfortable. It seems to me that an adventure must be defined as an undertaking whose end it is impossible to know.

That is why I applaud the youthful dramatist, the would-be adventurer, who breaks the pattern, who with mounting excitement writes the farewell note and slips out the window at dead of night to set off afoot for the railroad yards to board a freight bound for California. I believe I know how he feels. More important, I know that he is not running away from something so much as he is running toward something: toward life; toward himself; toward an end that cannot be known.

I wish him well. His chances of finding what he seeks are never good, but they are at least better than the chances of those who stay at home, placidly accepting patterns they never made, or chose.

[1]*Churchill:* Winston Churchill, famous twentieth century British politician (1874-1965); Prime Minister during World War II

[2]*Amy Lowell:* poet and critic (1874-1925), the quoted line comes from her famous poem, "Patterns"

Questions and Comments

1. In the second paragraph (p. 126), Keats writes of an "emptiness" inside him, and that he was "fearful." What was it that he and his companion were beginning to discover about their conceptions of the world and people after two weeks away from home?

2. Almost everyone dreams of running away. Each dreams of what it would be like, what would happen, what adventures would occur. Compare the boys' dreams with what actually happened.

3. What was so ironic about the author and Ralph's meeting Louis and Phillip?

4. What did Smollett mean by "matter-money" (p. 132)? Why did the author say, "... it was the source of our strength and the source of our weakness."? How did this realization differ from the discovery made two weeks after leaving home?

5. The author defines an adventure as, "... an undertaking whose end it is impossible to know." Did his adventure fulfill this definition? How?

6. If anyone were to ask John Keats if his running away was worthwhile, what would he say? Would he advise others to run away? Why or why not?

Word Study

1. "Mis" in *misgivings* means "ill, mistaken, wrong." What might the word mean in as it is used on p. 126?

2. *Pudgy* means "short and fat." Explain what the author means by describing a suburb as "pudgy with Buicks and Packards."

3. The following words appear in the essay and are worthy of study because they are quite commonly used by writers of adult nonfiction and fiction:

illiterates	demoralizing
perpetual	infuriating
nondescript	intrigued
bisected	arrogant
lethal	derisively
dubiously	inconsequential
derelicts	cyclical
virtually	retrospect
premonition	fumigated
fallacy	placidly

The following words also appear in the essay but are less commonly used:

ubiquitous	centrifugal
comestible	cardinal

Make a list of those words whose meanings you know, then find the sentence in the essay where the word appears and see if your definition makes sense. Look up the words you don't know in the dictionary and select a definition from the dictionary which best suits the sentence in which the word is used.

4. Look up these words: *chattel, gondola, alchemy, sadistic.* They have unusual derivations and stories behind them.

Composition

1. Almost everyone has a particular place in mind when they dream of running away. In a composition, first name the place or region you would run to. Describe what you think it is like and why you chose that place above all others.

2. "We were not running away from life but into it." You may react to this quote in two ways. First, did it turn out to be true for the boys in the essay? Why or why not? Second, apply the quote to yourself and define for yourself the difference between "running away from" and "running into" life.

3. Find and read Amy Lowell's poem, "Patterns." Show how its central meaning relates to the essay.

4. Explain in your own words, Churchill's quote: "Without a measureless and perpetual uncertainty, the drama of human life would be destroyed." Respond to it in a paragraph.

5. At bottom, this essay is really about two people attempting a first step in finding out who they are, what they are, and where they are going with their lives. Can you describe any experiences or occurrences in your own life which have assisted you in the discovery of your personal identity? In what ways have you learned important things about yourself, vital to your future plans concerning your education, career, and personal goals?

Joan Baez, (1941-   ) began her career as a folksinger in coffeehouses in 1958. She soon moved on to folk festivals, college recitals, concert halls, tours, and popular recordings. In addition to her musical fame, Joan Baez also became known for her strong political stands. She refused to pay war taxes in 1964. She was arrested in 1967 for civil disobedience in opposing the draft. And in 1975 she visited Hanoi, Vietnam. She is the founder of the Institute for the Study of Nonviolence, Palo Alto, California. In addition to her American tours and concerts, Joan Baez has appeared regularly on television and has toured in Europe. She has authored two books, *Daybreak* and *Coming Out*.

MEDITATION

Joan Baez

WHAT we mean at the school when we say meditation is really very simple to explain. And close to impossible to do. We mean to pay attention. To pay attention, but not to concentrate, to be still, and at the same time, to let go. To stop rehearsing, stop the fantasies. Look with your eyes. I don't know what is there for you to see. Listen with your ears. Everything is alive. Perhaps you can hear it being alive. Sit there. You might hypnotize yourself into a kind of calm, but if it is by a process of exclusion, I'm not so sure that it doesn't close some doors which should be left open. Don't expect a thing. When you expect something, you will be disappointed. Sit there. Don't smoke. Why must you smoke? Don't thumb a magazine. Perhaps you will begin to realize that you have only this one moment. That's all. The other moments have already left. The ones just ahead may never arrive. Suddenly there are a million places you would rather be. At the movies, on the beach, in a hot tub . . . There are a million things you could be doing. Eating, sleeping, reading, doing the laundry . . . Your thoughts will be about what happened earlier in the day, or ten years ago.

When all these thoughts crowd into your mind, as they will over and over and over, you are missing the minute. And by missing the minute, you are missing everything, because all you have is that minute. But don't chastise yourself. That too is a waste of time. If you like, pay attention to the fantasy, the daydream. Maybe you can learn from it. On the other hand, try not to analyze it. Just look at it. Pay attention to it.

Paying attention is not to try and reach another level, another plane, a higher state. You see how difficult it is just to sit on the ground for five minutes without yanking at the grass or getting sleepy? I do not doubt that one can have a spiritual experience, but I'm convinced that to the degree that it is induced it will be fabricated, and therefore deceptive. (Perhaps that explains in part my total lack of interest in drugs. I feel that I know there is no shortcut to enlightenment.) And it is so easy to kid oneself, because of the way we limit our lives to unthreatening trivialities, and the way ugliness and violence are imposed upon us in this century: Who wouldn't want to have a supernatural experience?

A well-known Indian philosopher, Krishnamurti, says that the only real creativity takes place when the mind is still. And how do we turn a shallow noisy little racing brook into a quiet lake, deep and reflecting and still . . . so still that the falling of a leaf upon it can make it tremble with excitement. There are only clues. He says that you have begun once the intent is there. If you have a strong enough desire for stillness, then you will find a way to it. And neither can I be much help to you, for what may be my most successfully attempted techniques for quieting the noise in my mind might not work for you at all.

Why bother to be still? Why bother to pay attention? At the school, specifically, we have a few reasons for making silence a part of the day's activities. (We feel that an imposed silence is far from ideal, but better than no silence at all.) One reason is that the models we've picked as our idea of men who knew what it was to grow up, like Jesus, Buddha, Gandhi, spent much of their lives in silent reflection and prayer. If you have an infected ear, you go to an ear, nose and throat man. If your eyesight begins to fail you, you visit an optometrist (unless, of course, you are a Christian Scientist, in which case you might often have more insight into sickness than others of us would like to admit). If your spirit is sick, or weak, or numb, or even dying or dead— . . . —shouldn't you at least attempt to put your faith in someone who had a few credentials? I mean if a child is sick, we don't take him to a veterinarian. Why do we so easily follow the ways of life of the loveless and fearful and spiritually stunted? Because it is easier, I suppose. It's not a simple thing to grow up.

Another reason for our attempting daily silences is that the Quakers, odd bunch of stuffed shirts that they might be, have existed as an organization for over three hundred years, during which time they have continuously been involved in peace action work, and have never given in to condoning murder. They do not pick the wars they will fight in, but they have picked the way in which they will fight, and their fight is against violence in all its forms. Anyone's violence. There have of course been men who have left the fold and gone off to fight conventional wars in the conventional sense, but the Quaker church has never given in to support violence, no matter what violence was being called at the time—self-defense, making the world safe for democracy, or simply, a "popular war." The Quaker way of worship consists of silence. Anyone in the meeting house may speak if the spirit moves him, but there is no minister. There is "that of God in every man." We thought that the silences might have to do with their insight into nonviolence.

Sometimes I think that it is enough to say that if we don't sit down and shut up once in a while we'll lose our minds even earlier than we had expected. Noise is an imposition on sanity, and we live in very noisy times.

To me, the difference between meditation and prayer is this: If your mind is ever to become still, you will find that the dialogue in your mind has stopped. I think the attempt at quiet requires a state of alertness, of waiting, of complete receptivity. It would be difficult to approach this state when there is still the local activity of a monologue . . . even if it is a monologue with God.

So. Not concentration, not monologue, or day-dreaming, or analyzing, or any certain sitting posture, or self-hypnosis . . . but the endless task of trying to pay attention.

Gandhi said that meditation is as essential to the nonviolent soldier as drill practice is to a conventional soldier. Christ said, "Be still and know that I am God." Buddha once stood up to give a sermon and said nothing. Try it for ten minutes a day. I can promise you nothing.

Questions and Comments

1. "To pay attention" and "to be still" seem almost impossible states of mind to attain as defined by Joan Baez. However, in trying to attain such a state, other interesting things can happen. What might they be?

2. Why do you think Baez dismisses smoking and drugs in her meditation process?

3. What does Joan Baez mean when she writes, ". . . shouldn't you . . . put your faith in someone who had a few credentials?" Who has "credentials" according to Baez?

4. How does Joan Baez distinguish between her form of meditation and prayer?

Word Study

1. *Chastise*, p. 142, comes from the Old French word *chastier*, which derived from the Latin word *castigare* meaning "to punish," (*castus* "pure" + *agere* "to drive"). Literally then, it means "to drive pure." What do you think it means in the article? Check the dictionary.

2. On page 142 there is the sentence, "I do not doubt that one can have a spiritual experience, but I'm convinced that to the degree that it is *induced* it will be *fabricated*, and therefore *deceptive*." The three italicized words are the key to a rather profound thought here. Parts of them appear in rather easy and simple words: intro*duced*, *fabric*, re*ceptive*. From these clues and other clues of your own, figure out the meaning of the sentence. Check your work with the dictionary.

3. *Trivialities, credentials,* and *condoning* should be reasonably easy to figure out from context. Check your dictionary.

Composition

1. Write a reaction, pro or con, to "Meditation," basing your arguments upon personal experience.

2. If you take time occasionally "to be still," describe how you approach these moments and what kind of place or environment you prefer.

3. If you have ever experienced a "supernatural moment" describe such a moment giving the specific details.

4. Why do you think Joan Baez closes her article with an almost negative sentence, "I can promise you nothing."? In view of the entire article does this seem entirely true? Discuss these questions in a paragraph or two.

John Knyveton was born in 1729 into a world which firmly believed fresh air was harmful, baths were dangerous, bleeding was a panacea for all illnesses, and generating pus was a necessary step toward healing. "Hair-raising" best describes the excerpts from *The Diary of a Surgeon—1751-1752*. The fact that the incidents are all true heightens the terror. Perhaps even more shocking is the fact that much of the medical theory and practice of the eighteenth century persisted up until the beginning of the twentieth.

All those who have ever felt they were born a century too late need only read Dr. Knyveton's diary to be reassured that they were most likely saved from a horrible nightmare. By the way, dentists in Knyveton's time burned out cavities with a red-hot wire and filled them with molten lead or gold, if the patient could stand it.

from THE DIARY OF A SURGEON—1751-1752

John Knyveton

September 19

WOKE early this morning by the cries of Milk-O![1] and the noise of market carts entering the town. Rose hastily in some excitement and to view through my window, being pleased to find thereat a fine prospect of trees and meadows, which Mr. Hunt later informs me are the Tottenham Fields, and beyond them the hills of Highgate and Hampstead; the last of interest to a Physician, as from them bubble certain

[1] *Milk-O:* cry of the street vendor selling milk

springs whose waters are very healthful for the stone[1] and surfeit,[2] and the like complaints. They are much sought after, I learn, by the gallants and ladies of the town, who seek in them to renew that Youth they dissipate so elegantly at routes[3] and gaming. Did not gaze long, my attention being catched by a wench lacing herself at the window of a neighbouring house the saucy quean smiling at me. Upon which with remembrance of certain of my uncle's advice, did retire and taking out the second volume of Doctor Sydenham's Treatise did read therein with much comfort and profit until summoned down by my host to break my fast.[4]

Am to pay him 10/6[5] per week for lodging and board, washing to be extra and I doubt not that he will have a hard bargain of it the Lord having favoured me with a hearty relish for my vittles. Much discourse at meat concerning my brother, now practising in Yorkshire, and who did lodge with Mr. Hunt some three years back when himself studying for the golden mantle of Æsculapius.[6] Mr. Hunt warns me that if I am to be much abroad it will be as well to buy myself a cudgel or better small sword as to the west of us beyond the Marylebone Gardens thieves and gentlemen of the road do swarm in great abundance attracted thereto by the many houses of the rich in that quarter, and they do pass even in day into the streets of the town to the great annoyance of the passers by. He informs me that quite recently some few months back the coach of my Lady Albemarle[7] was robbed in Great Russell

[1] *stone:* kidney stones

[2] *surfeit:* the condition of eating and drinking to excess—a hangover

[3] *routes:* parties

[4] *break my fast:* eat breakfast

[5] *10/6:* ten shillings and six pence. Twenty shillings made a pound. Twelve pence made one shilling, and twenty-one shillings equalled one guinea.

[6] *golden mantle of Æsculapius:* license of doctor or surgeon. Æsculapius was the Greek god of medicine.

[7] *my Lady Albemarle:* "My" is simply an expression and does not mean the narrator even knows the woman.

Street in broad day by nine men, the King compensating her for her loss the next day by giving her a gold watch and chain, very fine. And so to take my leave and into the street with many directions from my worthy host and his spouse as how to find my way to Infirmary Hall where I am to bring the knowledge imparted by my dear uncle in my four years apprenticeship to its full completion. On my way thither called at the house of Doctor Urquehart the anatomist, with whom I am to take Anatomy and Chirurgery or Surgery as it is more commonly called, to find the doctor already gone ahead to the Hall. Noted that he had a tolerable fine house with a large outbuilding at the back, which I doubt not is his dissecting room and with which I hope to become well acquaint before my time is served. And so on through the Park, where I saw some gentlemen very fine riding.

Infirmary Hall a very large building and with the swarm of beggars and quack salvers[1] about its gates I was hard put to it to find the entrance. This I did at last however by enquiring the way of a short youth with a disgraceful cravat who informed me he had been very drunk the night before. I offered to bleed him but with great flow of language he informed me that he was a doctor himself and quite capable of treating his own complaints, and so I introduced myself to him, his choler abating to find I was pursuing the same quest as he. With him to the lobby of the Infirmary where we found the lecturers for this session exhibiting their cards and questing for members for their lectures. My short friend informs me that Doctor Urquehart is one of the best teachers of Anatomy in London town and I found his knowledge very useful, as it saved me from the importunities of other teachers whose skill and knowledge was as small as their conceit was great. Arranged however with one gentleman in a fine peruke to take a course in Vegetable and Animal Anatomy and Physiology this to help me with my Materia Medica[2]

[1] *salvers:* A salver is a person who saves, or heals.

[2] *Materia Medica:* medical knowledge of the sources, nature, properties, and preparation of medical remedies, or drugs

and thereby parted with the sum of five guineas. Doctor Urquehart was then performing an amputation of the thigh upon a porter brought in that morning from Covent Garden with a compounded fracture of the left femur the result of a kick from a horse. My new found friend enquiring whether I had seen much surgery takes me through a long corridor with a heavy mephitic stench to a room at the far end lit by a large sky-light. Here we found my future teacher already begun upon his patient, the latter being tied down upon a large table, not so clean as the one my uncle uses for such purposes, but then in such a place they perform more operations in one week than my uncle performs in a year. The patient being a poor man had few friends able to make him drunk and so he being a well developed specimen many ropes were necessary to control his struggles. Amongst those holding him my friend the drunk gentleman pointed out a once famous pugilist and a very big man suspected of having taken the High Toby[1] but who was employed by Doctor Urquehart and shielded by him from the law because he could lift a coffin from its bed single-handed; a useful accomplishment in these otherwise enlightened days, when the poor surgeon must rely for the advancement of his art upon the fruit of the gallows-tree[2] and what he can snatch from the graveyards.

The incisions of Doctor Urquehart placed high up on the thigh there was considerable trouble from the mass of muscle to find the great arteries, which the Doctor for his own advancement wished to ligature with cords, though I learn that in such Institutions it is quite common to cauterise them only, with a hot iron or with boiling tar. Thus from the plunging of the patient who seemed unable to comprehend that it was done for his own good and the clumsiness of the Infirmary surgeon Mr. Jamie who was more foxed[3] than my friend ten minutes elapsed before the leg lay on the floor,

[1] *High Toby:* highway robbery by thieves on horseback

[2] *fruit of the gallows-tree:* Surgeons were dependent upon hangings for corpses so they might perform vivisection and study the human body.

[3] *foxed:* intoxicated

and much blood was shed. I wished to enquire from my short friend what the chances of recovery were, knowing that in such a place they must surely be very small if indeed existent at all, but after one attempt gave it up as the screams of the porter made speech impossible. Later he was removed and sawdust thrown over the floor and on the bigger blood blots on the walls—here again I saw the difference of town and country practice for my uncle could not use much sawdust as the carrier[1] would not consider it the worth of carriage.

Much edified, I turned to find my friend gone, and so to introduce myself to the Doctor then turning down his cuffs and tying a knot in his bob-wig, which had become disarranged, and to give him my letter of introduction from my uncle. He received me kindly for my uncle's sake but could not then spare me much time, as he had much work to perform that morning and was due at a tea-drinking at some fashionable salon the same afternoon. He requests me to call again at his house tomorrow morning, and so as I could not find my former guide and feeling rather lost and solitary amongst such a hive out into the street and to a walk in the Park. Strolled through the Mall—so a wayfarer informed it was called—a vastly fine place and into St. James Park, where I was much edified by a fine sight of Westminster Abbey rising from the ancient trees that surround it. Dined at a tavern and so home tired to an early bed.

September 25

This day wet and the streets very unpleasant the rain dripping off the roof gables and collecting in pools amongst the broken cobbles. To my great pleasure Doctor Urquehart after this morning's lecture confesses himself well pleased with my progress and with him and the other young gentlemen to Infirmary Hall. George Blumenfield[2] not at the lec-

---

[1] *carrier:* one who carries loads

[2] *George Blumenfield:* fellow student with Knyveton at Dr. Urquehart's

ture but waiting for us at the porch and so with us into the wards. Doctor Urquehart at the entry changes his peruke for at tie-wig and puts on a short coat as his fine full skirted one would brush the walls and sweep from them the lice and other insects which infect them. The wards at first sight rather curious; the beds of moderate width and containing not more than three to four patients, but these placed the feet of one to the head of another so that each receives not the tainted effluvium of their respective complaints. In the infants wards there were of course any from six to eight in one bed. Pregnant women have their own ward to which they are taken when the pains seize them, but from the press[1] those in the earlier stages are frequently put to lie with those about to die, so that comfort is had by both. The air rather foul, especially in the surgical ward, which lies at the end of the great Hall where all the general cases lie, but this of course no more than can be expected since the windows cannot be allowed open. For the safety of those that minister to them it is customary for these to carry some prophylactic which can be held to the nostrils; the attendants as a rule carry a sponge soaked in vinegar and those in the Surgical room a cresset[2] of smoking sulphur held in an iron cup at the end of an iron wand. All these things I noted later.

The Doctor had a number of operations awaiting, so with him to that room which I had visited the first day. Here I found Mr. Jamie the Infirmary surgeon and his assistant removing a wen[3] from the shoulder of an elderly woman of great strength of character. I admired the fortitude with which she bore the first cuts and afterwards rose from the table and walked to her bed. A number of well known Doctors and Surgeons present, I found to see my teacher attempt the removal of a broken jaw from a carrier. The man being bound and the assistants leaning their weight upon him Doc-

[1] *press:* crowding

[2] *cresset:* an iron holder for burning oil or pitchy wood

[3] *wen:* a small skin tumor

tor Urquehart and a gentleman from another Hospital cut down through the Masseteric Muscle[1] on the left side to the Mandible[2] and endeavoured to remove the broken portion. But after some twenty minutes they had to desist as the tongue had become involved and the patient had lost about two pints of blood, and the surgeon from the other Hospital therefore bound the broken fragment with wire and the patient was removed and given instructions to keep quiet. Saw the Doctor remove a foot very neatly also a finger from a sempstress and then with him to the wards where we arrived in time to see Mr. Rickard the Infirmary Physician order the removal of a case of Rising of the Lights or Phthisica Pneumonica.[3] So with the other gentlemen to see the autopsy on this case the Doctor proving in a merry and generous mood. The lungs riddled with exuviæ of Nature's effort to expel the morbific humours, very instructive, and so back with him to the Surgical Wards where we saw some of his patients of the previous days all of them doing well the wounds suppurating healthily. So out and it being late in the afternoon to dine lightly at a coffee house and then to walk beneath the trees in St. James Park pondering on all that I had seen and so home to supper and bed.

Questions and Comments

1. What interesting information about daily life in eighteenth-century London does the author give?

[1] *Masseteric Muscle:* muscle which governs mastication or chewing

[2] *Mandible:* lower jaw bone

[3] *Rising of the Lights or Phthisica Pneumonica:* respiratory disorder such as consumption or pneumonia

2. How would you describe the narrator's attitude toward Doctor Urquehart's surgery?

3. What facts about the hospital described would we consider horrendous today?

4. Knyveton emerges as a very real human being with feelings like all people. What are some of these feelings? In what ways is Knyveton unique?

5. Why might keeping a diary be such an important part of Knyveton's life?

6. How would you describe Knyveton's style of writing? What is its effect on the reader?

Word Study

1. *Vittles* is a dialect form of *victuals*. If *victuals* is unfamiliar to you, then look it up in a dictionary.

2. *Choler* historically referred to the bile, which was considered the source of irritable behavior in a person. Look up its present meaning.

3. *Peruke, cravat, bob-wig,* and *tie-wig* are terms hardly if ever used today. A peruke was a wig, and a bob-wig, or tie-wig, was a shorter version of the normally long peruke. A cravat is not in the wig category. What is it?

4. Read the following words in context and guess at their meaning before looking them up in a dictionary: *importunities* (page 148), *effluvium* (page 151), *prophylactic* (page 151), *exuviae* (page 152), *morbific* (page 152).

5. *Ligature* and *cauterise* are both contemporary medical terms that most laymen know. Look up their meanings in a dictionary.

6. Give the meaning of the following words using clues from the context:

". . . a *cudgel* or small sword . . ." (page 147)

". . . a heavy *mephitic* stench . . ." (page 149)

". . . his patients . . . all of them doing well the wounds *suppurating* heathily." (page 152)

Composition

1. Keep your own diary for a few days in the Knyveton fashion. Don't forget that, like him, you are a student and therefore school will comprise much of what you enter in your diary.

2. In a brief essay compare twentieth-century hospitals and doctors with those of the eighteenth century described by Knyveton.

For biographical information on Joan Baez, see page 141, the introduction to "Meditation."

THE WATER LEAVES

Joan Baez

Mɪᴍɪ and I were hanging around the Club 47 coffeehouse in Harvard Square.[1] We were on the way home from Newport,[2] '67. We were seeking old friends from eight years before, but also new faces, lots of new faces lined up in the warm New England evening. They let a blind girl in so she could find a seat. I watched the ticket lady hold her hand out timidly to return the change, not wanting to bump the blind girl's hand. When her things were in order the blind girl took the change and began calculating where she would sit, tapping a radar route around the tables and chairs. I went up to her and helped her find a seat.

"This is sort of comfy," I said, showing her the chair. "You're at the back, but on the aisle."

"Thank you very much," she said, sitting down and folding up her funny collapsible metal cane. Then she faced me and said, "Excuse me, but your voice sounds vaguely familiar . . ."

I told her my name and she let out a squeal.

"I'm Paula. Remember me? From Perkins[3]? Gee, that was eight years ago! Gee, it's good to see you!"

I sat down with her and we chatted. She asked about

[1]*Harvard Square:* a square near Harvard in Cambridge

[2]*Newport:* coastal city in Rhode Island; formerly the site of an annual jazz festival

[3]*Perkins:* a school for the blind

Mimi, and I called Mimi over. Paula grabbed her cane and purse and jumped up to hug her. Of course, I thought, I had heard stories about the devoted blind kids who had showed up at 47 every time Mimi and Dick were on the bill. Paula fell into an enraptured chat with Mimi, who sat with her head tilted, watching the funny blind girl's face.

"We went to the Winter Festival. It was terrible," she was telling Mimi. "We were in a snowstorm and my eyes were freezing. I thought I would die!"

"Your eyes were freezing?"

"Oh," she said, dropping her head back and facing me, and indicating her eyes by tapping her fingertips around her cheekbones. "These are just shell. See?" I saw two identical clear blue eyes. One of them was sunk a little in the socket.

"You mean glass?" I asked, and then looked closer and saw that her eyes were making almost imperceptible jerking motions in every direction, and that where we have the little dip next to the nose where gnats and sleep settle, Paula had an open place. In that place existed not the miraculous network of an eye, but something more like a dark cavern.

"Yes, they're glass," she said. "When it's really cold they get freezing and press against the socket and it's killing." She showed Mimi her eyes.

"Anyway," she went on, "the Festival was a big bore, except for Pete Seeger, of course." Her face broke into that magnificent odd smile which had never been checked in a mirror.

"Tell me," I said, "what you think of Perkins."

"Well," she said, trying to figure out how I felt about it.

"I was fired from there, myself," I said, to give her free rein. "For sitting on the boys' side, and taking one boy's watch home to be fixed. But it was really because I didn't wear shoes enough of the time, and because I loved the kids. I thought the school was set up for the kids. But it wasn't. It was set up for the teachers and housemothers."

"*You're* not kidding," said Paula in a low voice. "I didn't even know how to go *out* till I left Perkins and took a cane course." She took the folded-up metal off her lap and flipped it into the air and it snapped itself into a cane, as though it were a magic wand.

"Wow!" Mimi and I were impressed. "That's something. Do you like the cane?"

"Oh, I love it. It makes me much more independent than if I had a dog. You know, you're always having to tie the dog to something when you go into a store. This way I'm free to go anywhere I want, whenever I want."

Mimi and I played with the cane for a while.

Perkins Institute for the Blind. Stupid Perkins. Stuffy housemothers and overeducated teachers. Turn out nice clean well-behaved blind types. I wondered how Paula had survived, and then I began remembering the kids. I had worked with the kindergarteners. I was in charge of seven children, twenty hours a day, six days a week. And I lasted for two months.

Little Archie, the problem child, eight operations on his eyes by the age of six, cleft palate, no taste buds or sense of smell, chewed his vitamins up in the morning, dropped his glass eye in the oatmeal and cried in noisy sorrow that he'd lost his eye . . . I felt sick trying to wash his face the first day, because both his eye sockets were infected and oozing . . . so at the breakfast table I couldn't eat, and when the head housemother said, "Is something wrong?" I said, "Archie's face, it's sort of icky . . ." and began to cry.

"Oh goodness, dear, we can't let a little thing like that get us down," she said brightly, and she took Archie off to wash his face and threw up her breakfast.

Archie's mother was always the first parent to drop him at the school on Sunday afternoons and the last to pick him up on Fridays, and the housemothers didn't

give a damn about him in between because he was a bad
boy and all the operations had made him hard to look at.
I begged the women to quit calling him a bad boy, and
said I would spend extra time with him. It turned out that
Archie didn't know how to hug. So every time he came
around I'd grab all the children I could find and be hug-
ging them when he got near. He had a tiny bit of vision in
his one eye if he poked it with his fist, and he'd climb up
over the kids to find out what was happening. I'd be saying, "Oh Gail, what a lovely hug, thank you!" and so
Archie, with one fist jammed into his good eye, was beginning to see that he'd been missing something that
looked like fun. And then one night after I'd put him to
bed, and we'd said the horrible little Perkins prayer, I
gave Archie a kiss on the forehead and said good-night,
and as I got up to go he said, "Hey, Miss Joan, don't I
get a hug?" and after we'd had a big warm hug there was
a fiendish smile on his funny cockeyed face on the pillow,
and he said, "You know what, Miss Joan? You're a good
kid."

There was odd Lila, who had had polio and thought
that she still couldn't raise her arms. She held her elbows
close to her sides and rolled her poor head around day
and night and was bald in spots and matty haired at the
back of her skull. She screamed in her sleep, wet her bed,
and pretended she couldn't speak. The truth was that no
one knew how much she could hear or say, because she
wouldn't respond to testing, or teasing, or just plain loud
noises. Still, every night when we had songs, I would sing
"Takes a Worried Man to Sing a Worried Song," sub-
stituting, in every chorus, the name of each child in place
of the word "man," and every night I would watch carefully when I sang Lila's name, and she would just roll
her head and bang her fists together. One afternoon I was
carrying her around in my arms, chatting to her as if she
could hear, and I noticed that she was smiling, some-

thing she never did. Suddenly, in perfect rhythm and perfect tune, she sang softly, "Takes a worried Lila, to sing a worried song, Takes a worried Lila, to sing a worried song . . ." I didn't say anything to her, I just walked fast to where the head housemother was, and pointed very subtly at Lila.

"I'm worried now, but I won't be worried long," sang Lila, finishing up the verse just as the housemother was taking in her breath to say, "Oh, and who do we have here?" and leaning over to wipe off the lunch table. But by the time she had stopped bustling and had stood up to give us her attention, Lila had stopped singing and was smiling a viciously happy smile.

"Never mind," I said, and the housemother never-minded.

I walked off and jiggled Lila up and down a few times.

"So we goofed, huh, Lila?" I said, but Lila had stopped smiling and gone back to rolling her head, and in the time I was at Perkins, I never heard her sing or speak again.

Ming Lo was flown in from Chicago. He didn't walk. He spun in circles down the school hall. He knew two words, "Aunty" and "eat." If he was left alone for more than thirty seconds at night he would call out, in the most heartbreaking voice, "Aunty! Aunty!" So for a while we took night shifts holding Ming's hand, so that he could go to sleep and get some relief from the new unfamiliar hell into which someone had dropped him.

Ming was a compulsive eater, bed-wetter, and stripper, and as he grew used to the new life with all his Caucasian aunties, he felt free to slip out of his bed at nap time, spin out into the hall, strip all his clothes off, do pee-pee on the floor, and lie down in it, like a great fat Buddha gone mad, not just smiling, but laughing until he hurt. I always hoped to find him first, because the women slapped his hand and said, "Dirty Ming," and chalked one more thing up to "unmanageable and incurable," which they preferred to think he was, because he was too time-consuming and strange to keep at Perkins.

He figured out the word "cookie" after the first week and one incredible nap time I heard rustlings in my room, and I started down the hall, putting it all together just in time to see Ming twirl out of my room, leaving a trail of cookie chunks behind him. He had sniffed out a huge tin of English cookies, and in his splendid but hurried one-man orgy, he couldn't eat the cookies fast enough so what he hadn't time to chew and swallow, he'd mashed and crumbled and gooed and sat in and thrown over the entire room, and for the few minutes that he was free to indulge, Ming must have been an ecstatically happy boy.

One weekend I stayed at school to take care of Ming. The grounds at Perkins were beautiful and full of autumn. The air was getting sharp and cold, and Ming and I were alone in the kitchen. We were sitting at a stainless steel table near the window. I looked out at the brown leaves and the squirrels and the gray sky, and the stone wall that surrounded Perkins. And then I looked at Ming where he sat, three feet away from me, smiling to himself and playing with a spoon, his sightless black eyes slicing into his round face the design on the F-hole guitar. I looked back out the window and was swept over with that unspeakable sadness which seems to come so easily in a New England fall, and I let my eyes fill up and the tears fall free in silence, and suddenly in that sword-sharp loneliness, there was a motion at my side. Ming had put down his spoon and with compassion written out on his forehead, was reaching his arms to comfort me. "Miss Joan cry?" he said. "Miss Joan cry?"

Cindy was glass-fragile and white as an angel. When she was born she weighed two and a half pounds, and they put her in an incubator.[1] When she came out there were little grayish clouds on her eyes, and her parents realized that Cindy could stare at the sun without blinking.

Cindy walked backwards down the hall, patting the wall with her hands and stopping now and then to rock back and forth, shaking her head from side to side, frowning like a little blindfolded rockinghorse. To touch her or call her name would stop her dead still and leave her exposed and waiting.

"Look up at me, Cindy," I said. "You have such a beautiful smile, and I want to see it. When your head is down I can't see your face."

Cindy threw her head back and smiled experimentally. Her skin was translucent and tiny blue veins ran under her chin.

"Thank you, Cindy. Do you know that you are very beautiful when you smile?" and she looked pleased, but she wasn't ready to talk yet, and nobody had taught her how to nod her head.

One day, again in the autumn, when brown and yellow leaves covered the playground, I saw Cindy under a big maple tree, inching forward in her rocking walk, waving her hands all around her like feelers. She was throwing her head back and smiling, and her lips were moving. I walked quietly toward the tree, and as I approached I heard her say, "Cindy's walking on water leaves. Cindy's walking on water leaves." When I got too close she sensed me, and stopped, and waited.

"Cindy," I said.

"I'm walking on the water leaves," she answered.

"I see. Is it fun?"

"Miss Joan, this is my elbow," she said, smacking her elbow with her other hand.

"Want to see my elbow?" I asked. She smiled and threw

[1]*incubator:* a box-like apparatus for the maintenance of controlled conditions especially for the housing of premature or sick babies

her head back and began struggling in my direction.

"Miss Joan, who put my room upstairs?"

"Come on, Cindy. Come over here," I answered. And after she had fought her way through the webs of open air and found my hand, she gave it a tug, and we both sat down on the water leaves to chat.

Questions and Comments

1. The "water leaves" reference comes at the end of the essay. Why did Joan Baez give that title to the entire piece?

2. "And I lasted for two months." What reasons does the essay give for Baez's working at Perkins for only two months?

3. The essay contains some horrible details of human disfigurement and suffering. Would not the essay have more popular appeal if those details were omitted or softened? Why or why not?

4. According to this article, what is the most important trait people must have if they are to successfully care for handicapped children?

5. Explain whether you think this article is optimistic or pessimistic in its view of humanity.

Word Study

1. Go back to page 156 and see which of the following words is most synonomous to *imperceptible:* sickening, invisible, impossible, strange. Check your choice in the dictionary.

2. If you study the paragraph on page 160 where *ecstatically* comes at the very end, you should be able to guess its meaning. Now look up the meaning in the dictionary; notice particularly the Greek origin of this word and its original meaning.

Composition

1. There is a movement in education to "mainstream" handicapped children; that is, to send them to regular public schools with non-handicapped children. Write your personal reacton to this concept.

2. Would you be interested in working in a school such as Perkins? Why or why not?

3. Public institutions such as prisons, mental hospitals, schools for the handicapped, and training centers for the retarded, often suffer from lack of funds, overburdened staff, crowded conditions, and political scandal. There are, of course, notable exceptions. Look into the situation at a local public institution in or near your community and write a report of your findings. Your local newspaper would have some information. Also, it may be possible for you to visit the institution.

4. Do a study of your community resources for the mentally and physically handicapped and gather your information in a written report.

Jonathan Swift was a shrewd observer of life and people. He hated hypocrisy and injustice and wherever he saw these things he turned his satiric pen against them.

Swift wrote "A Modest Proposal" in 1729, a time of great economic turmoil in Ireland. The passing of various laws caused a departure from a primarily agricultural economy. Cattle became the prized commodity raised by landowners, and for the Irish peasantry the conversion of every possible acre of arable land into pasture land meant absolute ruin. The export of farm crops gradually ceased, and life became a constant struggle against starvation. In 1729 it was calculated that there were nearly 35,000 professional beggars strolling about the country.

A MODEST PROPOSAL

For Preventing the Children of Poor People From Being a Burthen to Their Parents or Country, and for Making Them Beneficial to the Public

Jonathan Swift

IT is a melancholy object to those, who walk through this great town[1] or travel in the country, when they see the streets, the roads, and cabin-doors, crowded with beggars of the female sex, followed by three, four, or six children, *all in rags,* and importuning every passenger for an alms. These mothers instead of being able to work for their honest livelihood, are forced to employ all their time in strolling, to beg sustenance for their helpless infants, who, as they grow up,

[1] *this great town:* Dublin, Ireland

164

either turn thieves for want of work, or leave their dear Native Country to fight for the Pretender in Spain[1] or sell themselves to the Barbadoes.[2]

I think it is agreed by all parties, that this prodigious number of children, in the arms, or on the backs, or at the heels of their mothers, and frequently of their fathers, is in the present deplorable state of the kingdom, a very great additional grievance; and therefore whoever could find out a fair, cheap and easy method of making these children sound useful members of the commonwealth would deserve so well of the public, as to have his statue set up for a preserver of the nation.

But my intention is very far from being confined to provide only for the children of professed beggars, it is of a much greater extent, and shall take in the whole number of infants at a certain age, who are born of parents in effect as little able to support them, as those who demand our charity in the streets.

As to my own part, having turned my thoughts, for many years, upon this important subject, and maturely weighed the several schemes of other projectors, I have always found them grossly mistaken in their computation. It is true a child, just dropped from its dam,[3] may be supported by her milk for a solar year with little other nourishment, at most not above the value of two shillings, which the mother may certainly get, or the value in scraps, by her lawful occupation of begging, and it is exactly at one year old that I propose to provide for them, in such a manner, as, instead of being a charge upon their parents, or the parish, or wanting food and raiment for the rest of their lives, they shall, on the contrary, contribute to the feeding and partly to the clothing of many thousands.

[1] *Pretender in Spain:* James Stuart, son of James II. A Spanish expedition under Alberoni attempted unsuccessfully to dethrone George I and replace him with James Stuart.

[2] *Barbadoes:* British Colony in the West Indies that used slaves.

[3] *dam:* mother

There is likewise another great advantage in my scheme, that it will prevent those voluntary abortions, and that horrid practice of women murdering their bastard children, alas, too frequent among us, sacrificing the poor innocent babes, I doubt, more to avoid the expense, than the shame, which would move tears and pity in the most savage and inhuman breast.

The number of souls in this kingdom being usually reckoned one million and a half, of these I calculate there may be about two hundred thousand couples whose wives are breeders, from which number I subtract thirty thousand couples, who are able to maintain their own children, although I apprehend there cannot be so many under the present distresses of the kingdom, but this being granted, there will remain an hundred and seventy thousand breeders. I again subtract fifty thousand for those women who miscarry, or whose children die by accident, or disease within the year. There only remain an hundred and twenty thousand children of poor parents annually born: The question therefore is, how this number shall be reared, and provided for, which, as I have already said, under the present situation of affairs, is utterly impossible by all the methods hitherto proposed, for we can neither employ them in handicraft, or agriculture; we neither build houses, (I mean in the country) nor cultivate land: they can very seldom pick up a livelihood by stealing till they arrive at six years old, except where they are of towardly parts,[1] although, I confess they learn the rudiments much earlier, during which time, they can however be properly looked upon only as *probationers*,[2] as I have been informed by a principal gentleman in the County of Cavan,[3] who protested to me, that he never knew above one or two instances under the age of six, even in a part of the kingdom so renowned for the quickest proficiency in that art.

[1] *of towardly parts:* extremely intelligent or fast learners
[2] *probationers:* apprentices or students
[3] *County of Cavan:* county in the Northern Republic of Ireland, in Ulster Province

I am assured by our merchants, that a boy or a girl, before twelve years old, is no saleable commodity, and even when they come to this age, they will not yield above three pounds,[1] or three pounds and half-a-crown[2] at most on the Exchange, which cannot turn to account either to the parents or the kingdom, the charge of nutriment and rags having been at least four times that value.

I shall now therefore humbly propose my own thoughts, which I hope will not be liable to the least objection.

I have been assured by a very knowing American of my acquaintance in London, that a young healthy child well nursed is at a year old a most delicious, nourishing, and wholesome food, whether stewed, roasted, baked, or boiled, and I make no doubt that it will equally serve in a fricassee, or a ragout.

I do therefore humbly offer it to public consideration, that of the hundred and twenty thousand children, already computed, twenty thousand may be reserved for breed, whereof only one fourth part to be males, which is more than we allow to sheep, black-cattle, or swine, and my reason is that these children are seldom the fruits of marriage, a circumstance not much regarded by our savages, therefore one male will be sufficient to serve four females. That the remaining hundred thousand may at a year old be offered in sale to the persons of quality, and fortune, through the kingdom, always advising the mother to let them suck plentifully in the last month, so as to render them plump, and fat for a good table. A child will make two dishes at an entertainment for friends, and when the family dines alone, the fore or hind quarter will make a reasonable dish, and seasoned with a little pepper or salt will be very good boiled on the fourth day, especially in winter.

I have reckoned upon a medium,[3] that a child just born will weigh 12 pounds, and in a solar year if tolerably nursed increaseth to 28 pounds.

I grant this food will be somewhat dear, and therefore

[1]*pound:* the basic monetary unit of the United Kingdom
[2]*half-a-crown:* British coin worth one-eighth of a pound
[3]*upon a medium:* on the average

very proper for landlords, who, as they have already de-
voured most of the parents, seem to have the best title to the
children. . . .

I have already computed the charge of nursing a beggar's
child (in which list I reckon all cottagers,[1] labourers, and
four-fifths of the farmers) to be about two shillings *per
annum*, rags included, and I believe no gentleman would
repine to give ten shillings for the carcass of a good fat child,
which, as I have said will make four dishes of excellent nu-
tritive meat, when he hath only some particular friend, or
his own family to dine with him. Thus the Squire[2] will learn
to be a good landlord, and grow popular among his tenants,
the mother will have eight shillings net profit, and be fit for
work till she produces another child.

Those who are more thrifty (as I must confess the times require) may flay[3] the carcass; the skin of which, artificially
dressed, will make admirable gloves for ladies, and summer
boots for fine gentlemen.

As to our City of Dublin, shambles[4] may be appointed for
this purpose, in the most convenient parts of it, and butchers
we may be assured will not be wanting, although I rather
recommend buying the children alive, and dressing them hot
from the knife, as we do roasting pigs.

A very worthy person, a true lover of his country, and
whose virtues I highly esteem, was lately pleased, in discours-
ing on this matter, to offer a refinement upon my scheme.
He said, that many gentlemen of this kingdom, having of
late destroyed their deer, he conceived that the want of venison might be well supplied by the bodies of young lads and
maidens, not exceeding fourteen years of age, nor under
twelve, so great a number of both sexes in every country
being now ready to starve, for want of work and service: and
these to be disposed of by their parents if alive, or otherwise
by their nearest relations. But with due deference to so ex-

[1] *cottagers:* those who live in cottages; probably small farmers
[2] *Squire:* country gentleman and lord in charge of a country estate
[3] *flay:* strip off the skin
[4] *shambles:* a slaughtering house

cellent a friend, and so deserving a patriot, I cannot be altogether in his sentiments; for as to the males, my American
acquaintance assured me from frequent experience, that
their flesh was generally tough and lean, like that of our
schoolboys, by continual exercise, and their taste disagree-
able, and to fatten them would not answer the charge. Then
as to the females, it would, I think with humble submission,
be a loss to the public, because they soon would become
breeders themselves: And besides, it is not improbable that
some scrupulous people might be apt to censure such a practice, (although indeed very unjustly) as a little bordering
upon cruelty, which, I confess, hath always been with me the
strongest objection against any project, however so well intended.

But in order to justify my friend, he confessed that this ex-
pedient was put into his head by the famous Psalmanazar, a
native of the island Formosa, who came from thence to London, above twenty years ago, and in conversation told my
friend, that in his country when any young person happened
to be put to death, the executioner sold the carcass to persons of quality, as a prime dainty, and that, in his time, the
body of a plump girl of fifteen, who was crucified for an attempt to poison the emperor, was sold to his Imperial Majesty's Prime Minister of State, and other great Mandarins of
the Court, in joints from the gibbet, at four hundred crowns.
Neither indeed can I deny, that if the same use were made of
several plump young girls in this town, who, without one
single groat[1] to their fortunes, cannot stir abroad without a
chair, and appear at the playhouse, and assemblies in foreign
fineries, which they never will pay for, the kingdom would
not be the worse.

Some persons of a desponding spirit are in great concern
about that vast number of poor people, who are aged, diseased, or maimed, and I have been desired to employ my
thoughts what course may be taken, to ease the nation of so
grievous an encumbrance. But I am not in the least pain
upon that matter, because it is very well known, that they

[1] *groat:* an old English silver coin worth fourpence

are every day dying, and rotting, by cold, and famine, and filth, and vermin, as fast as can be reasonably expected. And as to the younger labourers they are now in almost as hopeful a condition. They cannot get work, and consequently pine away for want of nourishment, to a degree, that if at any time they are accidentally hired to common labour, they have not strength to perform it; and thus the country and themselves are happily delivered from the evils to come.

I have too long digressed, and therefore shall return to my subject. I think the advantages by the proposal which I have made are obvious and many, as well as of the highest importance. . . .

Secondly, The poorer tenants will have something valuable of their own, which by law may be made liable to distress, and help to pay their landlord's rent, their corn and cattle being already seized, and *money a thing unknown.*

Thirdly, Whereas the maintenance of an hundred thousand children, from two years old, and upwards, cannot be computed at less than ten shillings a piece *per annum,* the nation's stock will be thereby increased fifty thousand pounds *per annum,* besides the profit of a new dish, introduced to the tables of all gentlemen of fortune in the kingdom, who have any refinement in taste, and the money will circulate among ourselves, the goods being entirely of our own growth and manufacture.

Fourthly, The constant breeders, besides the gain of eight shillings sterling *per annum,* by the sale of their children, will be rid of the charge of maintaining them after the first year.

Fifthly, This food would likewise bring great custom to taverns, where the vintners will certainly be so prudent as to procure the best receipts for dressing it to perfection, and consequently have their houses frequented by all the fine gentlemen, who justly value themselves upon their knowledge in good eating; and a skilful cook, who understands how to oblige his guests will contrive to make it as expensive as they please.

Sixthly, This would be a great inducement to marriage,

which all wise nations have either encouraged by rewards, or enforced by laws and penalties. It would increase the care and tenderness of mothers toward their children, when they were sure of a settlement for life, to the poor babes, provided in some sort by the public to their annual profit instead of expense. We should see an honest emulation among the married women, which of them could bring the fattest child to the market; men would become as fond of their wives, during the time of their pregnancy, as they are now of their mares in foal, their cows in calf, or sows when they are ready to farrow, nor offer to beat or kick them (as it is too frequent a practice) for fear of a miscarriage.

Many other advantages might be enumerated: For instance, the addition of some thousand carcasses in our exportation of barrelled beef; the propagation of swine's flesh, and improvement in the art of making good bacon, so much wanted among us by the great destruction of pigs, too frequent at our tables, which are no way comparable in taste, or magnificence to a well-grown, fat yearling child, which roasted whole will make a considerable figure at a Lord Mayor's feast, or any other public entertainment. But this, and many others I omit being studious of brevity.

Supposing that one thousand families in this city, would be constant customers for infants' flesh, besides others who might have it at merry-meetings, particularly weddings and christenings, I compute that Dublin would take off annually about twenty thousand carcasses, and the rest of the kingdom (where probably they will be sold somewhat cheaper) the remaining eighty thousand.

I can think of no one objection, that will possibly be raised against this proposal, unless it should be urged that the the number of people will be thereby much lessened in the kingdom. This I freely own, and was indeed one principal design in offering it to the world. I desire the reader will observe, that I calculate my remedy *for this one individual Kingdom of Ireland, and for no other that ever was, is, or, I think, ever can be upon earth.* Therefore let no man talk to me of other expedients: *Of taxing our absentees at five shil-*

lings a pound: Of using neither clothes, nor household furniture, except what is of our own growth and manufacture: Of utterly rejecting the materials and instruments that promote foreign luxury: Of curing the expensiveness of pride, vanity, idleness, and gaming in our women: Of introducing a vein of parsimony, prudence and temperance: Of learning to love our Country, wherein we differ even from LAPLANDERS,[1] *and the inhabitants of* TOPINAMBOO:[2] *Of quitting our animosities and factions. . . : Of being a little cautious not to sell our country and consciences for nothing: Of teaching landlords to have at least one degree of mercy toward their tenants. Lastly of putting a spirit of honesty, industry and skill into our shopkeepers, who, if a resolution could now be taken to buy our native goods, would immediately unite to cheat and exact upon us in the price, the measure, and the goodness, nor could ever yet be brought to make one fair proposal of just dealing, though often and earnestly invited to it.*

Therefore I repeat, let no man talk to me and the like expedients, till he hath at least some glimpse of hope that there will ever be some hearty and sincere attempt to put them in practice.

But as to myself, having been wearied out for many years with offering vain, idle, visionary thoughts, and at length utterly despairing of success, I fortunately fell upon this proposal, which as it is wholly new, so it hath something solid and real, of no expense and little trouble, full in our own power, and whereby we can incur no danger in *disobliging* ENGLAND. For this kind of commodity will not bear exportation, the flesh being of too tender a consistence, to admit a long continuance in salt, *although perhaps I could name a country, which would be glad to eat up our whole nation without it.*

After all I am not so violently bent upon my own opinion, as to reject any offer, proposed by wise men, which shall be found equally innocent, cheap, easy and effectual. But before

[1]*Laplanders:* a people of northern Scandinavia and parts of Russia
[2]*Topinamboo:* a district of Brazil

something of that kind shall be advanced in contradiction to my scheme, and offering a better, I desire the author, or authors will be pleased maturely to consider two points. First, as things now stand, how they will be able to find food and raiment for an hundred thousand useless mouths and backs. And secondly, there being a round million of creatures in human figure, throughout this kingdom, whose whole subsistence put into a common stock, would leave them in debt two millions of pounds sterling adding those, who are beggars by profession, to the bulk of farmers, cottagers and labourers with their wives and children, who are beggars in effect. I desire those politicians, who dislike my overture, and may perhaps be so bold to attempt an answer, that they will first ask the parents of these mortals, whether they would not at this day think it a great happiness to have been sold for food at a year old, in the manner I prescribe, and thereby have avoided such a perpetual scene of misfortunes, as they have since gone through, by the oppression of landlords, the impossibility of paying rent without money or trade, the want of common sustenance, with neither house nor clothes to cover them from the inclemencies of the weather, and the most inevitable prospect of entailing the like, or greater miseries upon their breed for ever.

I profess in the sincerity of my heart that I have not the least personal interest in endeavouring to promote this necessary work, having no other motive than the *public good of my country, by advancing our trade, providing for infants, relieving the poor, and giving some pleasure to the rich.* I have no children, by which I can propose to get a single penny; the youngest being nine years old, and my wife past child-bearing.

Questions and Comments

1. At what point in the essay does Swift first suggest what his

proposal might be? What problem in Ireland prompted him to make such a proposal?

2. Why does Swift say that this food will be very proper for landlords? What criticism of the landlords is he making?

3. In what paragraph does Swift reflect the attitude of people toward the aged and disabled citizens of Ireland? What do you think his attitude is toward the situation of the elderly?

4. What advantages does the author claim will grow out of his proposal?

5. What do you think Swift's real feelings are for the children and the old people of Ireland? What emotions do you think he is trying to inspire in the reader?

6. Swift states the problem and his solution to it very matter-of-factly and with great detail. Why? What effect does he achieve by writing in this manner?

7. After giving his solution to the problem Swift lists some other expedients which he has rejected. What are those expedients? What do you think Swift really thinks of them?

Word Study

1. Guess the meanings of the italicized words before looking them up in a dictionary:

"... beggars ... *importuning* every passenger for *alms* ..." (page 164)

"These mothers instead of being able to work ... are forced to employ all their time in strolling, to beg *sustenance* for their helpless infants. ..." (page 164)

"... wanting food and *raiment* for the rest of their lives ..." (page 165)

"And besides, it is not improbable that some *scrupulous* people might be apt to censure such a practice, (although indeed very unjustly) as a little bordering upon cruelty, which, I confess, hath always been with me the strongest objection against any project..." (page 169)

"... I have been desired to employ my thoughts what course may be taken, to ease the nation of so grievous an *encumbrance*." (page 169)

"We should see an honest *emulation* among the married women. . . ." (page 171)

2. Swift mentions serving a *fricassee* or a *ragout*. What are these dishes?

3. Swift mentions a young girl who was crucified for attempting to poison the emperor and whose body was sold from the *gibbet*. What is a gibbet?

4. The word *vintner* is derived from the Latin *vinetum* meaning "vineyard." What do you think the word *vintner* means? See page 170.

5. *Parsimony* on page 172 comes from the Latin *parsimonia* meaning "thrift or frugality." Does Swift use it in its original Latin sense?

Composition

1. Quoting examples from the selection, write a composition in which you closely analyze the satirical technique of Swift. Conclude your analysis with your estimate of the effectiveness of such a technique.

2. Basically, Swift's proposal is not a solution to the Irish situation. Rather it is a way of criticizing it. In a brief essay discuss what aspects of life in Ireland Swift was criticizing.

3. Here's an opportunity to be as cutting, bitter, and satirical as Swift in your attack of something. Get as angry as Swift probably would about some current item in the newspaper, a current social problem, a local school issue, or local political problem. Do not forget that controlled anger is the effective kind.

Louis (Studs) Terkel (1912-) graduated from Chicago University and the Chicago Law School. He has been an actor, a disc jockey, sports commentator, and television emcee, in addition to being a writer. This interview with Cesar Chavez comes from Terkel's book, *Hard Times*, a title he took from a book written by Charles Dickens. The subtitle of Terkel's book is, "An Oral History of the Great Depression." Terkel interviewed politicians, artists, writers, racketeers, farmers, businesspeople, even a six-day bicycle racer for the content of *Hard Times*. His particular skill in interviewing was that his subjects did all the talking; the reader is hardly aware that an interviewer exists.

Other books by Terkel are *Division Street* and *Giants of Jazz*.

CESAR CHAVEZ

Studs Terkel

OH, I remember having to move out of our house. My father had brought in a team of horses and wagon. We had always lived in that house, and we couldn't understand why we were moving out. When we got to the other house, it was a worse house, a poor house. That must have been around 1934. I was about six years old.

It's known as the North Gila Valley, about fifty miles north of Yuma. My dad was being turned out of his small plot of land. He had inherited this from his father, who had homesteaded it. I saw my two, three other uncles also moving out. And for the same reason. The bank had fore-closed on the loan.

If the local bank approved, the Government would guarantee the loan and small farmers like my father would

176

continue in business. It so happened the president of the bank was the guy who most wanted our land. We were surrounded by him: he owned all the land around us. Of course, he wouldn't pass the loan.

One morning a giant tractor came in, like we had never seen before. My daddy used to do all his work with horses. So this huge tractor came in and began to knock down this corral, this small corral where my father kept his horses. We didn't understand why. In the matter of a week, the whole face of the land was changed. Ditches were dug, and it was different. I didn't like it as much.

We all of us climbed into an old Chevy that my dad had. And then we were in California, and migratory workers. There were five kids—a small family by those standards. It must have been around '36. I was about eight. Well, it was a strange life. We had been poor, but we knew every night there was a bed *there*, and that *this* was our room. There was a kitchen. It was sort of a settled life, and we had chickens and hogs, eggs and all those things. But that all of a sudden changed. When you're small, you can't figure these things out. You know something's not right and you don't like it, but you don't question it and you don't let that get you down. You sort of just continue to move.

But this had quite an impact on my father. He had been used to owning the land and all of a sudden there was no more land. What I heard . . . what I made out of the conversations between my mother and my father—things like, we'll work this season and then we'll get enough money and we'll go buy a piece of land in Arizona. Things like that. Became a habit. He never gave up hope that some day he would come back and get a little piece of land.

I can understand very, very well this feeling. These conversations were sort of melancholy. I guess my brothers and my sisters could also see this very sad look on my father's face.

That piece of land he wanted . . . ?

No, never. It never happened. He stopped talking about that some years ago. The drive for land, it's a very powerful drive.

When we moved to California, we would work after school. Sometimes we wouldn't go. "Following the crops," we missed much school. Trying to get enough money to stay alive the following winter, the whole family picking apricots, walnuts, prunes. We were pretty new, we had never been migratory workers. We were taken advantage of quite a bit by the labor contractor and the crew pusher. In some pretty silly ways. (Laughs.)

Sometimes we can't help but laugh about it. We trusted everybody that came around. You're traveling in California with all your belongings in your car: it's obvious. Those days we didn't have a trailer. This is bait for the labor contractor. Anywhere we stopped, there was a labor contractor offering all kinds of jobs and good wages, and we were always deceived by them and we always went. Trust them.

Coming into San Jose, not finding—being lied to, that there was work. We had no money at all, and had to live on the outskirts of town under a bridge and dry creek. That wasn't really unbearable. What was unbearable was so many families living in just a quarter of a mile. And you know how kids are. They'd bring in those things that really hurt us quite a bit. Most of those kids were middle-class families.

We got hooked on a real scheme once. We were going by Fresno on our way to Delano. We stopped at some service station and this labor contractor saw the car. He offered a lot of money. We went. We worked the first week: the grapes were pretty bad and we couldn't make much. We all stayed off from school in order to make some money. Saturday we were to be paid and we didn't get paid. He came and said the winery hadn't paid him. We'd have money next week. He gave us $10. My dad took the $10 and went to the store and bought $10 worth of groceries. So we worked another week and in the middle of the second week, my father was asking him for his last week's pay, and he had the same excuse. This went on and we'd get $5 or $10 or $7 a week for about four weeks. For the whole family.

So one morning my father made the resolution no more work. If he doesn't pay us, we won't work. We got in a car and went over to see him. The house was empty. He had left. The winery said they had paid him and they showed us where they had paid him. This man had taken it.

Labor strikes were everywhere. We were one of the strikingest families, I guess. My dad didn't like the conditions, and he began to agitate. Some families would follow, and we'd go elsewhere. Sometimes we'd come back. We couldn't find a job elsewhere, so we'd come back. Sort of beg for a job. Employers would know and they would make it very humiliating. . . .

Did these strikes ever win?

Never.

We were among these families who always honored somebody else's grievance. Somebody would have a personal grievance with the employer. He'd say I'm not gonna work for this man. Even though we were working, we'd honor it. We felt we had to. So we'd walk out, too. Because we were prepared to honor those things, we caused many of the things ourselves. If we were picking at a piece rate and we knew they were cheating on the weight, we wouldn't stand for it. So we'd lose the job, and we'd go elsewhere. There were other families like that.

Sometimes when you had to come back, the contractor knew this . . . ?

They knew it, and they rubbed it in quite well. Sort of shameful to come back. We were trapped. We'd have to do it for a few days to get enough money to get enough gas.

One of the experiences I had. We went through Indio, California. Along the highway there were signs in most of the small restaurants that said "White Trade Only." My dad read English, but he didn't really know the meaning. He went in to get some coffee—a pot that he had, to get some coffee for my mother. He asked us not to come in, but we followed him anyway. And this young waitress said, "We don't serve Mexicans here. Get out of here." I was there, and I saw it and heard it. She paid no more attention. I'm sure for the rest of her life she never thought of it again. But every time we thought of it, it hurt us. So we got back in the car and we had a difficult time trying—in fact, we never got the coffee. These are sort of unimportant, but they're . . . you remember 'em very well.

One time there was a little diner across the tracks in Brawley. We used to shine shoes after school. Saturday was a good day. We used to shine shoes for three cents, two cents. Hamburgers were then, as I remember, seven cents. There was this little diner all the way across town. The moment we stepped across the tracks, the police stopped us. They would let us go there, to what we called "the American town," the Anglo town, with a shoe shine box. We went to this little place and we walked in.

There was this young waitress again. With either her boyfriend or someone close, because they were involved in conversation. And there was this familiar sign again, but we paid no attention to it. She looked up at us and she sort of—it wasn't what she said, it was just a gesture. A sort of gestsure of total rejection. Her hand, you know, and the way she turned her face away from us. She said: "Whattaya want?" So we told her we'd like to buy two hamburgers. She sort of laughed, a sarcastic sort of laugh. And she said, "Oh, we don't sell to Mexicans. Why don't you go across to Mexican town, you can buy 'em over there." And then she turned around and continued her conversation.

She never knew how much she was hurting us. But it stayed with us.

We'd go to school two days sometimes, a week, two weeks, three weeks at most. This is when we were migrating. We'd come back to our winter base, and if we were lucky, we'd get in a good solid all of January, February, March, April, May. So we had five months out of a possible nine months. We started counting how many schools we'd been to and we counted thirty-seven. Elementary schools. From first to eighth grade. Thirty-seven. We never got a transfer. Friday we didn't tell the teacher or anything. We'd just go home. And they accepted this.

I remember one teacher—I wondered why she was asking so many questions. (In those days anybody asked questions, you became suspicious. Either a cop or a social worker.) She was a young teacher, and she just wanted to know why we were behind. One day she drove into the camp. That was quite an event, because we never had a teacher come over. Never. So it was, you know, a very meaningful day for us.

This I remember. Some people put this out of their minds and forget it. I don't. I don't want to forget it. I don't want it to take the best of me, but I want it to be there because this is what happened. This is the truth, you know. History.

Questions and Comments

1. What simple and basic things does Chavez say he had come to depend on before he and his family became migratory workers?

2. Why would the Chavez family's desire for land be a "powerful drive"?

3. Explain how the labor contractors and crew pushers cheated the migratory workers? Why was it so easy to cheat the Chavez family?

4. At what cost did the Chavez family strike or honor grievances by other families?

5. One never forgets one's first experience as a victim of racial prejudice—even very young children. Put yourself in Chavez's position. Explain why it would be hard to forget.

6. Cesar Chavez has a very spotty educational background. What personal traits do you think helped him to rise above his educational background?

7. Why was it such a "meaningful day" for the migratory workers when the teacher came to visit the migratory worker camp?

8. Why does Cesar Chavez emphasize that he will not forget his childhood and his migratory worker days? Why is the "truth" and the "history" of that experience so important to him?

Word Study

1. *Migratory* is a key word in this interview. You should be able to define it by the end of the article. Using a dictionary check its meaning with two other words often confused with *migration: emigration* and *immigration*.

2. *Melancholy* describes the conversations between Chavez's mother and father, but could also describe the family's entire experience as migratory workers. Guess its meaning and then check it with the dictionary.

3. *Deceive* has some interesting synonyms: cheat, cozen, dupe, fool, gull, hoodwink trick, defraud, outwit, entrap, ensnare, betray, bamboozle. Which would fit the article best?

4. Find the passages in which the following words appear and using context clues guess at their meanings: *resolution* (p. 179), *agitate* (p. 179), *humiliating* (p. 179), *grievance* (p. 179).

Composition

1. Describe in an essay what alternatives would be open to you and your family if it suddenly had no means of income and no home.

2. Use the library and try to find the origins of anti-Mexican feelings in the United States. Organize your research findings in essay form.

3. Migratory workers are still an important factor in American farm industry. Using the library, find the states where such workers still exist in large numbers and chart the patterns of their migration. Have any changes taken place in the educational experiences of the children? Have conditions and wages improved? Organize your facts into a report you may give to the class. (You might also want to check back issues of newspapers for stories about Chavez's United Farm Workers Union.)

Steven M. Lovelady (1943–   ), now in charge of news coverage for *The Philadelphia Inquirer,* was a staff reporter for *The Wall Street Journal* when he wrote this selection (1969) about Stan Freberg. The author writes, ". . . the motivation for the piece was elemental: here was a wild man doing very well in a button-down business by going against common wisdom and practice at every instance. Every writer's idea of the ideal profile subject."

STAN FREBERG PROSPERS BY BROWBEATING CLIENTS, POKING FUN AT PRODUCTS

Steven M. Lovelady

"ALONG Madison Avenue," says Stanley Victor Freberg, "a rumor persists that I am hostile toward advertising. Let me clear that up right now. I am."

And how. Mr. Freberg, who is an adman himself, describes today's advertising as "that enormous bulk of audio-visual rubbish spewing forth from the massed media."

If Mr. Freberg doesn't talk like an adman, he certainly doesn't look or act like one either. Striding into button-down corporate board rooms in bell-bottom dungarees, lavender shirt and chukka boots, he transfixes executives with a wild-eyed glare described by one client as "scary, almost hypnotic." The effect is heightened by rimless, out-sized yellow sunglasses and a mop of Brillo pad hair.

The Freberg method is simple: Find out what most admen are doing and take the opposite tack. If this means poking a little fun at your client's product in ads, fine. If it means taking a swipe at the work of your rivals in the ad game, all the better. Also, don't take too much lip from the client.

STIRRING STRONG FEELINGS

This approach to advertising means that ex-comic Freberg now counts his critics "on the fingers of the Mormon Tabernacle Choir," as he puts it. Broadcasting Magazine has described him as "Dennis the Menace given a giant erector set to play havoc with," and one New York agency chief calls him "that insane idiot who has given all kinds of people the wrong idea about advertising." But Stan Freberg is cackling all the way to the bank.

At 42, Mr. Freberg has more clients beating on his doors than he can possibly handle and an income that puts him at or near the top of his profession. Dan Seymour, president of the J. Walter Thompson Co., the world's biggest ad agency, makes $272,000 a year; though Mr. Freberg won't say how much he makes, one who knows puts his annual personal income from advertising at between $500,000 and $750,000.

That's not bad for a Baptist minister's son who entered advertising only 12 years ago, after a network television executive told him that satire could never move consumer goods. Since then, Stan Freberg has used satire to peddle everything from potato chips (Bell brand) to religion (United Presbyterian Church). Clients agree that Mr. Freberg's work meets the acid test: When his ads begin to run, sales begin to shoot up.

HOLLYWOOD AND NEW YORK

He operates through two companies. One is Freberg

Ltd., an unlikely setup in Hollywood where the boss spends most of his time. The company has its own motto, Ars Gratia Pecuniae (Art for the Sake of Money), and its own Great Seal—which turns out to be a real seal, etched in brass, wearing sunglasses and whiskers. Freberg Ltd. consists of the owner, his wife Donna, and four aides.

Mr. Freberg recently opened a New York office under the name of Thyme Inc. According to him, it's a division of Parsley, Sage, Rosemary and Osborne. Thyme Inc.'s first client is P. Ballantine & Sons, a Newark, N.J., brewer whose beer sales skidded when it changed its formula in 1965. The company returned to the original formula in 1967, but sales continued to drop and Mr. Freberg was called in to tackle the problem.

He proposed that Ballantine not only admit the problem but make it the focus of the campaign. When one Ballantine executive timidly asked: "But isn't that a little bit negative?" Mr. Freberg roared: "A *little bit* negative? It's a great deal negative! Purge yourselves! Make a public confession! They'll love you for it!"

The executives went along, and the company's ads now feature a mournful Herman Ballantine telling his psychiatrist that his wife's dumb relatives changed the beer formula while he was on a cruise. When the analyst asks if sales fell off, Herman cries: "Fell off? Wouldn't 'plummeted' be a better word?" The ad goes on to explain that Herman has changed the formula back, but that nobody seems to know it yet.

PROMOTING PRUNES

Mr. Freberg's ads for Sunsweet prunes candidly announce that most people don't like prunes because they have ugly wrinkles and messy pits. Sunsweet then triumphantly reveals its development of a pitted prune and, amid stirring march music, vows continuing warfare on the wrinkles.

This sort of approach makes some clients nervous and other admen dubious; admitting that many people simply don't like your product is no way to sell, they maintain. Ballantine's ads have been blasted in the Brewer's Journal, a trade publication, and the company's former ad agency, Sullivan, Stauffer, Colwell & Baynes, quit rather than work with Mr. Freberg.

All of which bothers him not a bit. "The ads work," he says flatly. "They're honest, they're disarming. They get the public's sympathy. Besides, anyone who gagged on a Ballantine back in 1965 has to be told it's a different brew now." The brewing concern says it's still too soon to judge the effectiveness of the Freberg-devised ad campaign, but Sunsweet is more than satisfied. Its prune sales have increased fourfold since the campaign began six months ago.

Mr. Freberg, who cheerfully confesses to acute egomania[1] believes he is the best and most original adman alive and challenges one and all to find a single campaign of his that was a flop. Critics immediately point to his 1966 effort for Pacific Airlines, in which ads addressed to "you with the sweaty palms" assured the public that everyone, pilots included, was afraid to fly.

After only three months, the campaign folded. Critics say that's because it was scaring people off the airline and generating heavy pressure on Pacific from other carriers, who were concerned about ads that might put the safety of air travel in question. Mr. Freberg says the campaign was ended by a merger of Pacific into another carrier (now Air West) that didn't want to go along with the ads.

This sort of thing often seems to happen to Mr. Freberg. Many of his clients are relatively small companies that eventually are swallowed up by larger firms, which then dispense with the nettlesome Mr. Freberg. Accounts he has lost this way include Salada Tea, Contadina Tomato Paste and Chun King Chow Mein. Ballantine's also was acquired recently, but Mr. Freberg said he's felt "no tremors yet."

---

[1] *acute egomania:* excessive and intense faith in one's own abilities or talents

BARKING AT THE CLIENT

Still, most of the clients he has taken on have no quarrel
with the results they've obtained—though personal clashes
with the voluble Mr. Freberg are everyday occurrences. In
making presentations, he leans heavily toward bombast; he
does not persuade so much as overwhelm. "Most company
chiefs are used to agency types fawning over them and saying
things like, 'Look, J.B., if you don't like it we can run it
through again.' I bark at them like a top sergeant," he says.

Mr. Freberg also likes to play his clients film clips of what
he thinks are some of the worst commercials extant. Hop-
ping around the room, waving his arms and throwing objects at the screen, he will shout: "You're using up minutes
of people's lives! You have an obligation to put out as little
garbage as possible!"

One client confesses to a sense of awed helplessness
in the face of a Freberg presentation. Another, Jeno Paulucci, says: "I've had some awful, bloody fights with Stan.
He almost always wins."

Mr. Paulucci, who used to be president of the company
that made Chun King Chow Mein, remembers losing his
cool completely when Mr. Freberg showed him ad pro-
posals. Sample: As an announcer declares that "nine out
of 10 doctors prefer Chun King," the camera pans to the
MDs. Nine are Chinese, one is Caucasian.

The adman bet his client that the ads would boost sales
25% in six months. Mr. Paulucci took the bet. Four months
later, with sales already up 40%, he paid off—trudging along
Hollywood's La Cienega Boulevard in his $70 shoes, pull-
ing a rickshaw occupied by a chortling Stan Freberg. Mr.
Paulucci now is head of Jeno's Pizza Products, and his old
antagonist is still his adman.

GETTING HIS OWN WAY

Mr. Freberg seldom compromises with any of his customers. While he respects "a game client," he keeps tight

control of his campaigns. A clause in the contracts he executes with clients specifically stipulates that "What is funny is what Freberg says is funny." He retains the copyright to all his ads, and another contract clause denies clients the right to add to or delete from any of his creations.

Not surprisingly, all this is just too much for some clients, who invite Mr. Freberg in for a chat and then recoil in horror at his conditions and his ideas. In 1959, Plymouth executives, aghast at his suggestion that Plymouth openly name and criticize its competitors, handed him a check to pay off his contract and showed him to the door.

Some fellow admen would like to show him the way out of the business, too. Many agree with Robert Wilvers, head of the Jack Tinker Partners agency in New York, who says: "He's a very funny man, but advertising is more than making funny jokes. A joke is pointless unless it's relevant to the marketing problem. Too often, it can be a substitute for an idea. You've got to go beyond Freberg; humor is his only weapon."

Mr. Freberg retorts that climbing sales curves show his ideas work in the marketplace. As for his humor, he insists it is always related to a solution of a specific company problem or at least to the general problem of getting the viewer or reader into the store.

Still, he admits that he gets his biggest kicks out of devising ads that spoof other ads. As a novel offset to "the preposterous and unbelievable claims that fill the airwaves," he uses the Exaggeratedly Modest Claim. Jacobsen power lawnmowers, for example, are billed as "Faster Than Sheep!" A Sunsweet ad says: "Surveys prove the overwhelming majority of people prefer Sunsweet prunes to World War III!"

Says Mr. Freberg: "It's just a prune for crying out loud, it's not the Holy Grail.[1] So why not entertain a little?" The consumer is so appreciative of the low-key approach, he

[1]*Holy Grail:* in some biblical legends, was the platter—in others, the cup—used by Christ at the Last Supper

contends, that he runs out to buy the product.

For Westinghouse Electric Corp., Mr. Freberg has whipped up a college recruiting ad campaign that pokes fun at rival recruiting ads. In the usual non-Freberg pitch, corporations appeal to student idealism by playing up the corporate role in solving all sorts of social and economic problems; the mundane, day-by-day work any recruit must do is seldom mentioned.

But the star of Mr. Freberg's Westinghouse ads is engineering student Charlie Winfield, a man of narrow vision. Charlie puzzles recruiters; he does not want to help desalt the seas, uplift the ghetto or hurl man into space. All he seems to care about is "toastal engineering." Says Charlie, showing a sudden flicker of interest: "Get the raisins to keep from sticking on the little wire, and the caraway seeds will take care of themselves!"

UNFAIR TO GYPSIES

A hallmark of the Freberg school of advertising is the gag promotion that often accompanies an ad campaign. For Salada Tea, he invented a labor-management struggle between Salada and the fictitious American Federation of Gypsies, with each side taking full page ads in the New Yorker to solemnly explain their positions.

Despite the fact that the gypsy ad, signed by "Vladimir Krim, Head Gypsy," urged readers to protest to the non-existent Bureau of Gypsy Affairs in Washington, the New York Times was gulled by the promotion. It sent a reporter to Salada headquarters to look for picketing gypsies and to interview both sides.

More recently Mr. Freberg had his beer baron, Herman Ballantine, confide to his analyst that he had finally found a job his stupid relatives could handle—labeling beer bottles. Mr. Freberg then arranged to have 250,000 cases of Ballantine shipped to retail stores with the labels on upside down.

Though Mr. Freberg has a small staff at Thyme Inc. and

Freberg Ltd., he insists on doing all the creative work himself. Usually, he is juggling up to a dozen clients at once, each at a personal fee that starts at $50,000 a year "and works up very fast," according to one customer. He is on the run most of the time.

The Freberg day often begins before dawn, when the adman can be seen jogging through the moneyed streets of Beverly Hills, shouting: "All right! All you rich people out for volleyball!" Back at his 15-room mansion, health-food addict Freberg breakfasts on a dozen vitamin pills and picks up the phone.

For the rest of the day, he dashes from home to office to sessions with clients and agencies to film laboratories to shooting studios, trailing a lengthening string of missed telephone calls behind him. He enjoys working under pressure and can be a maddening perfectionist; he recently shot 72 takes of a Ballantine TV commercial before he was satisfied, keeping a studio crew of three dozen men well past midnight—and thereby saddling his client with a bill for quadruple overtime.

Questions and Comments

1. State the ways in which Stan Freberg departs from the usual approaches to advertising.

2. What evidence can you find in the article that proves Stan Freberg has "acute egomania"?

3. Stan Freberg treats his clients in ways different from other people in advertising. State what the different ways are.

4. What personal traits does Stan Freberg have that help make him successful?

5. Why do Stan Freberg advertisements appeal to consumers?

6. At one point the article hints at a Stan Freberg failure in advertising. What was the failure? Do you believe Stan Fre-

berg's explanation of why the advertising campaign was dropped? Why or why not?

Word Study

1. *Transfix* combines the Latin *trans* meaning "across" or "through" and *fixus* meaning to "fix" or "fasten." Find the sentence where it is used on page 184 and then define it in terms which fit that situation. Check your meaning in the dictionary.

2. *Purge, plummeted,* and *candidly,* are used in contexts which give away their meanings and are therefore good examples of how reading in itself builds vocabulary. Find the sentences using these words and discover their meanings.

3. *Voluble, bombast,* and *fawning* are words which either describe the way language can be used or the kind of language being used. Find the paragraph in which these three words are used and try to guess their meanings. Check with the dictionary.

4. Study the paragraphs in which *stipulate, mundane,* and *gulled* are used and find clues to their meaning in the paragraphs. Check your meanings in the dictionary.

Composition

1. Using the Stan Freberg approach, choose a popular brand-name product and write a thirty second script for a radio or television advertisement. (Timing must be exact for radio and television.)

2. Every school usually has a "character," someone who stands apart from the average conformists. Ask "the character" if you may interview him or her in order to do an article similar in approach to the Steven Lovelady article about Stan Freberg.

3. Select an advertisement you hate or are annoyed by. Examine the advertisement carefully and write in detail the reasons for your opinion.

4. Setting aside *what* Mr. Lovelady wrote, examine *how* he wrote his article. How did he sustain reader interest throughout? What devices did he use to make his article easy to read? To make it pleasurable? What are some traits of his style?

Aldous Huxley was an English-born writer who produced novels, essays, short stories, and biography of excellent quality. In 1932 he published a novel, *Brave New World,* which described a super-organized society of the future that abolished free will by methodical conditioning. Citizens of that future world were kept happy with pills which induced happiness, and the last vestiges of individualism and nonconformism were stamped out by autocratic government control. Huxley's book was reinforced in 1949 by Orwell's book of similar prophecy, *1984,* startling because it predicted that the society of *Brave New World* would assert itself six hundred years sooner than Huxley's book had predicted.

Huxley tended to agree that the process toward that "brave new world" was accelerating and so in 1958 wrote *Brave New World Revisited,* which provides a progress report on the processes described in 1932. It is an alarming book, and the following selection from it documents only one of the alarming aspects of this "brave new world."

BRAINWASHING

Aldous Huxley

In the two preceding chapters I have described the techniques of what may be called wholesale mind-manipulation, as practiced by the greatest demagogue and the most successful salesmen in recorded history. But no human problem can be solved by wholesale methods alone. The shotgun has its place, but so has the hypodermic syringe. In the chapters that follow I shall describe some of the more effective techniques for manipulating not crowds, not entire publics, but isolated individuals.

In the course of his epoch-making experiments on the conditioned reflex, Ivan Pavlov[1] observed that, when subjected to prolonged physical or psychic stress, laboratory animals exhibit all the symptoms of a nervous breakdown. Refusing to cope any longer with the intolerable situation, their brains go on strike, so to speak, and either stop working altogether (the dog loses consciousness), or else resort to slowdowns and sabotage (the dog behaves unrealistically, or develops the kind of physical symptoms which, in a human being, we would call hysterical). Some animals are more resistant to stress than others. Dogs possessing what Pavlov called a "strong excitatory" constitution break down much more quickly than dogs of a merely "lively" (as opposed to a choleric or agitated) temperament. Similarly "weak inhibitory" dogs reach the end of their tether much sooner than do "calm imperturbable" dogs. But even the most stoical dog is unable to resist indefinitely. If the stress to which he is subjected is sufficiently intense or sufficiently prolonged, he will end by breaking down as abjectly and as completely as the weakest of his kind.

Pavlov's findings were confirmed in the most distressing manner, and on a very large scale, during the two World Wars. As the result of a single catastrophic experience, or of a succession of terrors less appalling but frequently repeated, soldiers develop a number of disabling psychophysical symptoms. Temporary unconsciousness, extreme agitation, lethargy, functional blindness or paralysis, completely unrealistic responses to the challenge of events, strange reversals of lifelong patterns of behavior—all the symptoms, which Pavlov observed in his dogs, reappeared among the victims of what in the First World War was called "shell shock," in the Second, "battle fatigue." Every man, like every dog, has his own

[1] *Ivan Pavlov:* (1849-1936) Russian physiologist, famous for his experiments in cerebral activity by means of *conditioned reflex*. In one of his experiments Pavlov rang a bell each time he fed a dog. Eventually he rang the bell without feeding the dog; nevertheless the dog's saliva glands dripped saliva. Such a reflex is considered a "conditioned" one.

individual limit of endurance. Most men reach their limit after about thirty days of more or less continuous stress under the conditions of modern combat. The more than averagely susceptible succumb in only fifteen days. The more than averagely tough can resist for forty-five or even fifty days. Strong or weak, in the long run all of them break down. All, that is to say, of those who are initially sane. For, ironically enough, the only people who can hold up indefinitely under the stress of modern war are psychotics. Individual insanity is immune to the consequences of collective insanity.

The fact that every individual has his breaking point has been known and, in a crude unscientific way, exploited from time immemorial. In some cases man's dreadful inhumanity to man has been inspired by the love of cruelty for its own horrible and fascinating sake. More often, however, pure sadism was tempered by utilitarianism, theology or reasons of state. Physical torture and other forms of stress were inflicted by lawyers in order to loosen the tongues of reluctant witnesses; by clergymen in order to punish the unorthodox and induce them to change their opinions; by the secret police to extract confessions from persons suspected of being hostile to the government. Under Hitler, torture, followed by mass extermination, was used on those biological heretics, the Jews. For a young Nazi, a tour of duty in the Extermination Camps was (in Himmler's[1] words) "the best indoctrination on inferior beings and the subhuman races." Given the obsessional quality of the anti-Semitism which Hitler had picked up as a young man in the slums of Vienna, this revival of the methods employed by the Holy Office[2] against heretics and witches was inevitable. But in the light of the findings of Pavlov and of the knowledge gained by psychiatrists in the treatment of war neuroses, it seems a hideous and grotesque anachron-

[1]*Himmler:* Heinrich Himmler, head of the Gestapo, or Nazi secret police

[2]*Holy Office:* a group of enforcers of faith and morals of the Roman Catholic Church during the 15th and 16th centuries

ism. Stresses amply sufficient to cause a complete cerebral break down can be induced by methods which, though hatefully inhuman, fall short of physical torture.

Whatever may have happened in earlier years, it seems fairly certain that torture is not extensively used by the Communist police[1] today. They draw their inspiration, not from the Inquisitor[2] or the SS man,[3] but from the physiologist and his methodically conditioned laboratory animals. For the dictator and his policemen, Pavlov's findings have important practical implications. If the central nervous system of dogs can be broken down, so can the central nervous system of political prisoners. It is simply a matter of applying the right amount of stress for the right length of time. At the end of the treatment, the prisoner will be in a state of neurosis or hysteria, and will be ready to confess whatever his captors want him to confess.

But confession is not enough. A hopeless neurotic is no use to anyone. What the intelligent and practical dictator needs is not a patient to be institutionalized, or a victim to be shot, but a convert who will work for the Cause. Turning once again to Pavlov, he learns that, on their way to the point of final breakdown, dogs become more than normally suggestible. New behavior patterns can easily be installed while the dog is at or near the limit of its cerebral endurance, and these new behavior patterns seem to be ineradicable. The animal in which thay have been implanted cannot be deconditioned; that which it has learned under stress will remain an integral part of its make-up.

Psychological stresses can be produced in many ways. Dogs become disturbed when stimuli are unusually strong; when

---

[1]*Communist police:* (probably) refers to secret police in the Stalinist regime (1928–1953) of the Soviet Union

[2]*Inquisitor:* a member of the Spanish Inquisition of the 15th and 16th centuries who investigated charges of heresy, witchcraft, and blasphemy. Such Inquisitors could sentence people to death and torture.

[3]*SS man:* an officer of the terroristic Nazi police organization to enforce political obedience. SS men were noted for unrelenting cruelty to those who did not visibly follow the Nazi doctrines.

the interval between a stimulus and the customary response is unduly prolonged and the animal is left in a state of suspense; when the brain is confused by stimuli that run counter to what the dog has learned to expect; when stimuli make no sense within the victim's established frame of reference. Furthermore, it has been found that the deliberate induction of fear, rage or anxiety markedly heightens the dog's suggestibility. If these emotions are kept at a high pitch of intensity for a long enough time, the brain goes 'on strike.' When this happens, new behavior patterns may be installed with the greatest of ease.

Among the physical stresses that increase a dog's suggestibility are fatigue, wounds and every form of sickness.

For the would-be dictator these findings possess important practical implications. They prove, for example, that Hitler was quite right in maintaining that mass meetings at night were more effective than mass meetings in the daytime. During the day, he wrote, "man's will power revolts with highest energy against any attempt at being forced under another's will and another's opinion. In the evening, however, they succumb more easily to the dominating force of a stronger will."

Pavlov would have agreed with him; fatigue increases suggestibility. (That is why, among other reasons, the commercial sponsors of television programs prefer the evening hours and are ready to back their preference with hard cash.)

Illness is even more effective than fatigue as an intensifier of suggestibility. In the past, sickrooms were the scene of countless religious conversions. The scientifically trained dictator of the future will have all the hospitals in his dominions wired for sound and equipped with pillow speakers. Canned persuasion will be on the air twenty-four hours a day, and the more important patients will be visited by political soul-savers and mind-changers just as, in the past, their ancestors were visited by priests, nuns and pious laymen.

The fact that strong negative emotions tend to heighten suggestibility and so facilitate a change of heart had been observed and exploited long before the days of Pavlov. As **Dr.** William Sargant has pointed out in his enlightening book, *Battle for the Mind,* John Wesley's[1] enormous success as a preacher was based upon an intuitive understanding of the central nervous system. He would open his sermon with a long and detailed description of the torments to which, unless they underwent conversion, his hearers would undoubtedly be condemned for all eternity. Then, when terror and an agonizing sense of guilt had brought his audience to the verge, or in some cases over the verge, of a complete cerebral breakdown, he would change his tone and promise salvation to those who believed and repented. By this kind of preaching, Wesley converted thousands of men, women and children. Intense, prolonged fear broke them down and produced a state of greatly intensified suggestibility. In this state they were able to accept the preacher's theological pronouncements without question. After which they were reintegrated by words of comfort, and emerged from their ordeal with new and generally better behavior patterns ineradicably implanted in their minds and nervous systems.

The effectiveness of political and religious propaganda depends upon the methods employed, not upon the doctrines taught. These doctrines may be true or false, wholesome or pernicious—it makes little or no difference. If the indoctrination is given in the right way at the proper stage of nervous exhaustion, it will work. Under favorable conditions, practically everybody can be converted to practically anything.

We possess detailed descriptions of the methods used by the Communist police for dealing with political prisoners. From the moment he is taken into custody, the victim is subjected systematically to many kinds of physical and phychological stress. He is badly fed, he is made extremely uncomfortable, he is not allowed to sleep for more than a few hours

---

[1] *John Wesley:* founder of the Methodist Church in Great Britain and America

each night. And all the time he is kept in a state of suspense, uncertainty and acute apprehension. Day after day—or rather night after night, for these Pavlovian policemen understand the value of fatigue as an intensifier of suggestibility— he is questioned, often for many hours at a stretch, by interrogators who do their best to frighten, confuse and bewilder him. After a few weeks or months of such treatment, his brain goes on strike and he confesses whatever it is that his captors want him to confess. Then, if he is to be converted rather than shot, he is offered the comfort of hope. If he will but accept the true faith, he can yet be saved—not, of course, in the next life (for, officially, there is no next life), but in this.

Similar but rather less drastic methods were used during the Korean War on military prisoners. In their Chinese camps the young Western captives were systematically subjected to stress. Thus, for the most trivial breaches of the rules, offenders would be summoned to the commandant's office, there to be questioned, browbeaten and publicly humiliated. And the process would be repeated, again and again, at any hour of the day or night. This continuous harassment produced in its victims a sense of bewilderment and chronic anxiety. To intensify their sense of guilt, prisoners were made to write and rewrite, in ever more intimate detail, long autobiographical accounts of their shortcomings. And after having confessed their own sins, they were required to confess the sins of their companions. The aim was to create within the camp a nightmarish society, in which everybody was spying on, and informing against, everyone else. To these mental stresses were added the physical stresses of malnutrition, discomfort and illness. The increased suggestibility thus induced was skilfully exploited by the Chinese, who poured into these abnormally receptive minds large doses of pro-Communist and anti-capitalist literature. These Pavlovian techniques were remarkably successful. One out of every seven American prisoners was guilty, we are officially told, of grave collaboration with the Chinese authorities, one out of three of technical collaboration.

It must not be supposed that this kind of treatment is reserved by the Communists exclusively for their enemies. The young field workers, whose business it was, during the first years of the new regime, to act as Communist missionaries and organizers in China's innumerable towns and villages were made to take a course of indoctrination far more intense than that to which any prisoner of war was ever subjected. In his *China under Communism,* R. L. Walker describes the methods by which the party leaders are able to fabricate out of ordinary men and women the thousands of selfless fanatics required for spreading the Communist gospel and for enforcing Communist policies. Under this system of training, the human raw material is shipped to special camps, where the trainees are completely isolated from their friends, families and the outside world in general. In these camps they are made to perform exhausting physical and mental work; they are never alone, always in groups; they are encouraged to spy on one another; they are required to write self-accusatory autobiographies; they live in chronic fear of the dreadful fate that may befall them on account of what has been said about them by informers or of what they themselves have confessed. In this state of heightened suggestibility they are given an intensive course in theoretical and applied Marxism[1]—a course in which failure to pass examinations may mean anything from ignominious expulsion to a term in a forced labor camp or even liquidation. After about six months of this kind of thing, prolonged mental and physical stress produces the results which Pavlov's findings would lead one to expect. One after another, or in whole groups, the trainees break down. Neurotic and hysterical symptoms make their appearance. Some of the victims commit suicide, others (as many, we are told, as 20 per cent

---

[1]*Marxism:* the socialism of Karl Marx and Friedrich Engels, which views the class struggle as the fundamental force in history

of the total) develop a severe mental illness. Those who survive the rigors of the conversion process emerge with new and ineradicable behavior patterns. All their ties with the past—friends, family, traditional decencies and pieties—have been severed. They are new men, recreated in the image of their new god and totally dedicated to his service.

Throughout the Communist world tens of thousands of these disciplined and devoted young men are being turned out every year from hundreds of conditioning centers. What the Jesuits did for the Roman Church of the Counter Reformation, these products of a more scientific and even harsher training are now doing, and will doubtless continue to do, for the Communist parties of Europe, Asia and Africa.

In politics Pavlov seems to have been an old-fashioned liberal. But, by a strange irony of fate, his researches and the theories he based upon them have called into existence a great army of fanatics dedicated heart and soul, reflex and nervous system, to the destruction of old-fashioned liberalism, wherever it can be found.

Brainwashing, as it is now practiced, is a hybrid technique, depending for its effectiveness partly on the systematic use of violence, partly on skilful psychological manipulation. It represents the tradition of *1984* on its way to becoming the tradition of *Brave New World*. Under a long-established and well-regulated dictatorship our current methods of semiviolent manipulation will seem, no doubt, absurdly crude. Conditioned from earliest infancy (and perhaps also biologically predestined), the average middle- or lower-caste individual will never require conversion or even a refresher course in the true faith. The members of the highest caste will have to be able to think new thoughts in response to new situations; consequently their training will be much less rigid than the training imposed upon those whose business is not to reason why, but merely to do and die with the minimum of fuss. These upper-caste individuals will be members, still, of a wild species—the trainers and guardians, themselves only slightly conditioned, of a breed of completely domesticated animals. Their wildness will make it possible for them to become heretical and rebellious. When this happens, they will have to be either liquidated, or brainwashed back into orthodoxy, or (as in *Brave New World*) exiled to some island, where they can give no further trouble, except of course to one another. But universal infant conditioning and the other techniques of manipulation and control are still a few generations away in the future. On the road to the Brave New World our rulers will have to rely on the transitional and provisional techniques of brainwashing.

Questions and Comments

1. How does the first paragraph relate this essay to what Huxley has said in previous chapters and will say in later chapters?

2. What did Ivan Pavlov's experiments prove about animal behavior?

3. How did World War I and World War II show that Pavlov's findings applied to human behavior as well as animal behavior?

4. What examples does Huxley give of the use of physical torture to bring human beings to the breaking point? Why is torture not extensively used by the Communist police today?

5. What could a dictator who needed converts instead of "hopeless neurotics" learn from Pavlov?

6. What stresses are effective in increasing the suggestibility of a human being? What examples does Huxley give of their effectiveness?

7. What techniques of brainwashing were used on American prisoners of war during the Korean crisis?

8. What is the process used by the Chinese to produce fanatical preachers of government doctrine?

9. What distinction does Huxley make between "lower-caste" and "upper-caste" individuals?

10. What does Huxley predict will occur a few generations from now?

Word Study

1. On page 194 *demagogue* refers in particular to Hitler, former dictator of Germany, head of the Nazi party, and the man primarily responsible for World War II. Can you guess the meaning of *demagogue?* Check your guess in a dictionary.

2. Pavlov found that choleric or agitated dogs broke down more quickly than "lively" dogs, that "weak *inhibitory*" dogs broke down sooner than "calm *imperturbable*" dogs, and that even the "most *stoical*" dog broke down eventually. What do the italicized words mean?

3. Huxley includes lethargy in a list of psychophysical symptoms developed by soldiers. What does *lethargy* mean?

4. *Anachronism* derives from the Greek forms *ana*, "backward," and *chronos*, "time," together meaning "out of place in time." For example, an airplane flying overhead in a movie about the Old West would be considered an anachronism. To what does Huxley refer in his use of the word on page 196?

5. Give the meaning of the italicized words using clues in the context of the selection wherever possible.

"More often, however, pure *sadism* was tempered by utilitarianism, theology or reasons of state." (page 196)

". . . these new behavior patterns seem to be *ineradicable*." (page 197)

"These doctrines may be true or false, wholesome or *pernicious*—it makes little or no difference." (page 199)

". . . failure to pass examinations may mean anything from *ignominious* expulsion to a term in a forced labor camp or even *liquidation*." (page 201)

Composition

1. Write a composition in which you tell why you agree or disagree with Mr. Huxley's predictions for the future.

2. Take some aspect of modern life and show how it employs the techniques of brainwashing to condition people.

3. If you are disturbed by this essay, write a description of your hope for defense against it.

Mark Twain's nature turned inevitably toward making fun of something. Between 1892 and 1900, when Twain and his family lived mostly abroad, Europe had its turn as target for Twain's humorous bursts. "The Awful German Language," an appendix to *A Tramp Abroad*, is just one more shot at his European target.

The figure of Twain stands tall in the ranks of American writers. *Huckleberry Finn, Tom Sawyer,* and *Life on the Mississippi* are only a few of the priceless pieces which make up the monument of his complete written works.

Further proof of his greatness appeared in the 1960's, fifty years after his death, when a previously unpublished manuscript, *Letters to Earth,* immediately became a best seller. Here was the "last laugh" of a true master writer, exploding boisterously and irreverently among a new generation. Twain will go on speaking through his works to all future generations, assuming of course, that humanity retains its sense of humor.

THE AWFUL GERMAN LANGUAGE

Mark Twain

A little learning makes the whole world kin.—Proverbs xxxii, 7.

I WENT often to look at the collection of curiosities in Heidelberg Castle, and one day I surprised the keeper of it with my German. I spoke entirely in that language. He was greatly interested; and after I had talked awhile he said my German was very rare, possibly a "unique"; and wanted to add it to his museum.

If he had known what it had cost me to acquire my art, he would also have known that it would break any collector to buy it. Harris[1] and I had been hard at work on our German during several weeks at that time, and although we had made good progress, it had been accomplished under great difficulty and annoyance, for three of our teachers had died in the meantime. A person who has not studied German can form no idea of what a perplexing language it is.

Surely there is not another language that is so slip-shod and systemless, and so slippery and elusive to the grasp. One is washed about in it, hither and hither, in the most helpless way; and when at last he thinks he has captured a rule which offers firm ground to take a rest on amid the general rage and turmoil of the ten parts of speech, he turns over the page and reads, "Let the pupil make careful note of the following *exceptions*." He runs his eye down and finds that there are more exceptions to the rule than instances of it. So overboard he goes again, to hunt for another Ararat[2] and find another quicksand. Such has been, and continues to be, my experience. Every time I think I have got one of these four confusing "cases" where I am master of it, a seemingly insignificant preposition intrudes itself into my sentence, clothed with an awful and unsuspected power, and crumbles the ground from under me. For instance, my book inquires after a certain bird—(it is always inquiring after things which are of no sort of consequence to anybody): "Where is the bird?" Now the answer to this question,—according to the book,—is that the bird is waiting in the blacksmith shop on account of the rain. Of course no bird would do that, but then you must stick to the book. Very well, I begin to cipher out the German for that answer. I begin at the wrong end, necessarily, for that is the German idea. I say to myself, "*Regen,* (rain,) is masculine—or maybe it is feminine—or possibly neuter—it is

[1] *Harris:* Joel Chandler Harris, creator of the *Uncle Remus* stories for children, and a close friend of Twain

[2] *Ararat:* the supposed high resting place of Noah's Ark thought to be "secret" from anyone searching for those remains; a peak safe from all seekers

too much trouble to look, now. Therefore, it is either *der* (the) Regen, or *die* (the) Regen, or *das* (the) Regen, according to which gender it may turn out to be when I look. In the interest of science, I will cipher it out on the hypothesis that it is masculine. Very well—then *the* rain is *der* Regen, if it is simply in the quiescent state of being *mentioned,* without enlargement or discussion—Nominative case; but if this rain is lying around, in a kind of a general way on the ground, it is then definitely located, it is *doing something*— that is, *resting,* (which is one of the German grammar's ideas of doing something,) and this throws the rain into the Dative case, and makes it *dem* Regen. However, this rain is not resting, but is doing something *actively,*—it is falling,—to interfere with the bird, likely,—and this indicates *movement,* which has the effect of sliding it into the Accusative case and changing *dem* Regen into *den* Regen." Having completed the grammatical horoscope of this matter, I answer up confidently and state in German that the bird is staying in the blacksmith shop "wegen (on account of) *den* Regen." Then the teacher lets me softly down with the remark that whenever the word "wegen" drops into a sentence, it *always* throws that subject into the *Genitive* case, regardless of consequences—and that therefore this bird staid in the blacksmith shop "wegen *des* Regens."

N. B.[1] I was informed, later, by a higher authority, that there was an "exception" which permits one to say "wegen *den* Regen" in certain peculiar and complex circumstances, but that this exception is not extended to anything *but* rain.

There are ten parts of speech, and they are all troublesome. An average sentence, in a German newspaper, is a sublime and impressive curiosity; it occupies a quarter of a column; it contains all the ten parts of speech—not in regular order, but mixed; it is built mainly of compound words constructed by the writer on the spot, and not to be found in any dictionary—six or seven words compacted into one, with-

[1]*N. B.: nota bene* (Latin); note well, take notice

out joint or seam—that is, without hyphens; it treats of fourteen or fifteen different subjects, each enclosed in a parenthesis of its own, with here and there extra parentheses which
re-enclose three or four of the minor parentheses, making
pens within pens; finally, all the parentheses and re-paren-
theses are massed together between a couple of king-paren-
theses, one of which is placed in the first line of the majestic
sentence and the other in the middle of the last line of it—
after which comes the VERB, and you find out for the first
time what the man has been talking about; and after the
verb—merely by way of ornament, as far as I can make out,—
the writer shovels in *"haben sind gewesen gehabt haben geworden sein,"*[1] or words to that effect, and the monument is
finished. I suppose that this closing hurrah is in the nature of
the flourish to a man's signature—not necessary, but pretty.
German books are easy enough to read when you hold them
before the looking-glass or stand on your head,—so as to re-
verse the construction,—but I think that to learn to read and
understand a German newspaper is a thing which must always remain an impossibility to a foreigner.

Yet even the German books are not entirely free from attacks of the Parenthesis distemper—though they are usually
so mild as to cover only a few lines, and therefore when you
at last get down to the verb it carries some meaning to your
mind because you are able to remember a good deal of what
has gone before.

Now here is a sentence from a popular and excellent German novel,—with a slight parenthesis in it. I will make a perfectly literal translation, and throw in the parenthesis-marks
and some hyphens for the assistance of the reader,—though in
the original there are no parenthesis-marks or hyphens, and
the reader is left to flounder through to the remote verb the
best way he can:

[1] *haben . . . sein:* This is a senseless list of "to be" verbs in various forms.
German sentences often end with one, two, or three of the quoted forms.

"But when he, upon the street, the (in-satin-and-silk-cover-ed-now-very-unconstrainedly-after-the-newest-fashion-dressed) government counsellor's wife *met*," etc., etc.[1]

That is from "The Old Mamselle's Secret," by Mrs. Marlitt. And that sentence is constructed upon the most approved German model. You observe how far that verb is from the reader's base of operations; well, in a German newspaper they put their verb away over on the next page; and I have heard that sometimes after stringing along on exciting preliminaries and parentheses for a column or two, they get in a hurry and have to go to press without getting to the verb at all. Of course, then, the reader is left in a very exhausted and ignorant state.

We have the Parenthesis disease in our literature, too; and one may see cases of it every day in our books and newspapers: but with us it is the mark and sign of an unpractised writer or a cloudy intellect, whereas with the Germans it is doubtless the mark and sign of a practised pen and of the presence of that sort of luminous intellectual fog which stands for clearness among these people. For surely it is *not* clearness,—it necessarily can't be clearness. Even a jury would have penetration enough to discover that. A writer's ideas must be a good deal confused, a good deal out of line and sequence, when he starts out to say that a man met a counsellor's wife in the street, and then right in the midst of this so simple undertaking halts these approaching people and makes them stand still until he jots down an inventory of the woman's dress. That is manifestly absurd. It reminds a person of those dentists who secure your instant and breathless interest in a tooth by taking a grip on it with the forceps, and then stand there and drawl through a tedious anecdote before they give the dreaded jerk. Parentheses in literature and dentistry are in bad taste.

[1] *Author's note:* "Wenn er aber auf der Strasse der in Sammt und Seide gehüllten jetz sehr ungenirt nach der neusten mode gekleideten Regierungs-rathin begegnet."

The Germans have another kind of parenthesis, which they make by splitting a verb in two and putting half of it at the beginning of an exciting chapter and the *other half* at the end of it. Can any one conceive of anything more confusing than that? These things are called "separable verbs." The German grammar is blistered all over with separable verbs; and the wider the two portions of one of them are spread apart, the better the author of the crime is pleased with his performance. A favorite one is *reiste ab,*—which means, *departed.* Here is an example which I culled from a novel and reduced to English:

"The trunks being now ready, he—DE—after kissing his mother and sisters, and once more pressing to his bosom his adored Gretchen, who, dressed in simple white muslin, with a single tube-rose in the ample folds of her rich brown hair, had tottered feebly down the stairs, still pale from the terror and excitement of the past evening, but longing to lay her poor aching head yet once again upon the breast of him whom she loved more dearly than life itself, PARTED."

However, it is not well to dwell too much on the separable verbs. One is sure to lose his temper early; and if he sticks to the subject, and will not be warned, it will at last either soften his brain or petrify it. Personal pronouns and adjectives are a fruitful nuisance in this language, and should have been left out. For instance, the same sound, *sie,* means *you,* and it means *she,* and it means *her,* and it means *it,* and it means *they,* and it means *them.* Think of the ragged poverty of a language which has to make one word do the work of six,—and a poor little weak thing of only three letters at that. But mainly, think of the exasperation of never knowing which of these meanings the speaker is trying to convey. This explains why, whenever a person says *sie* to me, I generally try to kill him, if a stranger.

Now observe the Adjective. Here was a case where simplicity would have been an advantage: therefore, for no other reason, the inventor of this language complicated it all he

could. When we wish to speak of our "good friend or
friends," in our enlightened tongue, we stick to the one form
and have no trouble or hard feeling about it; but with the
German tongue it is different. When a German gets his
hands on an adjective, he declines it, and keeps on declining
it until the common sense is all declined out of it. It is as bad
as Latin. He says, for instance:

SINGULAR

Nominative—Mein gut*er* Freund,	my good friend.
Genitive—Mein*es* gut*en* Freund*es*,	of my good friend.
Dative—Mein*em* gut*en* Freund,	to my good friend.
Accusative—Mein*en* gut*en* Freund,	my good friend.

PLURAL

N.—Mein*e* gut*en* Freund*e*,	my good friends.
G.—Mein*er* gut*en* Freund*e*,	of my good friends.
D.—Mein*en* gut*en* Freund*en*,	to my good friends.
A.—Mein*e* gut*en* Freund*e*,	my good friends.

Now let the candidate for the asylum try to memorize
those variations, and see how soon he will be elected. One
might better go without friends in Germany than take all
this trouble about them. I have shown what a bother it is to
decline a good (male) friend; well, this is only a third of the
work, for there is a variety of new distortions of the adjective
to be learned when the object is feminine, and still another
when the object is neuter. Now there are more adjectives in
this language than there are black cats in Switzerland, and
they must all be as elaborately declined as the examples
above suggested. Difficult?—troublesome?—these words cannot describe it. I heard a Californian student in Heidelberg,
say, in one of his calmest moods, that he would rather decline two drinks than one German adjective.

The inventor of the language seems to have taken pleasure
in complicating it in every way he could think of. For instance, if one is casually referring to a house, *Haus,* or a

horse, *Pferd,* or a dog, *Hund,* he spells these words as I have indicated; but if he is referring to them in the Dative case, he sticks on a foolish and unnecessary *e* and spells them Hause, Pferde, Hunde. So, as an added *e* often signifies the plural, as the *s* does with us, the new student is likely to go on for a month making twins out of a Dative dog before he discovers his mistake; and on the other hand, many a new student who could ill afford loss, has bought and paid for two dogs and only got one of them, because he ignorantly bought that dog in the Dative singular when he really supposed he was talking plural,—which left the law on the seller's side, of course, by the strict rules of grammar, and therefore a suit for recovery could not lie.

In German, all the Nouns begin with a capital letter. Now that is a good idea; and a good idea, in this language, is necessarily conspicuous from its lonesomeness. I consider this capitalizing of nouns a good idea, because by reason of it you are almost always able to tell a noun the minute you see it. You fall into error occasionally, because you mistake the name of a person for the name of a thing, and waste a good deal of time trying to dig a meaning out of it. German names almost always do mean something, and this helps to deceive the student. I translated a passage one day, which said that "the infuriated tigress broke loose and utterly ate up the unfortunate fir-forest," *(Tannenwald).* When I was girding up my loins to doubt this, I found out that Tannenwald, in this instance, was a man's name.

Every noun has a gender, and there is no sense or system in the distribution; so the gender of each must be learned separately and by heart. There is no other way. To do this, one has to have a memory like a memorandum book. In German, a young lady has no sex, while a turnip has. Think what overwrought reverence that shows for the turnip, and what callous disrespect for the girl. See how it looks in print —I translate this from a conversation in one of the best of the German Sunday-school books:

"*Gretchen.* Wilhelm, where is the turnip?

"*Wilhelm*. She has gone to the kitchen.

"*Gretchen*. Where is the accomplished and beautiful English maiden?

"*Wilhelm*. It has gone to the opera."

To continue with the German genders: a tree is male, its buds are female, its leaves are neuter; horses are sexless, dogs are male, cats are female,—Tom-cats included, of course; a person's mouth, neck, bosom, elbows, fingers, nails, feet, and body, are of the male sex, and his head is male or neuter according to the word selected to signify it, and *not* according to the sex of the individual who wears it,—for in Germany all the women wear either male heads or sexless ones; a person's nose, lips, shoulders, breast, hands, hips, and toes are of the female sex; and his hair, ears, eyes, chin, legs, knees, heart, and conscience, haven't any sex at all. The inventor of the language probably got what he knew about a conscience from hearsay.

Now, by the above dissection, the reader will see that in Germany a man may *think* he is a man, but when he comes to look into the matter closely, he is bound to have his doubts; he finds that in sober truth he is a most ridiculous mixture; and if he ends by trying to comfort himself with the thought that he can at least depend on a third of this mess as being manly and masculine, the humiliating second thought will quickly remind him that in this respect he is no better off than any woman or cow in the land.

In the German it is true that by some oversight of the inventor of the language, a Woman is a female; but a Wife, (*Weib*,) is not,—which is unfortunate. A Wife, here, has no sex; she is neuter; so, according to the grammar, a fish is *he*, his scales are *she*, but a fishwife is neither. To describe a wife as sexless, may be called under-description; that is bad enough, but over-description is surely worse. A German speaks of an Englishman as the *Engländer;* to change the sex, he adds *inn*, and that stands for Englishwoman,— *Engländerinn*. That seems descriptive enough, but still it is not exact enough for a German; so he precedes the word with that article which indicates that the creature to follow is feminine, and writes it down thus: *"Die* Engländer*inn,"*—which means "the *she-Englishwoman."* I consider that that person is over-described.

Well, after the student has learned the sex of a great number of nouns, he is still in a difficulty, because he finds it impossible to persuade his tongue to refer to things as *"he"* and *"she,"* and *"him"* and *"her,"* which it has been always accustomed to refer to as *"it."* When he even frames a German sentence in his mind, with the hims and hers in the right places, and then works up his courage to the utterance-point, it is no use,—the moment he begins to speak his tongue flies the track and all those labored males and females come out as *"its."* And even when he is reading German to himself, he always calls those things *"it,"* whereas he ought to read in this way:

TALE OF THE FISHWIFE AND ITS SAD FATE[1]

It is a bleak Day. Hear the Rain, how he pours, and the Hail, how he rattles; and see the Snow, how he drifts along, and oh the Mud, how deep he is! Ah the poor Fishwife, it is stuck fast in the Mire; it has dropped its Basket of Fishes; and its Hands have been cut by the Scales as it seized some of the falling Creatures; and one Scale has even got into its Eye, and it cannot get her out. It opens its Mouth to cry for Help; but if any Sound comes out of him, alas he is drowned by the raging of the Storm. And now a Tomcat has got one of the Fishes and she will surely escape with him. No, she bites off a Fin, she holds her in her Mouth,—will she swallow her? No, the Fishwife's brave Mother-Dog deserts his Puppies and rescues the Fin,—which he eats, himself, as his Reward. O, horror, the Lightning has struck the Fishbasket; he sets him on

[1] *Author's note:* I capitalize the nouns, in the German (and ancient English) fashion.

Fire; see the Flame, how she licks the doomed Utensil with her red and angry Tongue; now she attacks the helpless Fishwife's Foot,—she burns him up, all but the big Toe, and even *she* is partly consumed; and still she spreads, still she waves her fiery Tongues; she attacks the Fishwife's Leg and destroys *it;* she attacks its Hand and destroys *her;* she attacks its poor worn Garment and destroys *her* also; she attacks its Body and consumes *him;* she wreathes herself about its Heart and *it* is consumed; next about its Breast, and in a Moment *she* is a Cinder; now she reaches its Neck,—*he* goes; now its Chin,—*it* goes; now its Nose,—*she* goes. In another Moment, except Help come, the Fishwife will be no more. Time presses,—is there none to succor and save? Yes! Joy, joy, with flying Feet the she-Englishwoman comes! But alas, the generous she-Female is too late: where now is the fated Fishwife? It has ceased from its Sufferings, it has gone to a better Land; all that is left of it for its loved Ones to lament over, is this poor smouldering Ash-heap. Ah, woful, woful Ash-heap! Let us take him up tenderly, reverently, upon the lowly Shovel, and bear him to his long Rest, with the Prayer that when he rises again it will be in a Realm where he will have one good square responsible Sex, and have it all to himself, instead of having a mangy lot of assorted Sexes scattered all over him in Spots.

There, now, the reader can see for himself that this pronoun-business is a very awkward thing for the unaccustomed tongue.

I suppose that in all languages the similarities of look and sound between words which have no similarity in meaning are a fruitful source of perplexity to the foreigner. It is so in our tongue, and it is notably the case in the German. Now there is that troublesome word *vermählt:* to me it has so close a resemblance,—either real or fancied,—to three or four other words, that I never know whether it means despised, painted, suspected, or married; until I look in the dictionary, and then I find it means the latter. There are lots of such words, and they are a great torment. To increase the difficulty there are words which *seem* to resemble each other, and yet do not; but they make just as much trouble as if they did. For instance, there is the word *vermiethen,* (to let, to lease, to hire); and the word *verheirathen,* (another way of saying to *marry*). I heard of an Englishman who knocked at a man's door in Heidelberg and proposed, in the best German he could command, to "verheirathen" that house. Then there are some words which mean one thing when you emphasize the first syllable, but mean something very different if you throw the emphasis on the last syllable. For instance, there is a word which means a run-away, or the act of glancing through a book, according to the placing of the emphasis; and another word which signifies to *associate* with a man, or to *avoid* him, according to where you put the emphasis,—and you can generally depend on putting it in the wrong place and getting into trouble.

There are some exceedingly useful words in this language. *Schlag,* for example; and *Zug.* There are three-quarters of a column of Schlags in the dictionary, and a column and a half of Zugs. The word Schlag means Blow, Stroke, Dash, Hit Shock, Clap, Slap, Time, Bar, Coin, Stamp, Kind, Sort, Manner, Way, Apoplexy, Wood-Cutting, Enclosure, Field, Forest-Clearing. This is its simple and *exact* meaning,—that is to say, its restricted, its fettered meaning; but there are ways by which you can set it free, so that it can soar away, as on the wings of the morning, and never be at rest. You can hang any word you please to its tail, and make it mean anything you want to. You can begin with *Schlag-ader,* which means artery, and you can hang on the whole dictionary, word by word, clear through the alphabet to *Schlag-wasser,* which means bilge-water,—and including *Schlag-mutter,* which means mother-in-law.

Just the same with *Zug.* Strictly speaking, Zug means Pull, Tug, Draught, Procession, March, Progress, Flight, Direction, Expedition, Train, Caravan, Passage, Stroke, Touch, Line, Flourish, Trait of Character, Feature, Lineament,

Chess-move, Organ-stop, Team, Whiff, Bias, Drawer, Propensity, Inhalation, Disposition: but that thing which it does *not* mean,—when all its legitimate pendants have been hung on, has not been discovered yet.

One cannot over-estimate the usefulness of Schlag and Zug. Armed just with these two, and the word *Also,* what cannot the foreigner on German soil accomplish? The German word *Also* is the equivalent of the English phrase "you know," and does not mean anything at all,—in *talk,* though it sometimes does in print. Every time a German opens his mouth an *Also* falls out; and every time he shuts it he bites one in two that was trying to *get* out.

Now, the foreigner, equipped with these three noble words, is master of the situation. Let him talk right along, fearlessly; let him pour his indifferent German forth, and when he lacks for a word, let him heave a *Schlag* into the vacuum; all chances are, that it fits it like a plug; but if it doesn't, let him promptly heave a *Zug* after it; the two together can hardly fail to bung the hole; but if, by a miracle, they *should* fail, let him simply say *Also!* and this will give him a moment's chance to think of the needful word. In Germany, when you load your conversational gun it is always best to throw in a *Schlag* or two and a *Zug* or two; because it doesn't make any difference how much the rest of the charge may scatter, you are bound to bag something with *them.* Then you blandly say *Also,* and load up again. Nothing gives such an air of grace and elegance and unconstraint to a German or an English conversation as to scatter it full of "Also's" or "you-knows."

In my note-book I find this entry:

July 1.—In the hospital, yesterday, a word of thirteen syllables was successfully removed from a patient,—a North-German from near Hamburg; but as most unfortunately the surgeons had opened him in the wrong place, under the impression that he contained a panorama, he died. The sad event has cast a gloom over the whole community.

That paragraph furnishes a text for a few remarks about one of the most curious and notable features of my subject,— the length of German words. Some German words are so long that they have a perspective. Observe these examples:

Freundschaftsbezeigungen.

Dilletantenaufdringlichkeiten.

Stadtverordnetenversammlungen.

These things are not words, they are alphabetical processions. And they are not rare; one can open a German newspaper any time and see them marching majestically across the page,—and if he has any imagination he can see the banners and hear the music, too. They impart a martial thrill to the meekest subject. I take a great interest in these curiosities. Whenever I come across a good one, I stuff it and put it in my museum. In this way I have made quite a valuable collection. When I get duplicates, I exchange with other collectors, and thus increase the variety of my stock. Here are some specimens which I lately bought at an auction sale of the effects of a bankrupt bric-a-brac hunter:

GENERALSTAATSVERORDNETENVERSAMMLUNGEN.

ALTERTHUMSWISSENSCHAFTEN.

KINDERBEWAHRUNGSANSTALTEN.

UNABHAENGIGKEITSERKLAERUNGEN.

WIEDERHERSTELLUNGSBESTREBUNGEN.

WAFFENSTILLSTANDSUNTERHANDLUNGEN.

Of course when one of these grand mountain ranges goes stretching across the printed page, it adorns and ennobles that literary landscape,—but at the same time it is a great distress to the new student, for it blocks up his way; he cannot crawl under it, or climb over it or tunnel through it. So he resorts to the dictionary for help; but there is no help there. The dictionary must draw the line somewhere,—so it leaves this sort of words out. And it is right, because these long things are hardly legitimate words, but are rather combinations of words, and the inventor of them ought to have been killed. They are compound words, with the hyphens left out. The various words used in building them are in the dictionary, but in a very scattered condition; so you can hunt the materials out, one by one, and get at the meaning at last, but it is a tedious and harassing business. I have tried this process upon some of the above examples. "Freundschaftsbezeigungen" seems to be "Friendship demonstrations," which is only a foolish and clumsy way of saying "demonstrations of friendship." "Unabhaengigkeitserklaerungen" seems to be "Independence declarations," which is no improvement upon "Declarations of Independence," as far as I can see. "Generalstaatsverordnetenversammlungen" seems to be "Generalstatesrepresentativesmeetings," as nearly as I can get at it,—a mere rhythmical, gushy euphuism for "meetings of the legislature," I judge. We used to have a good deal of this sort of crime in our literature, but it has gone out, now. We used to speak of a thing as a "never-to-be-forgotten" circumstance, instead of cramping it into the simple and sufficient word "memorable" and then going calmly about our business as if nothing had happened. In those days we were not content to embalm the thing and bury it decently, we wanted to build a monument over it.

But in our newspapers the compounding-disease lingers a little to the present day, but with the hyphens left out, in the German fashion. This is the shape it takes: instead of saying "Mr. Simmons, clerk of the county and district courts, was in town yesterday," the new form puts it thus: "Clerk of the County and District Court Simmons was in town yesterday." This saves neither time nor ink, and has an awkward sound besides. One often sees a remark like this in our papers: "*Mrs.* Assistant District Attorney Johnson returned to her city residence yesterday for the season." That is a case of really unjustifiable compounding; because it not only saves no time or trouble, but confers a title on Mrs. Johnson which she has no right to. But these little instances are trifles indeed, contrasted with the ponderous and dismal German system of piling jumbled compounds together. I wish to submit the following local item, from a Mannheim[1] journal, by way of illustration:

"In the daybeforeyesterdayshortlyafterelevno'clock Night, the inthistownstandingtavern called "The Wagoner" was downburnt. When the fire to the onthedownburninghouse-resting Stork's Nest reached, flew the parent Storks away. But when the bytheraging, firesurrounded Nest *itself* caught Fire, straightway plunged the quickreturning Mother-Stork into the Flames and died, her Wings over her young ones outspread."

Even the cumbersome German construction is not able to take the pathos out of that picture,—indeed it somehow seems to strengthen it. This item is dated away back yonder months ago. I could have used it sooner, but I was waiting to hear from the Father-Stork. I am still waiting.

"*Also!*" If I have not shown that the German is a difficult language, I have at least intended to do it. I have heard of an American student who was asked how he was getting along with his German, and who answered promptly: "I am not getting along at all. I have worked at it hard for three level months, and all I have got to show for it is one solitary German phrase,—'*Zwei glas*,' " (two glasses of beer). He paused a moment, reflectively, then added with feeling, "But I've got that *solid!*"

And if I have not also shown that German is a harassing and infuriating study, my execution has been at fault, and not my intent. I heard lately of a worn and sorely tried American student who used to fly to a certain German word for relief when he could bear up under his aggravations no longer,—the only word in the whole language whose sound was sweet and precious to his ear and healing to his lacerated spirit. This was the word *Damit*. It was only the *sound* that helped him, not the meaning;[2] and so, at last, when he

[1] *Mannheim:* important German city
[2] *Author's note:* It merely means, in its general sense, "*herewith.*"

learned that the emphasis was not on the first syllable, his only stay and support was gone, and he faded away and died.

I think that a description of any loud, stirring, tumultuous episode must be tamer in German than in English. Our descriptive words of this character have such a deep, strong, resonant sound, while their German equivalents do seem so thin and mild and energyless. Boom, burst, crash, roar, storm, bellow, blow, thunder, explosion; howl, cry, shout, yell, groan; battle, hell. These are magnificent words; they have a force and magnitude of sound befitting the things which they describe. But their German equivalents would be ever so nice to sing the children to sleep with, or else my awe-inspiring ears were made for display and not for superior usefulness in analyzing sounds. Would any man want to die in a battle which was called by so tame a term as a *Schlacht?* Or would not a consumptive feel too much bundled up, who was about to go out, in a shirt collar and a seal ring, into a storm which the bird-song word *Gewitter* was employed to describe? And observe the strongest of the several German equivalents for explosion,—*Ausbruch.* Our word Toothbrush is more powerful than that. It seems to me that the Germans could do worse than import it into their language to describe particularly tremendous explosions with. The German word for hell,—Hölle,—sounds more like *helly* than anything else; therefore, how necessarily chipper, frivolous and unimpressive it is. If a man were told in German to go there, could he really rise to the dignity of feeling insulted?

Having now pointed out, in detail, the several vices of this language, I now come to the brief and pleasant task of pointing out its virtues. The capitalizing of the nouns, I have already mentioned. But far before this virtue stands another,— that of spelling a word according to the sound of it. After one short lesson in the alphabet, the student can tell how any German word is pronounced, without having to ask; whereas in our language if a student should inquire of us "What does B, O, W, spell?" we should be obliged to reply, "Nobody can tell what it spells, when you set it off by itself,—you can only tell by referring to the context and finding out what it signifies,—whether it is a thing to shoot arrows with, or a nod of one's head or the forward end of a boat."

There are some German words which are singularly and powerfully effective. For instance, those which describe lowly, peaceful and affectionate home life; those which deal with love, in any and all forms, from mere kindly feeling and honest good will toward the passing stranger, clear up to courtship; those which deal with out-door Nature, in its softest and loveliest aspects,—with meadows, and forests, and birds and flowers, the fragrance and sunshine of summer, and the moonlight of peaceful winter nights; in a word, those which deal with any and all forms of rest, repose, and peace; those also which deal with the creatures and marvels of fairyland; and lastly and chiefly, in those words which express pathos, is the language surpassingly rich and effective. There are German songs which can make a stranger to the language cry. That shows that the *sound* of the words is correct,—it interprets the meanings with truth and with exactness; and so the ear is informed, and through the ear, the heart.

The Germans do not seem to be afraid to repeat a word when it is the right one. They repeat it several times, if they choose. That is wise. But in English when we have used a word a couple of times in a paragraph, we imagine we are growing tautological, and so we are weak enough to exchange it for some other word which only approximates exactness, to escape what we strongly fancy is a greater blemish. Repetition may be bad, but surely inexactness is worse.

There are people in the world who will take a great deal of trouble to point out the faults in a religion or a language, and then go blandly about their business without suggesting any remedy. I am not that kind of a person. I have shown that the German language needs reforming. Very well, I am ready to reform it. At least I am ready to make the proper sugges-

224 THE AWFUL GERMAN LANGUAGE

tions. Such a course as this might be immodest in another; but I have devoted upwards of nine full weeks, first and last, to a careful and critical study of this tongue, and thus have acquired a confidence in my ability to reform it which no mere superficial culture could have conferred upon me.

In the first place, I would leave out the Dative Case. It confuses the plurals; and besides, nobody ever knows when he is in the Dative Case, except he discover it by accident,— and then he does not know when or where it was that he got into it, or how long he has been in it, or how he is ever going to get out of it again. The Dative Case is but an ornamental folly,—it is better to discard it.

In the next place, I would move the Verb further up to the front. You may load up with ever so good a Verb, but I notice that you never really bring down a subject with it at the present German range,—you only cripple it. So I insist that this important part of speech should be brought forward to a position where it may be easily seen with the naked eye.

Thirdly, I would import some strong words from the English tongue,—to swear with, and also to use in describing all sorts of vigorous things in a vigorous way.[1]

Fourthly, I would reorganize the sexes, and distribute them according to the will of the Creator. This as a tribute of respect, if nothing else.

Fifthly, I would do away with those great long compounded words; or require the speaker to deliver them in sections, with intermissions for refreshments. To wholly do away with them would be best, for ideas are more easily received and digested when they come one at a time than when they come in bulk. Intellectual food is like any other; it is pleasanter and more beneficial to take it with a spoon than with a shovel.

[1] *Author's note: "Verdammt,"* and its variations and enlargements, are words which have plenty of meaning, but the *sounds* are so mild and ineffectual that German ladies can use them without sin. German ladies who could not be induced to commit a sin by any persuasion or compulsion, promptly rip out one of these harmless little words when they tear their dresses or don't like the soup. It sounds about as wicked as our "My gracious."

Sixthly, I would require a speaker to stop when he is done, and not hang a string of those useless "Haben sind gewesen gehabt haben geworden seins" to the end of his oration. This sort of gew-gaws undignify a speech, instead of adding a grace. They are therefore an offense, and should be discarded.

Seventhly, I would discard the Parenthesis. Also the re-Parenthesis, the re-re-parenthesis, and the re-re-re-re-re-re-parentheses, and likewise the final wide-reaching all-enclosing King-parenthesis. I would require every individual, be he high or low, to unfold a plain straightforward tale, or else coil it and sit on it and hold his peace. Infractions of this law should be punishable with death.

And eighthly and lastly, I would retain *Zug* and *Schlag*, with their pendants, and discard the rest of the vocabulary. This would simplify the language.

I have now named what I regard as the most necessary and important changes. These are perhaps all I could be expected to name for nothing; but there are other suggestions which I can and will make in case my proposed application shall result in my being formally employed by the government in the work of reforming the language.

My philological studies have satisfied me that a gifted person ought to learn English (barring spelling and pronouncing), in 30 hours, French in 30 days, and German in 30 years. It seems manifest, then, that the latter tongue ought to be trimmed down and repaired. If it is to remain as it is, it ought to be gently and reverently set aside among the dead languages, for only the dead have time to learn it.

Questions and Comments

1. Twain introduces the selection with a quotation he attributes to the Bible. Would you expect to find this quotation in the book of Proverbs? Why or why not?

2. How many forms for *the* are there in German? What are the three genders? What are the four cases?

3. According to Twain, where does the verb occur in a German sentence? What does this show about the German language?

4. What does Twain say is good about capitalizing all nouns? What problem is posed by capitalizing nouns?

5. What examples does Twain use to demonstrate the inconsistencies of German gender?

6. Which three German words does Twain take to task in particular? Why?

7. Why do compound words in German pose a problem?

8. In what two ways does Twain react to the sound of certain German words?

9. What does Twain say are some of the virtues of the German language?

10. What are some of the steps Twain would take to reform the German language?

Word Study

1. Twain cites three German words which have multiple meanings. Look up the English word *run* in an unabridged dictionary. How many meanings are there? What other common words with multiple meanings can you cite?

2. The meaning of *quiescent,* as in "quiescent state," may seem a bit difficult to guess, but think first of a common word which begins with *quie.* This should provide a good clue to the meaning of *quiescent.*

3. *Euphuism* (page 220), *tautological (page 223), and philological* (page 225) all relate to the study of language. Look up their meanings, and in particular note the etymology of *euphuism.*

4. English borrows heavily from the German language; for example, we say "gesundheit" after someone sneezes, we use "benzine" for cleaning, and we send our children to "kindergarten." How many other German words can you list which are part of the English language?

5. Here are some other words which should be looked up if you don't know them: *cipher* (page 207), *succor* (page 216), *ponderous* (page 220), *pathos* (page 221), *tumultuous* (page 222), *consumptive* (page 222), *gew-gaws* (page 225).

Composition

1. Point out those aspects of this selection you feel are particularly humorous and use them to analyze Twain's technique of humor.

2. Write an essay describing what you consider amusing or frustrating aspects of a language you are studying.

3. Write a brief essay describing some aspect of English which a foreigner might consider very amusing or frustrating, for example, the sounds represented by our *ough* spelling.

It is quite possible that the following article from Haya-kawa's *Language in Thought and Action* will open up a new world for you as important as anything you will ever study or discuss in high school. Semantics as defined by the author is "the study of human interaction through the mechanisms of linguistic communication." This definition of the author's specialty should not scare you. He goes on to say, "Today, the public is aware, perhaps to an unprecedented degree, of the role of verbal communication in human affairs. This awareness arises partly, of course, out of the urgency of the tensions everywhere existing between nation and nation, class and class, individual and individual, in a world that is changing with fantastic rapidity. It arises,too, out of the knowledge on the part of even the least reflective elements of the population that enormous powers for good or evil lie in the media of mass communication. Thoughtful people in all walks of life feel, therefore, the need of systematic help in the huge task that confronts all of us today, namely that of interpreting and evaluating the verbally received communications that pour in on us from all sides."

SYMBOLS

Samuel Hayakawa

This basic need, which certainly is obvious only in man, is the need of symbolization. The symbol-making function is one of man's primary activities, like eating, looking, or moving about. It is the fundamental process of the mind, and goes on all the time.

SUSANNE K. LANGER

Man's achievements rest upon the use of symbols.

ALFRED KORZYBSKI

THE SYMBOLIC PROCESS

Aɴɪᴍᴀʟѕ struggle with each other for food or for leadership, but they do not, like human beings, struggle with each other for things that *stand for* food or leadership: such things as our paper symbols of wealth (money, bonds, titles), badges of rank to wear on our clothes, or low-number license plates, supposed by some people to stand for social precedence. For animals, the relationship in which one thing *stands for* something else does not appear to exist except in very rudimentary form.[1]

The process by means of which human beings can arbitrarily make certain things *stand for* other things may be called the *symbolic process*. Whenever two or more human beings can communicate with each other, they can, by agreement, make anything stand for anything. For example, here are two symbols:

$$X \qquad Y$$

We can agree to let X stand for buttons and Y for bows; then we can freely change our agreement and let X stand for the Chicago White Sox and Y for the Cincinnati Reds; or let X stand for Chaucer and Y for Shakespeare, X for the CIO and Y for the AFL. *We are, as human beings, uniquely free to manufacture and manipulate and assign values to our symbols as we please.* Indeed, we can go further by making symbols that stand for symbols. If necessary we can, for instance, let the symbol M stand for all the X's in the above example (buttons, White Sox, Chaucer, CIO) and let N stand for all the Y's (bows, Cincinnati Reds, Shakespeare, AFL). Then we can make another symbol, T, stand for M and N, which would be an instance of a symbol of symbols of symbols. This freedom to create symbols of *any* assigned value and to create *symbols that stand for symbols* is essential to what we call the symbolic process.

Everywhere we turn, we see the symbolic process at work. Feathers worn on the head or stripes on the sleeve can be made to stand for military leadership; cowrie shells or rings of brass or pieces of paper can stand for wealth; crossed sticks can stand for a set of religious beliefs; buttons, elks' teeth, ribbons, special styles of ornamental haircutting or tattooing, can stand for social affiliations. The symbolic process permeates human life at the most primitive as well as at the most civilized levels. Warriors, medicine men, policemen, doormen, telegraph boys, cardinals, and kings wear costumes that symbolize their occupations. Savages collect scalps, college students collect membership keys in honorary societies, to symbolize victories in their respective fields. There are a few things that men do or want to do, possess or want to possess, that have not, in addition to their mechanical or biological value, a symbolic value.

All fashionable clothes, as Thorstein Veblen[1] has pointed out in his *Theory of the Leisure Class* are highly symbolic: materials, cut, and ornament are dictated only to a slight degree by considerations of warmth, comfort, or practicability. The more we dress up in fine clothes, the more we restrict our freedom of action. But by means of delicate embroideries, easily soiled fabrics, starched shirts, high heels, long and pointed fingernails, and other such sacrifices of comfort, the wealthy classes manage to symbolize, among other things, the fact that they don't have to work for a living. The not-so-wealthy, on the other hand, by imitating these symbols of wealth, symbolize their conviction that, even if they do work for a living, they are just as good as anybody else. Again, we select our furniture to serve as visible symbols of our taste, wealth, and social position; we trade in perfectly good cars for later models, not always to get better transportation, but to give evidence to the community that we can afford such luxuries. We often choose our residences on the basis of a feeling that it "looks well" to have a "good address." We like

---

[1] *Thorstein Veblen:* American social scientist (1857–1929) who wrote many books that keenly criticized established social and economic institutions

to put expensive food on our tables, not always because it tastes better than cheap food, but because it tells our guests that we wish to do them honor.

Such complicated and apparently unnecessary behavior leads philosophers, both amateur and professional, to ask over and over again, "Why can't human beings live simply and naturally?" Often the complexity of human life makes us look enviously at the relative simplicity of lives such as dogs and cats lead. But the symbolic process, which makes possible the absurdities of human conduct, also makes possible language and therefore all the human achievements dependent upon language. The fact that more things can go wrong with motorcars than with wheelbarrows is no reason for going back to wheelbarrows. Similarly, the fact that the symbolic process makes complicated follies possible is no reason for wanting to return to a cat-and-dog existence. A better solution is to understand the symbolic process so that instead of being its slaves we become, to some degree at least, its masters.

LANGUAGE AS SYMBOLISM

Of all forms of symbolism, language is the most highly developed, most subtle, and most complicated. It has been pointed out that human beings, by agreement, can make anything stand for anything. Now, human beings have agreed, in the course of centuries of mutual dependency, to let the various noises that they can produce with their lungs, throats, tongues, teeth, and lips systematically stand for specified happenings in their nervous systems. We call that system of agreements *language*. For example, we who speak English have been so trained that, when our nervous systems register the presence of a certain kind of animal, we may make the following noise: "There's a cat." Anyone hearing us expects to find that, by looking in the same direction, he will experience a similar event in his nervous system—one that will lead him to make an almost identical noise. Again, we have been so trained that when we are conscious of wanting food, we make the noise, "I'm hungry."

There is, as has been said, *no necessary connection between the symbol and that which is symbolized.* Just as men can wear yachting costumes without ever having been near a yacht, so they can make the noise, "I'm hungry," without being hungry. Furthermore, just as social rank can be symbolized by feathers in the hair, by tattooing on the breast, by gold ornaments on the watch chain, or by a thousand different devices according to the culture we live in, so the fact of being hungry can be symbolized by a thousand different noises according to the culture we live in: "J'ai faim," or "Es hungert mich," or "Ho appetito," or "Hara ga hetta," and so on.

However obvious these facts may appear at first glance, they are actually not so obvious as they seem except when we take special pains to think about the subject. Symbols and things symbolized are independent of each other; nevertheless, we all have a way of feeling as if, and sometimes acting as if, there were necessary connections. For example, there is the vague sense we all have that foreign languages are inherently absurd: foreigners have such funny names for things, and why can't they call things by their right names? This feeling exhibits itself most strongly in those English and American tourists who seem to believe that they can make the natives of any country understand English if they shout loud enough. Like the little boy who was reported to have said, "Pigs are called pigs because they are such dirty animals," they feel that the symbol is inherently connected in some way with the things symbolized. Then there are the people who feel that since snakes are "nasty, slimy creatures" (incidentally, snakes are *not* slimy), the word "snake" is a *nasty, slimy word.*

THE PITFALLS OF DRAMA

Naïveté regarding the symbolic process extends to symbols

other than words, of course. In the case of drama (stage, movies, radio), there appear to be people in almost every audience who never quite fully realize that a play is a set of fictional, symbolic representations. An actor is one who *symbolizes* other people, real or imagined: Frederic March may, in a given play, enact the role of (symbolize) a drunkard. The fact that Mr. March can do so with extraordinary realism proves nothing about his drinking habits, if any. Nevertheless, there are movie-goers who, instead of admiring Mr. March's skill in acting, begin to feel sorry for Mrs. March who is, alas, married to such a heavy drinker! Lewis Stone, who often plays the part of a judge, often gets letters from fans asking for legal advice. James Cagney, who plays "tough guy" roles, is often challenged to fight by men who say to him, "Think you're tough, do you? Lemme show you!" It was said some years ago that when Edward G. Robinson, who plays gangster roles with extraordinary vividness, visited Chicago, local hoodlums telephoned him at his hotel to pay their professional respects. One is reminded of the story of the actor, playing the part of a villain in a traveling theatrical troupe, who, at a particularly tense moment in the play, was shot by an overexcited cowpuncher in the audience. The cowpuncher of this story, however, is no more ridiculous than those thousands of people today, many of them adults, who write fan letters to a ventriloquist's dummy, or those goodhearted but impressionable people who send presents to the broadcasting station when two characters in a radio serial get married, or those astonishing patriots who rushed to recruiting offices to help defend the nation when, on October 30, 1938, the United States was "invaded" by an "army from Mars" in a radio dramatization.[1]

An extreme case of this kind is that of a woman who had a baby on the same day a fictitious baby was born to the heroine in her favorite soap-opera. She named her baby "Margaret" because the soap-opera "baby" was given that name.

[1]*radio dramatization:* this was Orson Welles's "War of the Worlds" broadcast

Some time later, the soap-opera "baby" "died." Thereupon the woman went into a state of inconsolable grief, being convinced that *her own baby* was dead. When her friends tried to convince her that *that* was her own baby, alive and howling right there beside her, she would not be consoled. "You can't fool me," she said. "Margaret is dead. I heard it on the radio." The woman was, of course, placed in a mental hospital—this was probably only one of many such misevaluations she was in the habit of making. Whatever else was wrong with her, one way of describing this particular misevaluation is to say that the words (in this case of the soap-opera) not only possessed for her the characteristics of reality, but *became a substitute reality completely shutting out the facts.*

THE WORD IS NOT THE THING

The above, however, are only the more striking examples of confused attitudes toward words and symbols. There would be little point in mentioning them if we were *uniformly and permanently aware* of the independence of symbols from things symbolized, as all human beings, in the writer's opinion, *can be* and *should be*.[1] But we are not. Most of us have, in some area or other of our thinking, improper habits of evaluation. For this, society itself is often to blame: most societies systematically encourage, concerning certain topics, the habitual confusion of symbols with things symbolized. For example, if a Japanese schoolhouse caught on fire, it used to be obligatory in the days of emperor-worship to try to rescue the emperor's *picture* (there was one in every schoolhouse), even at the risk of one's life. (If you got burned to death, you were posthumously ennobled.) In our society, we are encouraged to go into debt in order that we may dis-

[1] *Author's note:* Much of the make-believe activity of small children, even as young as two years, appears to arise from the spontaneous and joyous discovery of the symbolic process, involving clear distinctions between symbols and things symbolized and a pleasure in the independence and manipulability of symbols. A great deal of the natural wisdom of children is, however, snuffed out in the course of their education.

play, as symbols of prosperity, shiny new automobiles. Strangely enough, the possession of shiny automobiles even under these conditions makes their "owners" *feel* prosperous. In all civilized societies (and probably in many primitive ones as well), the symbols of piety, of civic virtue, or of patriotism are often prized above actual piety, civic virtue, or patriotism. In one way or another, we are all like the brilliant student who cheats in his exams in order to make Phi Beta Kappa:[1] it is so much more important to have the symbol than the things it stands for.

The habitual confusion of symbols with things symbolized, whether on the part of individuals or societies, is serious enough at all levels of culture to provide a perennial human problem. But with the rise of modern communications systems, there arises with peculiar urgency the problem of confusion of verbal symbols with realities. We are constantly being talked at, by teachers, preachers, salesmen, public relations counsels, governmental agencies, and moving-picture sound tracks. The cries of the hawkers of soft drinks, soap chips, and laxatives pursue us into our homes, thanks to the radio—and in some houses the radio is never turned off from morning to night. The mailman brings direct mail advertising. Billboards confront us on the highway, and we even take portable radios with us to the seashore.

We live in an environment shaped and largely created by hitherto unparalleled semantic influences: mass circulation newspapers and magazines which are given to reflecting, in a shocking number of cases, the weird prejudices and obsessions of their publishers and owners; radio programs, both local and network, almost completely dominated by commercial motives; public relations counsels, who are simply highly paid craftsmen in the art of manipulating and reshaping our semantic environment in ways favorable to their clients. It is an exciting environment, but fraught with danger: it is only

[1] *Phi Beta Kappa:* a national honor society for high scholastic distinction, founded in 1776

a slight exaggeration to say that Hitler conquered Austria by radio.

Citizens of a modern society need, therefore, more than ordinary "common sense"—which was recently defined by Stuart Chase[1] as that which tells you that the world is flat. They need to be scientifically aware of the powers and limitations of symbols, especially words, if they are to guard against being driven into complete bewilderment by the complexity of their semantic environment. The first of the principles governing symbols is this: The symbol is NOT the thing symbolized; the word is NOT the thing; the map is NOT the territory it stands for.

MAPS AND TERRITORIES

There is a sense in which we all live in two worlds. First, we live in the world of happenings about us which we know at first hand. But this is an extremely small world, consisting only of that continuum of the things that we have actually seen, felt, or heard—the flow of events constantly passing before our senses. So far as this world of personal experience is concerned, Africa, South America, Asia, Washington, New York, or Los Angeles do not exist if we have never been to these places. Chiang Kai-shek[2] is only a name if we have never seen him. When we ask ourselves how much we know at first hand, we discover that we know very little indeed.

Most of our knowledge, acquired from parents, friends, schools, newspapers, books, conversation, speeches, and radio, is received *verbally*. All our knowledge of history, for example, comes to us only in words. The only proof we have that the Battle of Waterloo[3] ever took place is that we have had

[1] *Stuart Chase:* American writer who specialized in economics but who wrote *The Tyranny of Words*, a book about semantics, in 1938

[2] *Chiang Kai-shek:* President of Taiwan (1948–1975), now deceased

[3] *Battle of Waterloo:* battle in which Napoleon was decisively defeated by the British and their allies, June 18, 1815

reports to that effect. These reports are not given us by people who saw it happen, but are based on other reports: reports of reports of reports, which go back ultimately to the first-hand reports given by people who did see it happening. It is through reports, then, and through reports of reports, that we receive most knowledge: about government, about what is happening in China, about what picture is showing at the downtown theater—in fact, about anything which we do not know through direct experience.

Let us call this world that comes to us through words the *verbal world,* as opposed to the world we know or are capable of knowing through our own experience, which we shall call the *extensional world.* (The reason for the choice of the word "extensional" will become clear later.) The human being, like any other creature, begins to make his acquaintance with the extensional world from infancy. Unlike other creatures, however, he begins to receive, as soon as he can learn to understand, reports, reports of reports, reports of reports of reports. In addition he receives inferences made from reports, inferences made from other inferences, and so on. By the time a child is a few years old, has gone to school and to Sunday school, and has made a few friends, he has accumulated a considerable amount of second- and third-hand information about morals, geography, history, nature, people, games—all of which information together constitutes his verbal world.

Now this verbal world ought to stand in relation to the extensional world as a *map* does to the *territory* it is supposed to represent. If a child grows to adulthood with a verbal world in his head which corresponds fairly closely to the extensional world that he finds around him in his widening experience, he is in relatively small danger of being shocked or hurt by what he finds, because his verbal world has told him what, more or less, to expect. He is prepared for life. If, however, he grows up with a false map in his head—that is, with a head crammed with false knowledge and superstition—he will constantly be running into trouble, wasting his efforts, and acting like a fool. He will not be adjusted to the world as it is; he may, if the lack of adjustment is serious, end up in a mental hospital.

Some of the follies we commit because of false maps in our heads are so commonplace that we do not even think of them as remarkable. There are those who protect themselves from accidents by carrying a rabbit's foot in the pocket. Some refuse to sleep on the thirteenth floor of hotels—this is so common that most big hotels, even in the capitals of our scientific culture, skip "13" in numbering their floors. Some plan their lives on the basis of astrological predictions. Some play fifty-to-one shots on the basis of dream books. Some hope to make their teeth whiter by changing their brand of tooth paste. All such people are living in verbal worlds that bear little, if any, resemblance to the extensional world.

Now, no matter how beautiful a map may be, it is useless to a traveler unless it accurately shows the relationship of places to each other, the structure of the territory. If we draw, for example, a big dent in the outline of a lake for, let us say, artistic reasons, the map is worthless. But if we are just drawing maps for fun without paying any attention to the structure of the region, there is nothing in the world to prevent us from putting in all the extra curlicues and twists we want in the lakes, rivers, and roads. No harm will be done *unless someone tries to plan a trip by such a map.*

Similarly, by means of imaginary or false reports, or by false inferences from good reports, or by mere rhetorical exercises, we can manufacture at will, with language, "maps" which have no reference to the extensional world. Here again no harm will be done unless someone makes the mistake of regarding such "maps" as representing real territories.

We all inherit a great deal of useless knowledge, and a great deal of misinformation and error (maps that were formerly thought to be accurate), so that there is always a portion of what we have been told that must be discarded. But the cultural heritage of our civilization that is transmitted to us—our socially pooled knowledge, both scientific and humane—has been valued principally because we have believed that it gives us accurate maps of experience. The analogy of verbal worlds to maps is an important one and will be referred to frequently throughout this book. It should be noticed at this point, however, that there are two ways of getting false maps of the world into our heads: first, by having them given to us; second, by making them up for ourselves by misreading the true maps given to us.

Questions and Comments

1. Why is a word a symbol? Why isn't the sound produced by pronouncing "urg" a symbol? What can you do which might make "urg" a symbol?

2. What is a symbol of a symbol?

3. What are some evidences of the symbolic process at work in everyday life?

4. What does the author mean when he suggests that instead of being slaves to the symbolic process we become to some degree its masters?

5. What are the "pitfalls of drama"? Why do they occur?

6. What danger does the author see in the rise of modern communications systems? What does he say citizens of a modern society need more than ever to combat this danger?

7. What does Stuart Chase mean when he says "Common sense . . . tells you that the world is flat"?

8. What does the author mean by the *verbal world* and the *extensional world*? Why is the verbal world like a map? What advice does the author give you about using such maps?

Word Study

1. Show how the Latin derivation helps to reveal the meaning of the following words:

   precedence from *praecedere* meaning "to go"

   rudimentary from *rudis* meaning "rude," "unwrought"

   permeates from *permeare* meaning "to go," "to pass"

   obligatory from *obligere* meaning "to bind"

   posthumously from *posthumus* meaning "late born," "last born"

   arbitrarily from *arbiter* meaning "to make a decision"

   perennial from *per annus* meaning "year"

2. *Fraught* is thought to come from Middle Dutch *vracht,* meaning "freight." What does it mean in "an exciting environment, but fraught with danger"?

Composition

1. In a brief essay discuss what any one of the following symbolizes to you: the American flag, a ten-dollar bill, a crown, a cross, a fraternity pin.

2. The author says, "The habitual confusion of symbols with things symbolized, whether on the part of individuals or societies, is serious enough at all levels of culture to provide a perennial human problem." Discuss what this statement means and how it affects you in your own life.

3. In a brief composition discuss some of your own "private" symbols which have meanings special only to yourself.

Herbert Matthews served as war correspondent for the *New York Times* during the Spanish Revolution in the 1930's. He wrote in his book *The Education of a Correspondent,* from which the following account is taken, "The life that civilization imposes on us is only a veneer. A man must go to meet his fate, wherever it may be, whenever it may come. The urge to go out and fight, to pit one's strength and wits against the forces of nature, to seek adventure, risk life and take joy in comradeship and danger—these are deep feelings, so deep that even I who love life and family and luxury and books have yielded to them. But I still say that it all means nothing if one cannot at the end turn back to where the heart is, and in that warm place seek to put into thought and language the lessons that have been so hardly learned."

In the Spanish Civil War the Loyalists, or government forces, were opposed by the Nationalists, or Rebels. General Francisco Franco headed the Nationalist forces. In November of 1936 volunteer brigades composed of men from many countries joined the Loyalists and helped save Madrid. However, with the help of thousands of Italian and German troops, the Nationalists triumphed and Franco became El Caudillo, the dictator, until he died in 1975.

TRAGEDY AT BARCELONA

Herbert Matthews

I HAD seen some fearful bombings in Madrid, but there was no blitz in the form in which we now know it. The capital had its own special form of calamity in the incessant shellings by the ring of German artillery around the city. I lived through and wrote about so many of them that the feelings they aroused became dulled, and it used to take all my ingenuity to find something new to say about them. The terror, destruction, and death were never less for Madrid, but for newspaper readers it was merely another shelling, and one got used to reading about such things. The callousness to suffering which World War II has made a commonplace, began in Spain. A newspaperman cannot sustain indignation or horror in others, and that was why the Rebels were able to ignore public opinion in their bombings and shellings. The first few times it was embarrassing to them that the civilized world was shocked and horrified by what they did, but Fascism knows that the way to deal with public opinion is to tell it lies and then to forget about it.

The penthouse which I and Sefton Delmer[1] had on the edge of the Retiro Park in Madrid provided a spectacular observation post for the night shellings which were so frequent in the autumn of 1937. There never was rhyme or reason for them, no system, no particular objective; it was totalitarian warfare along Italo-German lines. The idea was to strike terror into and break down morale in the rear guard. The terror was there, but to the eternal glory of Madrid it must be stated that the morale never wavered.

When I was not on my terrace watching the flashes of the guns along the whole horizon beyond the Manzanares[2] and hearing the screech of the incoming shells and feeling that sick sensation in the pit of the stomach, which means that you are afraid, I was in Hemingway's[3] room at the Florida Hotel. A little crowd of us used to gather there nearly every evening—Evan Shipman and Martin Hourihan (American Internationals then recovering from wounds), Martha Gellhorn,[4] Almuth Heilbrun (widow of a doctor in the International Brigade killed outside Huesca), and any American friends who happened to be in Madrid on leave. Hem-

[1]*Sefton Delmer:* friend of Matthews; foreign correspondent for *London Daily Express*

[2]*Manzanares:* river flowing near Madrid

[3]*Hemingway:* Ernest Hemingway, famous American novelist (1899–1961)

[4]*Martha Gellhorn:* foreign correspondent for *Collier's Weekly,* an American magazine no longer in print

ingway was certain that he had a "dead angle" and that we were safe in that room. It was a good thing to believe, anyway, so we would open the windows and turn on the Chopin "mazurka" record, just as they did in *The Fifth Column*.[1] Indeed, that was the time when the play was being written, and the ideas came in on those 3-, 6- and 9-inch shells which frequently shook the Florida to its foundations, but somehow never reached our room.

By March, 1938, we thought we knew all about bombing and shelling, but we were innocents. It took eighteen raids in forty-four hours on Barcelona to show us and the world what a weapon the airplane could be. Until the next war it remained the one classic example of what modern bombing could do to a city and the human beings in it. No people in mass had ever been called upon to suffer the physical and spiritual torture which the inhabitants of Barcelona endured in that maddening stretch of time during which bombers of a foreign nation which had no quarrel with Spain inflicted punishment on a defenseless city.

It began at 10:15 on Wednesday evening, March 16, 1938, under a full moon that seemed to hang in the center of the sky. That meant the raiders had excellent visibility, while the city's searchlights were paled under the glow. In any event, the antiaircraft defense was so pitifully inadequate that nothing could be done to stop the attacks. Prime Minister Neville Chamberlain[2] (and therefore all the others) had refused the Government's plea to be allowed at least to buy antiaircraft guns which they would guarantee to use only in the rear guard.

We could see even that night—or rather hear—wave on wave of planes coming over, for the same ones could not possibly have gone back to Majorca[3] and returned so quickly.

[1] *The Fifth Column:* play written by Ernest Hemingway. Four columns of Rebels were advancing on Madrid; Rebel sympathizers within the city comprised the "fifth column."

[2] *Neville Chamberlain:* Prime Minister of England at the time of this article

[3] *Majorca:* Spanish island in western Mediterranean Sea 145 miles east of Spanish coast

Only later, in Italy, did I learn that they came from Italy itself and from Sardinia,[1] as well as from Palma.[2] Understand that, to a considerable extent, this was an experiment. The air force had to teach its pilots how to make long raids, and besides, there was a new type of bomb to be tried out.

Between 10:15 and two in the morning there were eight raids, but it was not until the morning of the 17th that the full horror of what was happening penetrated the city. At night only those in immediate contact with the bombs and their destruction could know their message, but in the daytime you saw it with your own eyes, and it seared the eyeballs so that however much you tried to forget or however long you lived, the picture could not be erased. During the night we sat in the darkened offices of the press censorship, hearing the throb of the engines, the roar of the bombs, the crashing of houses and the tinkling of glass, trusting that the next bomb would not land on us and that the lights would go up and the telephone be restored long enough to permit us to get our stories over. We knew the bombs were being scattered all over the city; that the planes were flying too high to choose objectives; that an appalling amount of death and destruction was taking place. But you have to see things to feel them with full force.

The next day, St. Patrick's Day, I and a million others saw things which Dante[3] could not have imagined. Bombs can do more horrible things to the human body and spirit than the most fiendish tortures can devise. I did not get up for the first raid at 7:40, but when the next came at 10:25 I drove immediately to the center of the destruction, and what I saw made me realize that newspapermen had a mission that day: to tell the world what bombing means. My pen was dipped in blood for that dispatch.

---

[1] *Sardinia:* Italian island in Mediterranean Sea west of southern Italy

[2] *Palma:* chief city and port of Majorca

[3] *Dante:* famous poet of Renaissance Italy who composed the great classic *Divine Comedy,* in which one section, "The Inferno," describes Hell

I had been seeing the effects of bombs for more than a year, but it was immediately obvious to me that this was something different—not the ordinary high explosive, not the delayed fuse, but something intended to fall in the streets and break out flat, killing a maximum number of people. One bomb dropped in a square at the foot of the Paralelo, a busy cross-section in the lower part of the city not far from the port. The trees around had been snapped off a few inches from the ground; one would have thought they had been sawn off, but for the roughness of the break. It does no good to throw yourself down, when that type of bomb falls near you. I could tell where each person out of thirty or forty killed there had been standing, because of the isolated pools of blood. A street car had been wrecked, and everyone in it killed or wounded. A truck was still burning, and something black and shriveled that had been human had just been taken out and placed in a basket.

And then there was the noise—ambulances dashing up with men on the footboards blowing whistles, women screaming and struggling hysterically, men shouting. Up the block a house was burning fiercely. And all around, all over the city, everywhere I went were wrecked houses, dead, wounded and those intangibles of fear, horror, fury, mental and physical torture. The attacks were in one sense haphazard, for the bombs were dropped at random, without specific objectives. However, there was an obvious plan to be certain that every part of the city, from the richest quarter to the poorest, received its full measure of tragedy. It was not necessary to send many planes each time. The fearful damage done in the 1:55 P.M. raid on March 17 required only five Savoia-Marchetti bombers. That raid alone bore within itself more terror and ferocity than any previous raid in aviation's history.

The planes came along the axis of the Calle Cortes, a wide, fashionable avenue that cuts across the center of Barcelona. At a given moment one plane dropped two or three bombs (the Spanish experts could not determine how many) of the new type and of a size that could not have been less than 500 kilos each. At the same time, a number of 50-, 100- and 200-kilo bombs (the kilogram is 2.2 pounds) were released by the planes. The effect was like that of a combined earthquake and tornado. The best guess that could be made afterwards was that they were liquid-air bombs, for the destruction was caused by concussion and not by fragmentation of the bomb-casings. No pieces of casing were recovered, indicating that the shells were thin. The buildings on one side of the street were literally blown away, so that one could see through into the next street. One of the houses on the other side, which stood on a corner, was considered the strongest building in Barcelona, of huge blocks of stone around a steel framework six stories high. The part facing the spot where the bomb had fallen was torn apart, and blocks that could not have weighed less than a few tons each were scattered over a radius of two hundred yards.

The Paseo de Gracias cuts across the Calle Cortes at right angles, three blocks down. People standing at that intersection were bowled over like ninepins; some died through collapse of their lungs. Limbs of trees, six or eight inches thick, were torn off their trunks; nearly every window, from the Plaza Cataluña to the Calle Majorca, crashed. A little nearer to the scene, lampposts were blown down, trees torn up by the roots and set afire. A loaded bus which had been close to the main explosion was a grotesquely twisted mass of iron; the passengers had disappeared. Everywhere around were those viscous masses of blood which showed where human beings had been. A haze of smoke and dust hung over the scene for hours, as did an acrid smell of powder or some other chemical.

It was sheer madness. I happened to be eating lunch with Delmer's wife in the Hostal del Sol, which was about five blocks up toward the Diagonal, but fortunately not in a direct line. The windows bent in toward us, and the whole building shook exactly as if there were an earthquake. We were unharmed and others had been killed, but there never is any reason in a bombing—particularly totalitarian bombing of that sort—why you should not be the one killed. You feel that always, and it is nerve-racking. Any unusual noise makes your heart jump—horns of cars that sound like sirens, the banging of doors, the roar of automobile motors. I even saw a cat jump as if from an electric shock when a shopkeeper suddenly lowered his blinds. Bombs make a rushing, whistling, screaming sound when they come down, and that was what we kept hearing, sometimes actually, sometimes in imagination.

You see so many freakish things and they add so much to the horror! It is all horror, and one gets dazed from it—blood over pavements, bodies, all black and red, that seem the creation of a diseased mind; men, women, and children buried alive or screaming, in the wreckage of their houses, like trapped animals. I never saw so many weeping women. There was a house where nothing remained on the fifth floor except some clothes hanging on a rack. In another place the corner of a kitchen had somehow escaped, and we could see that the housewife had not had time to wash the dishes before she died. I saw a guard pick up somebody's finger; I saw a pool of blood topped with a man's beret; I saw an automobile whose occupants must literally have disappeared into the air. It was all a nightmare—the dead piled in trucks, gangs of salvage men digging in the ruins, stretchers stained red, street-cleaners sweeping up human fragments, a cock crowing lustily from atop a wrecked building, smoke, dust, powder—and blood everywhere, thick, sticky pools of blood, splotches and drops of it; wherever one looked there was something stained with blood.

I watched them take two wounded persons out of a building wrecked in the first bombing on the 17th. Both had been completely buried. The woman was screaming so weakly that we thought it was a child until they extricated her limp body. She seemed dead then, but they rushed her away to the hospital. The other was a fifteen-year-old boy. By some miracle he had not been crushed, although one could see that from his hair down to his bare feet he had been completely buried. His body did not seem to have been hurt, but something else was, for he could not control his movements or the twitching of his face or his shuddering.

The hospitals were quickly overcrowded. They were already burdened with wounded from the Aragon[1] front. Every autobus had been commandeered for ambulance purposes. Men stood on the running boards blowing whistles, to clear the way, and it was that never-ceasing shrill and piercing sound which seemed more characteristic of the day than anything else. In the afternoon I counted 328 dead lying side by side in the morgue of the clinical hospital, but there were other morgues. It was not possible to count the bodies buried in the wreckage. There could not have been less than 1,300 killed and 2,000 wounded in the eighteen raids. The Government never dared to give out even approximately truthful figures of bombing casualties, lest they should demoralize the populace.

But one does not assess such torture by deaths and wounds alone. Totalitarian bombing is meant to strike terror, to break the morale of the home front, to weaken resistance, because human beings are not built to withstand such horror. It is true that such bombings str ke error, terror that freezes the blood and drives one either hysterical or to the verge of hysteria. But then, too, one would not be human if it all did not cause rage—deep, burning rage. Those Spaniards had to yield to it in the end, because machines are stronger than bodies, but what they felt then must be still corroding within them like poison. Even I, re- reating in my mind those long hours of horror, cannot help feeling again the bitterness and

---

[1] *Aragon:* region of northeastern Spain

hatred against everything those Fascist bombers stood for, although more than seven years have passed. That was the sort of thing that taught me my politics.

Of course, such bombing is effective. Who can look at the results and not think, "That is what may happen to me next time"? If you had said to those weeping women on March 17 and 18, "Do you want your men to give up and stop this war?" who can doubt what they would have answered? The strain grew with each succeeding raid. Foreigners were deserting their hotels for the frontier as fast as they could. The Ritz Hotel was hit during the first raid on the 17th, to the satisfaction of those of us in the Majestic who knew the Ritz to be the home of war profiteers and friends of Franco. Certainly, bombing it helped the exodus. The American Consular and Embassy staffs stuck to their posts as they were to do until the end, but they had to move from the Plaza Cataluña to Tibidabo, on the hill. Even that district was bombed, for no part of the city was spared, but it was comparatively safe. We all had a sense of impending disaster. Before we made our rounds the second morning, Delmer, who had a true British contempt for sentiment or weakness, gave Isobel, his wife, some money, "in case something silly happens." The chambermaid said to me hysterically as I went out, "We are all going to be killed, all!" The clerk at the drugstore sighed as he handed over the headache medicine I badly needed. "Oh, for a plane to fly to France!" he said. "I don't want to die."

But life had to go on. After each raid the blood was washed off the streets, the car tracks were repaired, the wreckage was cleared away. Then the people—those who had not fled—waited for the next raid. In the lower quarters of the city they prepared to spend the night in the subways. So many went down that the men had to get out, leaving for the women and children what space there was. Others huddled in their cellars, knowing themselves safe from any but a direct hit.

We did not sleep that night of the 17th. The moon was still strong; the weather clear and windless—and we had three raids. Then three more raids the next day—and at three in the afternoon it ended. No one could ever explain why it ended. The raids were extraordinarily effective; Barcelona was not only terrorized but paralyzed. A continuation might have brought a general hysteria and a mass flight from the city. The Government spared a few precious combat planes from the front, but not enough for any real opposition, and the antiaircraft fire was pathetically inadequate. The Italians could have continued with impunity. At the time we made two guesses: first, that whatever, it did to Barcelona, it was arousing the Catalans[1] as they had not been stirred since Napoleon's time; and secondly, we flattered ourselves that the stories we sent had shocked world opinion to such an extent that the Rebel command decided it was not worth while to continue the bombing. After hearing what the Italians had to say after the war, I believe another reason has to be added, at least as a possibility: Franco refused to countenance the destruction of Barcelona, which he expected to capture in a short while.

Questions and Comments

1. According to the author, what purpose did the Italians have in their bombing of Spanish cities? What attitude of the Fascists toward human life does such a purpose expose?

2. What does Matthews mean when he says that to a considerable extent the terrible raids on Barcelona were an experiment?

[1] *Catalans:* the inhabitants of Catalonia, an eastern region of Spain

3. After witnessing the devastation of the bombings Matthews says he realized that journalists had a mission. What was the mission?

4. In what way did the bombings affect forever the author's political outlook?

5. What indication did Matthews give toward the end of the selection that the morale of the people was crumbling?

6. Blood and gore are frequently inserted in story and drama solely for the purpose of providing sensation. What is the purpose of the blood and gore passages in this selection?

7 Sometimes minute detail, clearly and unemotionally described, makes a piece of writing carry impact. What are some of the details in this piece which strike you as outstanding and unforgettable?

Word Study

1. The meanings of the italicized words in the following sentences should be easy to guess from their context.

   "The *callousness* to suffering which World War II has made a commonplace, began in Spain." (page 242)

   ". . . everywhere I went were wrecked houses, dead, wounded and those *intangibles* of fear, horror, fury, mental and physical torture." (page 245)

   ". . . but what they felt then must be still *corroding* within them like poison." (page 248)

2. The word *viscous* comes from the Latin *viscum,* meaning "mistletoe." The sticky gum from the mistletoe was spread on tree limbs and leaves to snare small birds. What does *viscous* as in "viscous masses of blood" mean?

3. The book in the Bible which describes Moses leading the Israelites to the Promised Land is Exodus. What does the word mean in "bombing it [the Ritz Hotel] helped the exodus"? What does *ex* mean? List at least ten more words which begin with *ex*.

Composition

1. Herbert Matthews claims, "You have to see things to feel them with full force." In a brief composition discuss to what degree he has succeeded in making you see and feel the horror of the bombings of Barcelona.

2. "Fascism" and "totalitarianism" are two terms that are important to this selection. Write a composition in which you point out the main features of these two philosophies and show how they contrast with the main features of democracy.

3. At some point in your life you may have witnessed or read about some terrible disaster, such as fire, flood, tornado, earthquake, or auto wreck. Write a brief account of the disaster, setting down as vividly as you can some of the unforgettable details of what you witnessed.

Pulitzer prizewinner Bruce Catton has written several famous books about the Civil War. *This Hallowed Ground* (1955) tells of the war from a Union point of view. The section which follows provides a marvelous contrast between Grant and Lee, then goes further to show how these two men represent "two separate visions of America." However, Mr. Catton never permits the reader to forget that both these men were first very exceptional human beings, demonstrating great compassion and intelligence as they quickly negotiated one of the most famous surrenders of all time.

from TWILIGHT IN VICTORY

Bruce Catton

UNTIL this Palm Sunday of 1865 the word Appomattox had no meaning. It was a harsh name left over from Indian days, it belonged to a river and to a country town, and it had no overtones. But after this day it would be one of the haunted possessions of the American people, a great and unique word that would echo in the national memory with infinite tragedy and infinite promise, recalling a moment in which sunset and sunrise came together in a streaked glow that was half twilight and half dawn.

The business might almost have been stage-managed for effect. No detail had been overlooked. There was even the case of Wilmer McLean, the Virginian who once owned a place by a stream named Bull Run and who found his farm overrun by soldiers in the first battle of the war. He sold out and moved to southern Virginia to get away from the war, and he bought a modest house in Appomattox Court House;

and the war caught up with him finally, so that Lee and Grant chose his front parlor—of all the rooms in America—as the place where they would sit down together and bring the fighting to an end.

Lee had one staff officer with him, and in Mr. McLean's front yard a Confederate orderly stood by while the war horse Traveler nibbled at the spring grass. Grant came with half a dozen officers of his own, including the famous Sheridan,[1] and after he and Lee had shaken hands and taken their seats these trooped into the room to look and to listen. Grant and Lee sat at two separate tables, the central figures in one of the greatest tableaus of American history.

It was a great tableau not merely because of what these two men did but also because of what they were. No two Americans could have been in greater contrast. (Again, the staging was perfect.) Lee was legend incarnate—tall, gray, one of the handsomest and most imposing men who ever lived, dressed today in his best uniform, with a sword belted at his waist. Grant was—well, he was U. S. Grant, rather scrubby and undersized, wearing his working clothes, with mud-spattered boots and trousers and a private's rumpled blue coat with his lieutenant general's stars tacked to the shoulders. He wore no sword. The men who were with them noticed the contrast and remembered it. Grant himself seems to have felt it; years afterward, when he wrote his memoirs, he mentioned it and went to some lengths to explain why he did not go to this meeting togged out in dress uniform. (In effect, his explanation was that he was just too busy.)

Yet the contrast went far beyond the matter of personal appearance. Two separate versions of America met in this room, each perfectly embodied by its chosen representative.

There was an American aristocracy, and it had had a great day. It came from the past and it looked to the past; it seemed almost deliberately archaic, with an air of knee

[1] *Sheridan:* Philip Henry Sheridan was the Union general in command of the Army of the Shenandoah.

breeches and buckled shoes and powdered wigs, with a leisured dignity and a rigid code in which privilege and duty
were closely joined. It had brought the country to its birth
and it had provided many of its beliefs; it had given courage
and leadership, a sense of order and learning, and if there
had been any way by which the eighteenth century could
possibly have been carried forward into the future, this class
would have provided the perfect vehicle. But from the day of
its beginning America had been fated to be a land of unending change. The country in which this leisured class had its
place was in powerful ferment, and the class itself had
changed. It had been diluted. In the struggle for survival it
had laid hands on the curious combination of modern machinery and slave labor, the old standards had been altered,
dignity had begun to look like arrogance, and pride of purse
had begun to elbow out pride of breeding. The single lifetime of Robert E. Lee had seen the change, although Lee
himself had not been touched by it.

Yet the old values were real, and the effort to preserve
them had nobility. Of all the things that went to make up
the war, none had more poignance than the desperate fight
to preserve these disappearing values, eroded by change from
within as much as by change from without. The fight had
been made and it had been lost, and everything that had
been dreamed and tried and fought for was personified in
the gray man who sat at the little table in the parlor at Appomattox and waited for the other man to start writing out
the terms of surrender.

The other man was wholly representative too. Behind him
there was a new society, not dreamed of by the founding
fathers: a society with the lid taken off, western man standing
up to assert that what lay back of a person mattered nothing
in comparison to what lay ahead of him. It was the land of
the mudsills, the temporarily dispossessed, the people who
had nothing to lose but the future; behind it were hard
times, humiliation and failure, and ahead of it was all the

world and a chance to lift oneself by one's bootstraps. It had few standards beyond a basic unformulated belief in the irrepressibility and ultimate value of the human spirit, and it could tramp with heavy boots down a ravaged Shenandoah Valley[1] or through the embers of a burned Columbia[2] without giving more than a casual thought to the things that were being destroyed. Yet it had its own nobility and its own standards; it had, in fact, the future of the race in its keeping, with all the immeasurable potential that might reside in a people who had decided that they would no longer be bound by the limitations of the past. It was rough and uncultivated and it came to important meetings wearing muddy boots and no sword, and it had to be listened to.

It could speak with a soft voice, and it could even be abashed by its own moment of triumph, as if that moment were not a thing to be savored and enjoyed. Grant seems to have been almost embarrassed when he and Lee came together in this parlor, yet it was definitely not the embarrassment of an underling ill at ease in a superior's presence. Rather it was simply the diffidence of a sensitive man who had another man in his power and wished to hurt him as little as possible. So Grant made small talk and recalled the old days in the Mexican War, when Lee had been the polished staff officer in the commanding general's tents and Grant had been an acting regimental quartermaster, slouching about like the hired man who looked after the teams. Perhaps the oddest thing about this meeting at Appomattox was that it was Grant, the nobody from nowhere, who played the part of gracious host, trying to put the aristocrat at his ease and, as far as might be, to soften the weight of the blow that was about to come down. In the end it was Lee who, so to speak, had to call the meeting to order, remarking (and the remark must have wrenched him almost beyond endurance) that

[1] *Shenandoah Valley:* area in northwestern Virginia drained by the Shenandoah River; scene of heavy fighting in the war

[2] *Columbia:* capital city of South Carolina, ravaged by the Union forces

they both knew what they were there for and that perhaps they had better get down to business. So Grant opened his orderly book and got out his pencil. He confessed afterward that when he did so he had no idea what words he was going to write.

He knew perfectly well what he was going to say, however, and with a few pauses he said it in straightforward words. Lee's army was to be surrendered, from commanding general down to humblest private. All public property would be turned over to the United States Army—battle flags, guns, muskets, wagons, everything. Officers might keep their side arms (Grant wrote this after a speculative glance at the excellent sword Lee was wearing) and their horses, but the army and everything it owned was to go out of existence.

It was not, however, to go off to a prison camp. Throughout the war Lincoln had stressed one point: the people of the South might have peace whenever they chose just by laying down their arms and going home. Grant made this official. Officers and men, having disarmed themselves, would simply give their paroles.[1] Then they could go to their homes . . . and here Grant wrote one of the greatest sentences in American history, the sentence that, more than any other thing, would finally make it impossible for any vengeful government in Washington to proceed against Confederate veterans as traitors. Having gone home, he wrote, officers and men could stay there, "not to be disturbed by the United States authorities so long as they observe their paroles and the laws in force where they may reside." When the powerful signature, "U. S. Grant," was signed under that sentence, the chance that Confederate soldiers might be hanged or imprisoned for treason went out of the window.

Having written all of this, Grant handed it over for Lee to read.

Lee's part was not easy. He made a business of getting out

[1]*paroles:* (their) word or oath

his glasses, polishing them carefully, crossing his legs, and adjusting himself. Once he borrowed a lead pencil to insert a word that Grant had omitted. When he had finished he raised a point. In the Confederate army, he said, horses for cavalry and artillery were not government issue; the soldiers themselves owned them. Did the terms as written permit these men to take their horses home with them? Grant shook his head. He had not realized that Confederate soldiers owned their steeds, and the terms he had written were explicit: all such animals must be turned in as captured property. Still—Grant went on to muse aloud; the last battle of the war was over, the war itself was over except for picking up the pieces, and what really mattered was for the men of the South to get back home and become civilians again. He would not change the written terms, but he supposed that most of Lee's men were small farmers anxious to return to their acres and get a crop in, and he would instruct the officers in charge of the surrender ceremonies to give a horse or a mule to any Confederate soldier who claimed to own one, so that the men would have a chance "to work their little farms." And in those homely words the great drama of Appomattox came to a close.

The draft of the terms having been agreed on, one of Grant's staff officers took the document to make a fair copy. The United States Army, it appeared, lacked ink, and to write the copy the officer had to borrow a bottle of ink from Lee's staff officer; a moment later, when the Confederate officer sat down to write Lee's formal acceptance, it developed that the Confederate army lacked paper, and he had to borrow from one of Grant's men. The business was finally signed and settled. Lee went out on the porch, looked off over the hills and smote his hands together absently while Traveler was being bridled, and then mounted and started to ride away. Grant and his officers saluted, Lee returned the salute, and there was a little silence while the man in gray rode off to join the pathetic remnant of an army that had just gone out of existence—rode off into mist and legend, to take his place at last in the folklore and the cherished memories of the nation that had been too big for him.

Grant stayed in character. He heard a banging of guns; Union artillerists were firing salutes to celebrate the victory, and Grant sent word to have all that racket stopped—those men in gray were enemies no longer but simply fellow countrymen (which, as Grant saw it, was what the war had all been about), and nothing would be done to humiliate them. Instead, wagonloads of Federal hardtack[1] and bacon would start moving at once for the Confederate camp, so that Lee's hungry men might have a square meal. Grant himself would return to Washington by the next train, without waiting to observe the actual laying down of arms. He was commanding general of the nation's armies, the war was costing four million dollars a day, and it was high time to start cutting expenses. Back in the Federal camp, Grant sat down in front of his tent to wait for the moment of departure. He seemed relaxed and in a mood to talk, and his officers gathered around him to hear what he would say about the supreme moment he had just been through. Grant addressed one of them, who had served with him in the Mexican War . . . "Do you remember that white mule old so-and-so used to ride, down in Mexico?" The officer nodded, being just then, as he confessed later, in a mood to remember the exact number of hairs in the mule's tail if that was what Grant wanted. So Grant chatted about the Mexican War, and if he had great thoughts about the piece of history he had just made he kept them to himself. Meanwhile the Army of the Potomac was alerted to be ready to move on if necessary. It was just possible it might have to march down into North Carolina and help Sherman[2] take care of Joe Johnston.[3]

[1] *hardtack:* a hard biscuit

[2] *Sherman:* General William Tecumseh Sherman had commanded the famous march through the South toward the sea.

[3] *Joe Johnston:* Joseph Eggleston Johnston was the Confederate general then in command of defenses in Georgia.

But this would not be needed. Lee was the keystone of the arch, and when he was removed the long process of collapse moved swiftly to its end. Johnston himself had no illusions. Much earlier he had confessed himself unable to do more against Sherman than annoy him. Now he was ready to do as Lee had done. What remained of the Confederate government—Jefferson Davis[1] and his iron determination, Cabinet ministers, odds and ends of government papers and funds— was flitting south, looking in vain for some refuge where it could start all over again, but there was no place where it could go. Far down in Alabama, General Wilson's[2] cavalry had taken Selma, the last remaining munitions center, had dismantled its productive apparatus with smooth, disciplined effectiveness, and had gone on to occupy Montgomery, where Davis once stood before a great crowd and heard an orator proclaim: "The man and the hour have met!" Mobile had been surrendered, and the Confederate troops in Mississippi and Alabama would lay down their arms as soon as the Federals could catch up with them. Beyond the Mississippi there still existed a Confererate army, but it might as well have been in Siberia. As an obvious matter of inescapable fact, the war was over.

Questions and Comments

1. What does the author mean when he refers to Appomattox as a "haunted possession" of the American people?

2. What details does the author point out to show the contrast between Grant and Lee?

3. What does the author mean by "the old values"? What is his attitude toward the old values?

[1] *Jefferson Davis:* President of the Confederacy
[2] *General Wilson:* James Harrison Wilson, a Union general

4. What were some of the traits of the "new society" or "western man"? What is the author's attitude toward this new society?

5. Why might General Grant have been embarrassed by General Lee's presence?

6. Why was the exchange of paper and ink such an interesting detail of the surrender?

7. What facts does the author provide which show that Grant was a person of practical nature?

8. Why does the author refer to Lee as "the keystone of the arch"?

Word Study

1. Show how the Latin derivation helps to reveal the meaning of the following words. Check your results with a dictionary.

incarnate from *incarnare* meaning "to make flesh"
poignance from *pungere* meaning "to pierce" or "to sting"
diffidence from *diffidentia* meaning "distrust"
erode from *erodere* meaning "to gnaw" or "to consume"
ferment from *fermento* meaning "to cause to rise"

2. The author speaks of the meeting of Grant and Lee as a great *tableau*. What is a tableau?

3. One meaning of *mudsill* is the lowest sill of a structure which rests on the earth or mud. What does *mudsill* mean as in "the land of the mudsills, the temporarily dispossessed, the people who had nothing to lose but the future"?

4. Give the meanings of the following words using clues from the context of the story. Check their meanings with your dictionary: *imposing* (page 254), *scrubby* (page 254), *wrenched* (page 256), *speculative* (page 259), *smote* (page 258).

Composition

1. In a brief composition discuss what you feel to be some of the most memorable details of this account of the surrender at Appomattox. Tell how the author was able to make these details vivid and unforgettable for the reader.

2. Discuss the author's concept of the "old values" giving way to the "new society." Show in what respects the process is still going on around you.

3. Pretend that you are a reporter covering some famous historical incident. Write an account of the incident for your newspaper. Try to report details accurately, vividly, and as freshly as if they were occurring right before your eyes.

This account of Lincoln's funeral is from "Vast Pageant, Then Great Quiet," which comprises Chapter 76 in Carl Sandburg's *Abraham Lincoln: The War Years,* Volume IV. Sandburg's mammoth biography of Lincoln stands today as one of the great documents of scholarly research—great because the scholarly fact-gathering and documentation were touched with the poet's craft. The account which follows includes all the facts but, growing from the facts through Sandburg's sure sense of style is a moving story of a nation still young, trying to grope its way through the tragedy of its first presidential assassination.

VAST PAGEANT,
THEN GREAT QUIET

Carl Sandburg

THERE was a funeral.

It took long to pass its many given points.

Many millions of people saw it and personally moved in it and were part of its procession.

The line of march ran seventeen hundred miles.

As a dead march nothing like it had ever been attempted before.

Like the beginning and the end of the Lincoln Administration, it had no precedents to go by.

It was garish, vulgar, massive, bewildering, chaotic.

Also it was simple, final, majestic, august.

In spite of some of its mawkish excess of show and various maudlin proceedings, it gave solemn unforgettable moments to millions of people who had counted him great, warm and lovable.

The people, the masses, nameless and anonymous numbers of persons not listed nor published among those present— these redeemed it.

They gave it the dignity and authority of a sun darkened by a vast bird migration.

They shaped it into a drama awful in the sense of having naïve awe and tears without shame.

They gave it the color and heave of the sea which is the mother of tears.

They lent to it the color of the land and the earth which is the breadgiver of life and the quiet tomb of the Family of Man.

Yes, there was a funeral.

From his White House in Washington—where it began— they carried his coffin and followed it nights and days for twelve days.

By night bonfires and torches lighted the right of way for a slow-going railroad train.

By day troops with reversed arms, muffled drums, multitudinous feet seeking the pivotal box with the silver handles.

By day bells tolling, bells sobbing the requiem, the salute guns, cannon rumbling their inarticulate thunder.

To Baltimore, Harrisburg, Philadelphia, New York, they journeyed with the draped casket to meet overly ornate catafalques.

To Albany, Utica, Syracuse, moved the funeral cortege always met by marchers and throngs.

To Cleveland, Columbus, Indianapolis, Chicago, they took the mute oblong box, met by a hearse for convoy to where tens of thousands should have their last look.

Then to Springfield, Illinois, the old home town, the Sangamon near by, the New Salem hilltop near by, for the final rest of cherished dust.

Thus the route and the ceremonial rites in epitome.

The weather was April and May but the smoke and haze was October and the feeling of the hour silent snow on the January earth of a hard winter.

The ground lay white with apple blossoms this April week. The redbird whistled. Through black branches shone blue sky. Ships put out from port with white sails catching the wind. Farmers spoke to their horses and turned furrows till sundown on the cornfield. Boys drew circles in cinder paths and played marbles. Lilac bushes took on surprises of sweet, light purple. In many a back yard the potato-planting was over. In this house was a wedding, in that one a newborn baby, in another a girl with a new betrothal ring. Life went on. Everywhere life went on.

In the East Room of the White House lay the body of a man, embalmed and prepared for a journey. Sweet roses, early magnolias, and the balmiest of lilies were strewn for an effect as though the flowers had begun to bloom even from his coffin. On a platform under·a canopy of folds and loops of black silk and crape rested the coffin. Six feet six was the coffin in length, one foot and a half across the shoulders. The wood was mahogany, lined with lead, covered with black broadcloth, at the sides four massive silver handles. Tassels, shamrock leaves, silver stars and silver cords could be seen on facings and edges. A shield with a silver plate had the inscription:

ABRAHAM LINCOLN
SIXTEENTH PRESIDENT OF THE UNITED STATES
BORN FEB. 12, 1809
DIED APRIL 15, 1865

On a pillow of white silk lay the head, on plaited satin rested the body, dressed in the black suit in which the first inaugural was delivered, with its references to "fellow citizens," to "my dissatisfied countrymen," to "better angels," as though even among angels there are the worse and the better. The chandeliers at each end of the East Room drooped with black alpaca. The eight grand mirrors of the room spoke sorrow with night-shade silk gauze. The doors, the windows too, drooped with black alpaca.

It was Tuesday, April 18, and outside surged the largest mass of people that ever thronged the White House lawn. In two columns they filed through the East Room, moving along the two sides of the coffin, many pale and limping soldiers out of the convalescent wards of the hospitals, many women and children sobbing and weeping aloud as they passed pausing only the slightest moment for a look. Those counting estimated twenty-five thousand. If it had been a hundred thousand or ten thousand the impression of any beholder would have been much the same. . . .

The services were over. The pallbearers took the silver handles. The bong of big bells on cathedrals struck and the little bells of lesser steeples chimed in, as across the spring sunshine came the tolling of all the church bells of Washington and Georgetown, and Alexandria across the river. Counting the minutes with their salutes came the hoarse boom of fort guns encircling the national capital and several batteries sent into the city.

Out of the great front door of the Executive Mansion for the last time went the mortal shape of Abraham Lincoln, sixteenth President of the United States. Six gray horses stood waiting with a black hearse fourteen feet long, seven feet wide, mounted eight feet from the ground. It moved under escort of regimental bands playing a dead march, cavalry, artillery, navy and marine detachments, infantry and drum corps with reversed arms and muffled drums. On the one-mile route to the Capitol pavements and curbs were packed with onlookers, who also filled every roof, window, doorway, balcony, and stairway. Sixty thousand spectators watched a parade of forty thousand mourners.

Marshal Ward Hill Lamon[1] and aides headed the civic procession, which included nearly all the high men of the Government, followed by department and bureau employees, State delegations, municipal officers, visiting firemen of the Perseverance Hose Company of Philadelphia, three hundred convalescents from Finley Hospital, representations from the Union League, the Mount Vernon Association, the Fenian Brotherhood, the Sons of Temperance, German glee clubs, a Catholic delegation of two hundred and fifty students and teachers from Gonzaga College, three hundred Italians of the 39th New York regiment carrying the national flags of Italy and the United States, several thousand "persons of African descent," as termed in the Emancipation Proclamation, their banner reading "We mourn our loss." A varied, kaleidoscopic, and human America followed a lost leader.

From his sickbed, sore with his dagger wounds, Secretary Seward[2] gazed from the window with mingled grief and thanks. In a group of marching Treasury bureau officials he could see a flag with a gash torn in it. This had caught the assassin's foot and broken his leg. Immediately behind the hearse Seward could see two grooms leading a horse, surmising this was the horse that had most often carried the body now in the hearse.

At Seventh Street a regiment of colored troops just arrived from the front, by a mistaken maneuver, wheeled about and found itself at the head and forefront of the procession, winning admiration by their marching order and skill in the manual of arms. At Fifteenth Street one of the horses of President Johnson's[3] carriage began rearing for a runaway and

[1] *Marshal Ward Hill Lamon:* U.S. Marshal of Washington, D.C.; former law partner of Lincoln

[2] *Seward:* William Henry Seward was appointed Secretary of State by Lincoln; served 1861–1869.

[3] *Johnson:* Vice-President Andrew Johnson became President on Lincoln's death, April 15, 1865.

the President and his companion Preston King alighted and took seats in another carriage. Neither these nor any other incidents hindered the smooth flow of a procession that stretched for miles, moving into Pennslyvania Avenue as a long breathing link of living persons connecting and welding the unity of the White House and the Capitol.

In the rotunda of the Capitol, under the great white dome that had come to its finished contruction while the war raged, twelve sergeants of the Veteran Reserve Corps carried the coffin to a huge catafalque. The honorary pallbearers ranged themselves in a circle. Generals, admirals, the President, the Cabinet, stood some ten feet from the coffin. Dr. Gurley[1] spoke a brief service. Lincoln's bodyguard, with an added company and officers, formed a cordon around the coffin. The building was cleared.

In silence during night watches the body of Lincoln lay with eyes never opening to see far above him the arches of the great dome that for him symbolized the Union. When in front of this building he had spoken his first inaugural, the parts and pieces of that dome lay scattered on the ground around him. He had seen them lifted up and woven and mortised and completed for his second inaugural. Then he stood vertical and looked up. Now he lay horizontal with eyelids beyond opening. In the night watches while the guard mount changed, whispering, quiet on soft feet, into midnight and past into daybreak, midway between House and Senate chambers, midway between those seats and aisles of heartbreak and passion, he lay a horizontal clay tabernacle.

In the morning of Thursday, April 20, at ten o'clock the doors opened in special consideration for wounded soldiers from the hospitals, weak and battered men, some with empty sleeves, others on crutches, to file by. Afterward came the public, at times three thousand to the hour, before mid-

---

[1] *Dr. Gurley:* Phineas D. Gurley, minister of New York Avenue Presbyterian Church, Washington, D.C.

night twenty-five thousand persons. Many had seen him in
the life, in buildings, on streets, in a carriage, on a horse,
breathing and speaking before an audience. Now they looked
at him, some in agreement and some not with the *New York
World* reporter who wrote: "Death has fastened into his fro-
zen face all the character and idiosyncrasy of life. He has not
changed one line of his grave, grotesque countenance, nor
smoothed out a single feature. The hue is rather bloodless
and leaden, but he was always sallow. . . . Whatever energy
or humor or tender gravity marked the living face is hardened into pulseless outline. . . . The white satin around it
reflects sufficient light upon the face to show that death is
really there."

The same reporter, George Alfred Townsend, described
the embalmer as having by a customary process drained the
blood from the body by the jugular vein, "and through a
cutting made on the inside of the thigh the empty blood vessels were charged with a chemical preparation which soon
hardened to the consistency of stone." Scalp and brain had
been removed, blood emptied from the chest. "All that we
see of Abraham Lincoln, so cunningly contemplated in this
splendid coffin, is a mere shell, an effigy, a sculpture. He lies
in a sleep, but it is the sleep of marble. All that made this
flesh vital, sentient and affectionate, is gone forever." This
was the factual and informative news version of what Dr.
Gurley in his prayer of the day before had set forth more
utterly: "For what is our life? It is even a vapor that appear-
eth for a little time and then vanisheth away. . . . We commit
its decaying remains to their kindred element, earth to earth,
ashes to ashes, dust to dust."

Some who gazed on the face remembered the poem he so
often recited for them, that old-rose-and-lavender keepsake of
a poem. For him it had a musk of smell and a dusk of light, a
weatherworn stain of hard walnut with a sunset smoke loiter-
ing and elusive in the faded grain of the wood. Before he

went to Congress, before the Mexican War, he said these
verses. Years later when President he said them. They carried
for him a music in the air now:

> The leaves of the oak and the willow shall fade,
> Be scattered around, and together be laid;
> As the young and the old, the low and the high,
> Shall crumble to dust and together shall lie. . . .
>
> The saint who enjoyed the communion of Heaven,
> The sinner who dared to remain unforgiven,
> The wise and the foolish, the guilty and just,
> Have quietly mingled their bones in the dust. . . .
>
> 'Tis the wink of an eye; 'tis the draught of a breath
> From the blossom of health to the paleness of death,
> From the gilded saloon to the bier and the shroud;
> O, why should the spirit of mortal be proud?[1]

Friday morning, April 21, just six days after the death in
the Peterson house on Tenth Street, President Johnson,
General Grant, Stanton[2] and other Cabinet members, saw
the coffin placed aboard a special burial car at the Washington depot—joined by another and smaller casket, that of the
son Willie, which had been disinterred and was to have burial in Springfield, Illinois, near his father. Railroad-yard en-
gine bells tolled and a far-stretching crowd stood with uncovered heads as the train of seven cars—with a scout pilot en-
gine ahead to test the roadway—moved out of Washington
for Baltimore.

Questions and Comments

1. The author uses words to describe the Lincoln funeral
   that appear to be contradictory. What are some of these
   words? In what sense are they contradictory? In what sense
   are they completely consistent?

[1] *The leaves . . . be proud:* from "Oh, Why Should the Spirit of Mortal Be
Proud?" by William Knox. The poem is also known as "Mortality."

[2] *Stanton:* Edwin Stanton was chosen as Secretary of War by Lincoln.

2. What function does the author say the thousands of silent spectators played in Lincoln's funeral?

3. What is the season of the year? What irony do you detect in a funeral occurring during this season of the year?

4. What picture do you get of Lincoln's appearance in life from George Townsend's description of him in death?

5. What insights into Lincoln's character and personal beliefs do you think are revealed by the poem we are told he was so fond of?

Word Study

1. Perhaps no other selection in this text contains so many difficult words. Sandburg's love of language is always profusely on display in his writing. What do the italicized words in the following sentences mean?

"It was *garish,* vulgar, massive, bewildering, chaotic."

"Also it was simple, final, majestic, *august.*"

"In spite of some of its *mawkish* excess of show and various *maudlin* proceedings, it gave solemn unforgettable moments to millions of people. . . ."

"By day troops with reversed arms, muffled drums, *multitudinous* feet seeking the *pivotal* box with the silver handles."

"By day bells tolling, bells sobbing the *requiem,* the salute guns, cannon rumbling their *inarticulate* thunder."

2. Some words peculiar to funerals have interesting stories behind them. Look up the derivation of *pallbearer* and *hearse.* What did they mean originally? *Coffin* has had many meanings through the years, one of them—the pastry lining of a pie. Look up some of its other meanings. *Catafalque* comes from the Italian meaning "scaffold," and refers to the structure upon which a coffin is laid. *Casket* means "coffin" only in the United States.

3. People are very touchy about funerals and death, having even invented special substitutes in language for "death."

For example, a person doesn't die, he "passes on." List other examples of such euphemistic expressions concerning death or dying.

4. Here are more words you may need to check in your dictionary: *epitome* (page 265), *alpaca* (page 266), *idiosyncrasy* (page 269), *sallow* (page 269), *sentient* (page 269), *disinterred* (page 270).

Composition

1. Much of this selection is highly poetic in form and language. In a composition point out the author's use of such poetic devices as repetition, rhythm, refrain, and figurative language. Which do you feel would be more effective as a method of describing a vast spectacle—a poetic account or a more prosaic account such as you might read in a newspaper? Give reasons for your answer.

2. In a brief composition discuss what you think are the author's feelings about Lincoln. Show how these feelings are revealed by the language he uses and the emotional tone of the selection.

Malcolm X (1925-1965) was born Malcolm Little in Omaha, Nebraska. Although only thirty-nine years old when he was assassinated, he had risen to national prominence as one of the greatest advocates of black nationalism in the United States. The road to the achievement of his leadership role contained such adverse events as his father's having been murdered when Malcolm was six, his mother's having a nervous breakdown when he was twelve (and he and his sisters and brothers being declared wards of the state), having no formal education beyond the ninth grade, and being imprisoned for stealing and carrying a gun when he was twenty-one. In 1965 he said to Alex Haley, "I have given to this book (his autobiography) so much of whatever time I have because I feel, and I hope, that if I honestly and fully tell my life's account, read objectively it might prove to be a testimony of some social value." He often spoke of dying violently and young—he was right. Three assassins cut him down with sixteen shotgun and pistol wounds in the chest on February 21, 1965, as he was about to make a speech in Harlem, New York City.

The material which follows appears toward the end of Malcolm X's autobiography and describes the ideas and changes in his basic philosophy. These changes followed his visit to Mecca, birthplace of Mohammed the Prophet, and holiest of cities to those in the Moslem faith; referred to as "Holy World" by Malcolm X.

from THE AUTOBIOGRAPHY OF MALCOLM X

Malcolm X and Alex Haley

I KEPT having all kinds of troubles trying to develop the kind of Black Nationalist organization I wanted to build for the American Negro. Why Black Nationalism? Well, in the competitive American society, how can there ever be any white-black solidarity before there is first some black solidarity? If you will remember, in my childhood I had been exposed to the Black Nationalist teachings of Marcus Garvey[1]—which, in fact, I had been told had led to my father's murder. Even when I was a follower of Elijah Muhammad,[2] I had been strongly aware of how the Black Nationalist political, economic and social philosophies had the ability to instill within black men the racial dignity, the incentive, and the confidence that the black race needs today to get up off its knees, and to get on its feet, and get rid of its scars, and to take a stand for itself.

One of the major troubles that I was having in building the organization that I wanted—an all-black organization whose ultimate objective was to help create a society in which there could exist honest white-black brotherhood—was that my earlier public image, my old so-called "Black Muslim" image, kept blocking me. I was trying to gradually reshape that image. I was trying to turn a corner, into a new regard by the public, especially Negroes; I was no less angry than I had been, but at the same time the true brotherhood I had seen in the Holy World had influenced me to recognize that anger can blind human vision.

Every free moment I could find, I did a lot of talking to key people whom I knew around Harlem, and I made a lot of speeches, saying: "True Islam taught me that it takes *all* of the religious, political, economic, psychological, and racial ingredients, or characteristics, to make the Human Family and the Human Society complete.

"Since I learned the *truth* in Mecca, my dearest friends

[1]*Marcus Aurelius Gàrvey:* Jamaican born black nationalism advocate who assumed the title, "Leader of the Negro Peoples of the World" (1887–1940)

[2]*Elijah Muhammad:* considered the "Messenger of Allah" by American Muslims

have come to include *all* kinds—some Christians, Jews, Buddhists, Hindus, agnostics, and even atheists! I have friends who are called capitalists, Socialists, and Communists! Some of my friends are moderates, conservatives, extremists—some are even Uncle Toms! My friends today are black, brown, red, yellow, and *white!*"

I said to Harlem street audiences that only when mankind would submit to the One God who created all—only then would mankind even approach the "peace" of which so much *talk* could be heard . . . but toward which so little *action* was seen.

I said that on the American racial level, we had to approach the black man's struggle against the white man's racism as a human problem, that we had to forget hypocritical politics and propaganda. I said that both races, as human beings, had the obligation, the responsibility, of helping to correct America's human problem. The well-meaning white people, I said, had to combat, actively and directly, the racism in other white people. And the black people had to build within themselves much greater awareness that along with equal rights there had to be the bearing of equal responsibilities.

I knew, better than most Negroes, how many white people truly wanted to see American racial problems solved. I knew that many whites were as frustrated as Negroes. I'll bet I got fifty letters some days from white people. The white people in meeting audiences would throng around me, asking me, after I had addressed them somewhere, "What *can* a sincere white person do?"

When I say that here now, it makes me think about that little co-ed I told you about, the one who flew from her New England college down to New York and came up to me in the Nation of Islam's restaurant in Harlem, and I told her that there was "nothing" she could do. I regret that I told her that. I wish that now I knew her name, or where I could telephone her, or write to her, and tell her what I tell white people now when they present themselves as being sincere, and ask me, one way or another, the same thing that she asked.

The first thing I tell them is that at least where my own particular Black Nationalist organization, the Organization of Afro-American Unity, is concerned, they can't *join* us. I have these very deep feelings that white people who want to join black organizations are really just taking the escapist way to salve their consciences. By visibly hovering near us, they are "proving" that they are "with us." But the hard truth is this *isn't* helping to solve America's racist problem. The Negroes aren't the racists. Where the really sincere white people have got to do their "proving" of themselves is not among the black *victims*, but out on the battle lines of where America's racism really *is*—and that's in their own home communities; America's racism is among their own fellow whites. That's where the sincere whites who really mean to accomplish something have got to work.

Aside from that, I mean nothing against any sincere whites when I say that as members of black organizations, generally whites' very presence subtly renders the black organization automatically less effective. Even the best white members will slow down the Negroes' discovery of what they need to do, and particularly of what they can do—for themselves, working by themselves, among their own kind, in their own communities.

I sure don't want to hurt anybody's feelings, but in fact I'll even go so far as to say that I never really trust the kind of white people who are always so anxious to hang around Negroes, or to hang around in Negro communities. I don't trust the kind of whites who love having Negroes always hanging around them. I don't know—this feeling may be a throwback to the years when I was hustling in Harlem and all of those red-faced, drunk whites in the afterhours clubs were always grabbing hold of some Negroes and talking about "I just want you to know you're just as good as I am—" And then they got back in their taxicabs and black limousines and went back downtown to the places where they lived and worked, where no blacks except servants had better get caught. But, anyway, I know that every time that whites join a black organization, you watch, pretty soon the blacks will be leaning on the whites to support it, and before you know it a black may be up front with a title, but the whites, because of their money, are the real controllers.

I tell sincere white people, "Work in conjunction with us—each of us working among our own kind." Let sincere white individuals find all other white people they can who feel as they do—and let them form their own all-white groups, to work trying to convert other white people who are thinking and acting so racist. Let sincere whites go and teach nonviolence to white people!

We will completely respect our white co-workers. They will deserve every credit. We will give them every credit. We will meanwhile be working among our own kind, in our own black communities—showing and teaching black men in ways that only other black men can—that the black man has got to help himself. Working separately, the sincere white people and sincere black people actually will be working together.

In our mutual sincerity we might be able to show a road to the salvation of America's very soul. It can only be salvaged if human rights and dignity, in full, are extended to black men. Only such real, meaningful actions as those which are sincerely motivated from a deep sense of humanism and moral responsibility can get at the basic causes that produce the racial explosions in America today. Otherwise, the racial explosions are only going to grow worse. Certainly nothing is every going to be solved by throwing upon me and other so-called black "extremists" and "demagogues[1]" the blame for the racism that is in America.

---

[1]*demagogues:* speakers who gain political power through taking advantage of social discontent

Sometimes, I have dared to dream to myself that one day, history may even say that my voice—which disturbed the white man's smugness, and his arrogance, and his complacency—that my voice helped to save America from a grave, possibly even a fatal catastrophe.

The goal has always been the same, with the approaches to it as different as mine and Dr. Martin Luther King's[1] nonviolent marching, that dramatizes the brutality and the evil of the white man against defenseless blacks. And in the racial climate of this country today, it is anybody's guess which of the "extremes" in approach to the black man's problems might *personally* meet a fatal catastrophe first—"non-violent" Dr. King, or so-called "violent" me.

Anything I do today, I regard as urgent. No man is given but so much time to accomplish whatever is his life's work. My life in particular never has stayed fixed in one position for very long. You have seen how throughout my life, I have often known unexpected drastic changes.

I am only facing the facts when I know that any moment of any day, or any night, could bring me death. This is particularly true since the last trip that I made abroad. I have seen the nature of things that are happening, and I have heard things from sources which are reliable.

To speculate about dying doesn't disturb me as it might some people. I never have felt that I would live to become an old man. Even before I was a Muslim—when I was a hustler in the ghetto jungle, and then a criminal in prison, it always stayed on my mind that I would die a violent death. In fact, it runs in my family. My father and most of his brothers died by violence—my father because of what he believed in. To come right down to it, if I take the kind of things in which I believe, then add to that the kind of temperament that I have, plus the one hundred per

[1]*Dr. Martin Luther King, Jr.:* black American minister (1929-1968). A dedicated worker for civil rights and an advocate of passive resistance; the victim of an assassin

cent dedication I have to whatever I believe in—these are ingredients which make it just about impossible for me to die of old age.

Questions and Comments

1. What does Malcolm X have to say to those white people who ask, "What can I do?"

2. Malcolm X does not want whites to join black organizations. What are his reasons? Do you agree that this approach is the way to solve the problem?

3. Would you describe Malcolm X's view of the black-white problem a broad point of view or a narrow one? Explain your response.

4. What are the reasons for Malcolm X's believing he will die young and die violently?

Word Study

1. *Agnostics* and *atheists*, on page 275, are both related to people's faith in God. Check the meaning of each in the dictionary, and be sure to understand the slim line of meaning which separates one from the other. Other words in this same category are: theistic, deistic, freethinker, unbeliever, and infidel.

2. *Racism* as opposed to *race* and *racial* is a key word in this article, first appearing on page 275. Read the passage in which it appears and try to guess its meaning; then check with a dictionary.

3. *Smugness, arrogance,* and *complacency* (page 278) are the attitudes which Malcolm X hopes his voice will disturb in the white people who possess them. If these words lie at the root of prejudice between races, what do you think they mean? Check your meanings against the dictionary's.

Composition

1. Malcolm X said in his *Autobiography* that the matter of black oppression is an international problem, not simply an American problem. Write a personal reaction to this statement, drawing on your knowledge of current affairs and history.

2. Malcolm X once said he felt safer and more secure with people who did not hide their prejudice and who said openly, "I don't like blacks." In a paragraph or two explain why he might have felt that way.

3. Using the library, try to find information about the roots of prejudice. In America the question involves Native Americans, blacks, Mexicans, Puerto Ricans, women, religions, and national origins. Organize the information you find into a written report.

4. What evidence on the national scene today proves that the black-white situation still has not been resolved? Organize your evidence into a written report. Include indications of improvement.

"I am that gadfly which the god has attached to the state, and all day long and in all places am always fastening upon you, arousing and persuading and reproaching you. You will not easily find another like me, and therefore I would advise you to spare me." So spoke Socrates in 399 B.C. at his trial in Athens, when he was accused of corrupting the city's youth.

Socrates is still a gadfly today and continues to "corrupt" youth because his ideas still live in the written word, preserved by his brilliant student, Plato. Socrates never wrote himself, but his teachings, as preserved by Plato, are among the most outstanding in philosophical thought.

The following selections from Plato's *Apology* and *Phaedo* show not only the profound intellect of Socrates but also his marvelous integrity as a great human being.

from APOLOGY
and PHAEDO

Plato

from APOLOGY

Not much time will be gained, O Athenians, in return for the evil name which you will get from the detractors of the city, who will say that you killed Socrates, a wise man; for they will call me wise even although I am not wise when they want to reproach you. If you had waited a little while, your desire would have been fulfilled in the course of nature. For I am far advanced in years,[1] as you may perceive, and not

---

[1] *far advanced in years:* Socrates was in his seventies.

far from death. I am speaking now only to those of you who
have condemned me to death. And I have another thing to
say to them: You think that I was convicted through
deficiency of words—I mean, that if I had thought fit to leave
nothing undone, nothing unsaid, I might have gained an acquittal. Not so; the deficiency which led to my conviction
was not of words—certainly not. But I had not the boldness
or impudence or inclination to address you as you would
have liked me to address you, weeping and wailing and la-
menting, and saying and doing many things which you have
been accustomed to hear from others, and which, as I say, are
unworthy of me. But I thought that I ought not to do anything common or mean in the hour of danger: nor do I now
repent of the manner of my defence, and I would rather die
having spoken after my manner, than speak in your manner
and live. For neither in war nor yet at law ought any man to
use every way of escaping death. For often in battle there is
no doubt that if a man will throw away his arms, and fall on
his knees before his pursuers, he may escape death; and in
other dangers there are other ways of escaping death, if a
man is willing to say and do anything. The difficulty, my
friends, is not in avoiding death, but in avoiding
unrighteousness; for that runs faster than death. I am old
and move slowly, and the slower runner has overtaken me,
and my accusers are keen and quick, and the faster runner,
who is unrighteousness, has overtaken them. And now I depart hence condemned by you to suffer the penalty of death,
and they, too, go their ways condemned by the truth to suffer
the penalty of villany and wrong; and I must abide by my
award—let them abide by theirs. I suppose that these things
may be regarded as fated—and I think that they are well.

And now, O men who have condemned me, I would fain
prophesy to you; for I am about to die, and that is the hour
in which men are gifted with prophetic power. And I prophesy to you who are my murderers, that immediately after my

death punishment far heavier than you have inflicted on me will surely await you. Me you have killed because you wanted to escape the accuser, and not to give an account of your lives. But that will not be as you suppose: far otherwise. Foɪ I say that there will be more accusers of you than there are now; accusers whom hitherto I have restrained: and as they are younger they will be more severe with you, and you will be more offended at them. For if you think that by killing men you can avoid the accuser censuring your lives, you are mistaken; that is not a way of escape which is either possible or honorable; the easiest and the noblest way is not to be crushing others, but to be improving yourselves. This is the prophecy which I utter before my departure, to the judges who have condemned me.

Friends, who would have acquitted me, I would like also to talk with you about this thing which has happened, while the magistrates are busy, and before I go to the place at which I must die. Stay then awhile, for we may as well talk with one another while there is time. You are my friends, and I should like to show you the meaning of this event which has happened to me. O my judges—for you I may truly call judges—I should like to tell you of a wonderful circum- stance. Hitherto the familiar oracle within me has constantly been in the habit of opposing me even about trifles, if I was going to make a slip or error about anything; and now as you see there has come upon me that which may be thought, and is generally believed to be, the last and worst evil. But the oracle made no sign of opposition, either as I was leaving my house and going out in the morning, or when I was going up into this court, or while I was speaking, at anything which I was going to say; and yet I have often been stopped in the middle of a speech; but now in nothing I either said or did touching this matter has the oracle opposed me. What do I take to be the explanation of this? I will tell you. I regard this as a proof that what has happened to me is a good, and that those of us who think that death is an evil are in error. This is a great proof to me of what I am saying, for the customary sign would surely have opposed me had I been going to evil and not to good.

Let us reflect in another way, and we shall see that there is great reason to hope that death is a good, for one of two things: either death is a state of nothingness and utter unconsciousness, or, as men say, there is a change and migration of the soul from this world to another. Now if you suppose that there is no consciousness, but a sleep like the sleep of him who is undisturbed even by the sight of dreams, death will be an unspeakable gain. For if a person were to select the night in which his sleep was undisturbed even by dreams, and were to compare with this the other days and nights of his life, and then were to tell us how many days and nights he had passed in the course of his life better and more pleasantly than this one, I think that any man, I will not say a private man, but even the great king, will not find many such days or nights, when compared with the others. Now if death is like this, I say that to die is gain; for eternity is then only a single night. But if death is the journey to another place, and there, as men say, all the dead are, what good, O my friends and judges, can be greater than this? If indeed when the pilgrim arrives in the world below, he is delivered from the professors of justice in this world, and finds the true judges who are said to give judgment there, Minos and Rhadamanthus and Æacus and Triptolemus, and other sons of God who were righteous in their own life, that pilgrimage will be worth making. What would not a man give if he might converse with Orpheus and Musæus and Hesiod and Homer?[1] Nay, if this be true, let me die again and again. I, too, shall have a wonderful interest in a place where I can converse with Palamedes, and Ajax the son of Telamon, and other heroes of old, who have suffered death through an unjust

[1]*Orpheus . . . Homer:* These names and subsequent names mentioned here by Socrates are famous Greek artists of ancient times. They represent models for areas of human accomplishment: music, poetry, war, travel, and adventure.

judgment; and there will be no small pleasure, as I think, in comparing my own sufferings with theirs. Above all, I shall be able to continue my search into true and false knowledge; as in this world, so also in that; I shall find out who is wise, and who pretends to be wise, and is not. What would not a man give, O judges, to be able to examine the leader of the great Trojan expedition; or Odysseus or Sisyphus, or numberless others, men and women too! What infinite delight would there be in conversing with them and asking them questions! For in that world they do not put a man to death for this; certainly not. For besides being happier in that world than in this, they will be immortal, if what is said is true.

Wherefore, O judges, be of good cheer about death, and know this of a truth—that no evil can happen to a good man, either in life or after death. He and his are not neglected by the gods; nor has my own approaching end happened by mere chance. But I see clearly that to die and be released was better for me; and therefore the oracle gave no sign. For which reason, also, I am not angry with my accusers, or my condemners; they have done me no harm, although neither of them meant to do me any good; and for this I may gently blame them.

Still I have a favor to ask of them. When my sons are grown up, I would ask you, O my friends, to punish them, and I would have you trouble them, as I have troubled you, if they seem to care about riches, or anything, more than about virtue; or if they pretend to be something when they are really nothing—then reprove them, as I have reproved you, for not caring about that for which they ought to care, and thinking that they are something when they are really nothing. And if you do this, I and my sons will have received justice at your hands.

The hour of departure has arrived, and we go our ways—I to die, and you to live. Which is better, God only knows.

from PHAEDO

When he had done speaking, Crito said: And have you any commands for us,[1] Socrates—anything to say about your children, or any other matter in which we can serve you?

Nothing particular, he said: only, as I have always told you, I would have you to look to yourselves; that is a service which you may always be doing to me and mine as well as to yourselves. And you need not make professions; for if you take no thought for yourselves, and walk not according to the precepts which I have given you, not now for the first time, the warmth of your professions will be of no avail.

We will do our best, said Crito. But in what way would you have us bury you?

In any way that you like; only you must get hold of me, and take care that I do not walk away from you. Then he turned to us, and added with a smile: I cannot make Crito believe that I am the same Socrates who have been talking and conducting the argument; he fancies that I am the other Socrates whom he will soon see, a dead body—and he asks, How shall he bury me? And though I have spoken many words in the endeavor to show that when I have drunk the poison I shall leave you and go to the joys of the blessed— these words of mine, with which I comforted you and myself, have had, as I perceive, no effect upon Crito. And therefore I want you to be surety[2] for me now, as he was surety for me at the trial: but let the promise be of another sort; for he was my surety to the judges that I would remain, but you must be my surety to him that I shall not remain, but go away and depart; and then he will suffer less at my death, and not be grieved when he sees my body being burned or buried. I would not have him sorrow at my hard lot, or say at the buri-

[1] *have you any commands for us:* Phaedo, Simmias, Cabes, Crito, and Apollodorus were present at Socrates' death. References to Echecrates are of direct address and made by Phaedo as he tells Echecrates of Socrates' death.

[2] *surety:* one who pledges, and accepts certain responsibilities, for another

al, Thus we lay out Socrates, or, Thus we follow him to the grave or bury him; for false words are not only evil in themselves, but they infect the soul with evil. Be of good cheer, then, my dear Crito, and say that you are burying my body only, and do with that as is usual, and as you think best.

When he had spoken these words, he arose and went into the bath chamber with Crito, who bade us wait; and we waited, talking and thinking of the subject of discourse, and also of the greatness of our sorrow; he was like a father of whom we were being bereaved, and we were about to pass the rest of our lives as orphans. When he had taken the bath his children were brought to him—(he had two young sons and an elder one); and the women of his family also came, and he talked to them and gave them a few directions in the presence of Crito; and he then dismissed them and returned to us.

Now the hour of sunset was near,[1] for a good deal of time had passed while he was within. When he came out, he sat down with us again after his bath, but not much was said. Soon the jailer, who was the servant of the Eleven, entered and stood by him, saying: To you, Socrates, whom I know to be the noblest and gentlest and best of all who ever came to this place, I will not impute the angry feelings of other men, who rage and swear at me when, in obedience to the authorities, I bid them drink the poison—indeed I am sure that you will not be angry with me; for others, as you are aware, and not I, are the guilty cause. And so fare you well, and try to bear lightly what must needs be; you know my errand. Then bursting into tears he turned away and went out.

Socrates looked at him and said: I return your good wishes, and will do as you bid. Then, turning to us, he said, How charming the man is: since I have been in prison he has always been coming to see me, and at times he would talk to

[1] *hour . . . near:* Greek custom directed that death such as Socrates was to suffer should occur at sunset.

me, and was as good as could be to me, and now see how generously he sorrows for me. But we must do as he says, Crito; let the cup be brought, if the poison is prepared: if not, let the attendant prepare some.

Yet, said Crito, the sun is still upon the hilltops, and many a one has taken the draught late, and after the announcement has been made to him, he has eaten and drunk, and indulged in sensual delights; do not hasten, then, there is still time.

Socrates said: Yes, Crito, and they of whom you speak are right in doing thus, for they think that they will gain by the delay; but I am right in not doing thus, for I do not think that I should gain anything by drinking the poison a little later; I should be sparing and saving a life which is already gone: I could only laugh at myself for this. Please then to do as I say, and not to refuse me.

Crito, when he heard this, made a sign to the servant; and the servant went in, and remained for some time, and then returned with the jailer carrying the cup of poison. Socrates said: You, my good friend, who are experienced in these matters, shall give me directions how I am to proceed. The man answered: You have only to walk about until your legs are heavy, and then to lie down, and the poison will act. At the same time he handed the cup to Socrates, who in the easiest and gentlest manner, without the least fear or change of color or feature, looking at the man with all his eyes, Echecrates, as his manner was, took the cup and said: What do you say about making a libation out of this cup to any god? May I, or not? The man answered: We only prepare, Socrates, just so much as we deem enough. I understand, he said: yet I may and must pray to the gods to prosper my journey from this to that other world—may this, then, which is my prayer, be granted to me. Then holding the cup to his lips, quite readily and cheerfully he drank off the poison. And hitherto most of us had been able to control our sorrow; but now when we saw him drinking, and saw too that he had finished the draught, we could no longer forbear, and in spite of myself my own tears were flowing fast; so that I covered my face and wept over myself, for certainly I was not weeping over him, but at the thought of my own calamity in having lost such a companion. Nor was I the first, for Crito, when he found himself unable to restrain his tears, had got up and moved away, and I followed; and at that moment, Apollodorus, who had been weeping all the time, broke out into a loud cry which made cowards of us all. Socrates alone retained his calmness: What is this strange outcry? he said. I sent away the women mainly in order that they might not offend in this way, for I have heard that a man should die in peace. Be quiet, then, and have patience.

When we heard that, we were ashamed, and refrained our tears; and he walked about until, as he said, his legs began to fail, and then he lay on his back, according to the directions, and the man who gave him the poison now and then looked at his feet and legs; and after a while he pressed his foot hard and asked him if he could feel; and he said, no; and then his leg, and so upwards and upwards, and showed us that he was cold and stiff. And he felt them himself, and said: When the poison reaches the heart, that will be the end. He was beginning to grow cold about the groin, when he uncovered his face, for he had covered himself up, and said (they were his last words)—he said: Crito, I owe a cock to Asclepius;[1] will you remember to pay the debt? The debt shall be paid, said Crito; is there anything else? There was no answer to this question; but in a minute or two a movement was heard, and the attendants uncovered him; his eyes were set, and Crito closed his eyes and mouth.

Such was the end, Echecrates, of our friend, whom I may truly call the wisest, and justest, and best of all the men whom I have ever known.

---

[1] *Asclepius:* Greek god of medicine and of healing. The usual offering to him was a cock—to return thanks (or pay the doctor's bill) after recovery from an illness.

Questions and Comments

1. To whom does Socrates address his first remarks?

2. How might Socrates have achieved an acquittal? Why did he not do this?

3. What does Socrates say is more difficult to avoid than death? Why?

4. Why isn't killing an effective way to eliminate accusers according to Socrates?

5. What reason does Socrates have for believing that his actions and words in court were correct?

6. What does Socrates consider to be the two alternatives in death? How does this position affect his attitude toward death?

7. What request does Socrates make to his friends with regard to his sons?

8. Why is Socrates somewhat indifferent about the disposal of his body?

9. What beliefs do you think helped Socrates to remain calm in the face of death?

10. What reason does Phaedo give for his tears?

11. What do Socrates' last words tell us about him?

Word Study

1. In Greek and Roman times an oracle was the medium by which a god revealed divine purpose or hidden knowledge. *Oracle* comes from the Latin *orare,* meaning "to speak." What other English words derive from this Latin word?

2. *Intimation* comes from the Latin *intimare,* meaning "to make known." What is an intimation?

3. Socrates asks, "What do you say about making a libation out of this cup to any god?" How does the context (page 278) help to reveal the meaning of *libation*?

4. Here are some other words which should be looked up if you don't know them: *censuring* (page 283), *reprove* (page 285), *precepts* (page 286), *impute* (page 287), *draught* (page 289), *forbear* (page 289).

Composition

1. Discuss Socrates' attitude toward death and show how this attitude helped him to overcome any fear he might have had.

2. Write a brief analysis of the character of Socrates from some of the ideas he puts forth in *Apology* and *Phaedo*.

3. Compare Socrates with Joan of Arc or some other figure in history who was executed for his or her beliefs.